CALIFORNIA

GO MATH

Middle School Grade 6

Solutions Key

Cover Image Credits: Malibu Beach ©John B. Mueller Photography/Flickr/Getty Images

Printed in the U.S.A.

ISBN 978-0-544-20722-6

4 5 6 7 8 9 10 0982 22 21 20 19 18 17 16 15 14

4500472650 B C D E F G

Table of Contents

Table of Contents

UNIT 6 Relationships in Geometry

UNIT 7 Measurement and Data

Solutions Key
Numbers

MODULE 1 *Integers*

Are You Ready?

1. 471 > 468
2. 5,005 < 5,050
3. 398 > 389
4. 10,973 < 10,999
5. 8,471 < 9,001
6. 108 > 95
7. 177 > 156 > 99 > 87
8. 603 > 600 > 591 > 589
9. 3,056 > 2,650 > 2,605 > 2,088
10. 10,415 > 1,037 > 1,029 > 995
11.

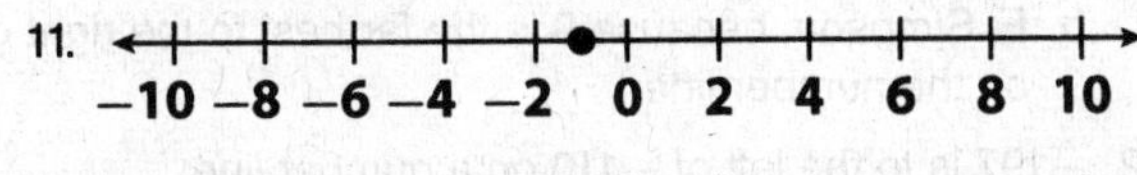

12.

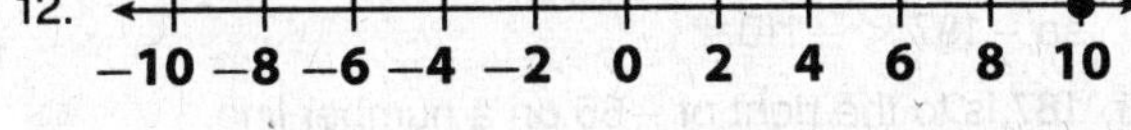

13.

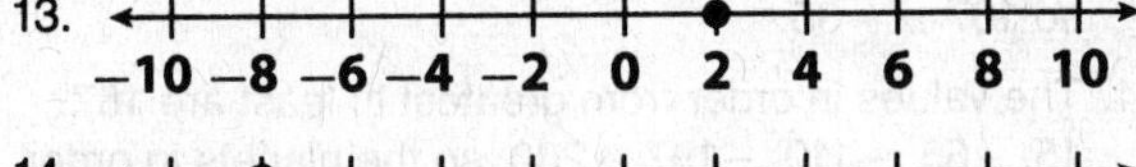

14.

−10 −8 −6 −4 −2 0 2 4 6 8 10

LESSON 1.1

Your Turn

6.
7.

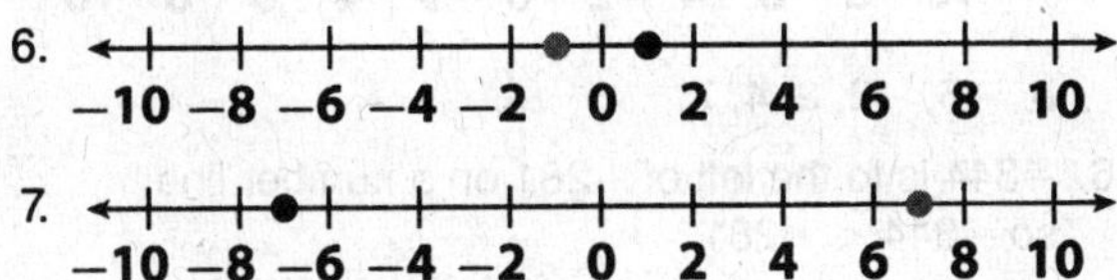

8. The opposite of 10 is −10.
9. The opposite of −5 is 5.
10. The opposite of 0 is 0.
11. 4; the opposite of 4 is −4, so the opposite of the opposite of 4 is the same as the opposite of −4, which is 4.

Guided Practice

1.

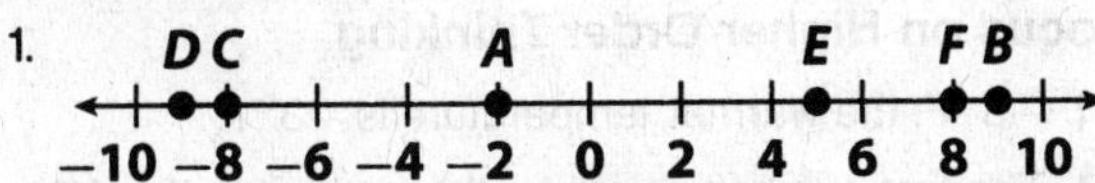

2. −2 is the opposite of 2

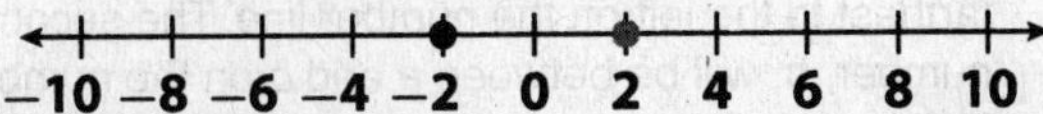

3. 8 is the opposite of −8

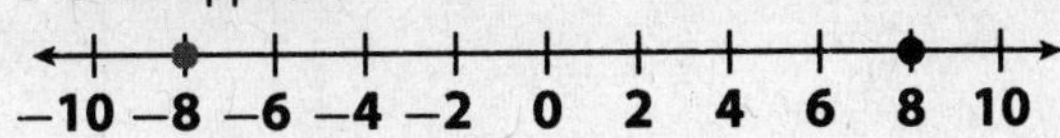

4. 0 is the opposite of 0

5. The opposite of 4 is −4.
6. The opposite of −11 is 11.
7. The opposite of 3 is −3.
8. The opposite of −3 is 3.
9. The opposite of 0 is 0.
10. The opposite of 22 is −22.
11. The amount decreased by $450 − $420 = $30, which can be represented as a change of −$30.

Independent Practice

12. a. A, C, and E have a negative charge.
    b. A and D; B and E; −3 and +3 are opposites, and +1 and −1 are opposites.
    c. C; the opposite of −2 is +2, but that number is not in the table.
13. The opposite of −17 is 17.
14. −4 is 4 units to the left of 0.
15. 2; the opposite of 2 is −2, so the opposite of the opposite of 2 is the same as the opposite of −2, which is 2.
16. 15 is 15 units to the right of 0.
17. 12 is 12 units to the right of 0.
18. The opposite of −19 is 19.
19. a. gain; a positive number represents a gain
    b. Lady; Zeus's weight change is 2 and Lady's is −2.
    c. Lady and Rocky
    d. Sparky's; a change of 0 indicates no change in weight.
    e. −6; the opposite of 6 is −6.
    f. No; a −6 pound change means Lucky lost 6 pounds.
20. 12 units, the opposite of 6 is −6, and both numbers are 6 units away from 0, so the distance between them is 12 units.
21. 4 units, the opposite of −2 is 2, and both numbers are 2 units away from 0, so the distance between them is 4 units.
22. 0 units, the opposite of 0 is 0, and the distance between 0 and 0 is 0.
23. 14 units, the opposite of −7 is 7, and both numbers are 7 units away from 0, so the distance between them is 14 units.
24. a. 7 points; Timothy's score is −25, and the opposite of −25 is 25. In order to have 25 points, Shawna needs 7 more points.

b. Kaylynn; Timothy's score is 25 away from 0, Shawna's score is 18 away from 0, and Kaylynn's score is 14 away from 0.

c. Shawna; she is the only player with a positive score.

Focus on Higher Order Thinking

25. −9; it is 9 units away from 0 on a number line, and 6 is only 6 units away from 0.

26. Its opposite is *k* units to the right of 0 on the number line.

27. Cindy assumed the original integer is always positive. But if the original integer is negative, its opposite will be positive. Also, if the original integer is 0, its opposite will be 0.

28. The opposites are 10 and 4; −10 is 3 units to the left of −7, and 10 is the opposite of −10. −4 is 3 units to the right of −7, and 4 is the opposite of −4.

LESSON 1.2

Your Turn

2. −10 −8 −6 −4 −2 0 2 4 6 8 10

4, 2, 0, −3, −5, −6

3. −10 −8 −6 −4 −2 0 2 4 6 8 10

−10, −6, −1, 0, 2, 5, 8, 9

4. −10 is to the left of −2 on a number line, so −10 < −2.

5. −6 is to the left of 6 on a number line, so −6 < 6.

6. −7 is to the right of −8 on a number line, so −7 > −8.

7. −2 > −18; −18 < −2

8. −39 < 39; 39 > −39

Guided Practice

1. a. A C D E B

−10 −8 −6 −4 −2 0 2 4 6 8 10

b. −9 is to the left of the other temperatures on the number line, so it is the lowest, or coldest, temperature. City A was coldest. 10 is to the right of the other temperatures on the number line, so it is the greatest, or warmest, temperature. City B was warmest.

2. When graphed on a number line, the numbers are in this order: −9, −6, −3, 0, 1, 4, 8

3. When graphed on a number line, the numbers are in this order: −65, −13, −7, 7, 34, 55, 62

4. −17 > −22; −22 < −17

5. −9 is to the left of 2 on a number line, so −9 < 2.

6. −1 is to the right of −3 on a number line, so −1 >−3.

7. −8 is to the left of −4 on a number line, so −8 < −4.

8. −2 is to the right of −6 on a number line, so −2 > −6.

9. a. −3 is to the left of 2 on a number line, so −3 < 2.

b. 0 is to the right of −4 on a number line, so 0 > −4.

10. Sample answer: Temperatures in degrees Celsius can be 0° (freezing point for water), positive (above 0°), or negative (below 0°). You might compare two daily temperatures: 3 °C > −3 °C.

Independent Practice

11. a. A R L S B E

−10 −8 −6 −4 −2 0 2 4 6 8 10

b. E. Simpson, because 9 is the farthest to the right on the number line.

12. −197 is to the left of −110 on a number line, so −197 < −110.

13. 167 is to the right of −65 on a number line, so 167 > −65.

14. The values in order from greatest to least are 167, 15, −65, −110, −197, −200, so the planets in order of average surface temperature from greatest to least are Mercury, Earth, Mars, Jupiter, Uranus, Neptune.

15. a. C B D E A

−10 −8 −6 −4 −2 0 2 4 6 8 10

b. −5, −2, 2, 4, 7

16. −344 is to the left of −281 on a number line, so −344 < −281.

17. 377 is to the right of 249 on a number line, so 377 > 249.

18. 249 is to the right of −344 on a number line, so 249 > −344.

19. −344 is the farthest to the left on a number line, so Argentina has the lowest elevation.

20. Lisa won the game because she had the lowest score.

Focus on Higher Order Thinking

21. −3 °F; the warmer temperature is −3 °F.

22. The first number, *a*, will be the farthest to the right on the number line. The third number, *c*, will be farthest to the left on the number line. The second number, *b*, will be between *a* and *c* on the number line.

23. $-10, -3, 5, 16$ and $-3, 5, -10, 16$; both lists end with 16 because 16 is the greatest number and is farthest from zero. This would not be true for the second group of numbers because in that list, the least number, -16, would be at the beginning of the first list, not at the end.

LESSON 1.3

Your Turn

4. The temperature at night reached 13 °F below zero.
5. 12, because -12 is 12 units away from 0 on a number line.
6. 91, because 91 is 91 units away from 0 on a number line.
7. 55, because -55 is 55 units away from 0 on a number line.
8. 0, because 0 is 0 units away from 0 on a number line.
9. 88, because 88 is 88 units away from 0 on a number line.
10. 1, because 1 is 1 unit away from 0 on a number line.

Guided Practice

1. If a number is negative, then the number is less than its absolute value.
2. a. $-\$10$; it is a fee, so it represents a change of $-\$10$ in the amount of money Ryan has.

   b.

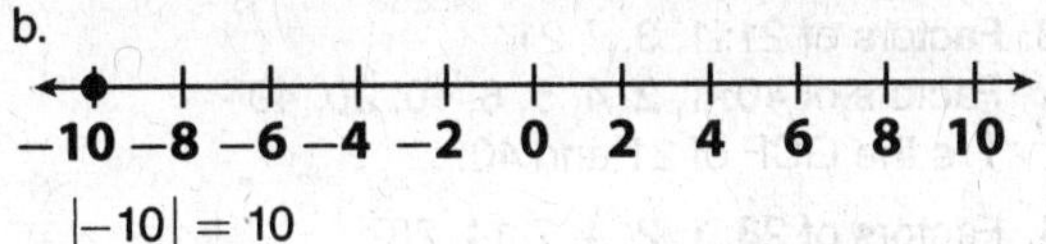

   $|-10| = 10$

3. a. Leo needs to earn more than 100 points.

   b. Gabrielle starts with 20 more points than Leo, so she needs to earn fewer than Leo to have a positive score.

   c. Sinea starts with 50 less points than Leo, so she needs to earn more than 50 points to have a higher score than Leo.
4. When a number is nonnegative, the absolute value of the number is equal to the number.

Independent Practice

5. The first week his balance changed by $+\$80$. The second week his balance changed by $-\$85$.
6. $-\$67$, because the absolute value of -67 is greater than the absolute value of 34.
7. a. February and March represent positive numbers, because Bertrand bought posters. January and April represent negative numbers, because Bertrand sold posters.

   b. April; He sold 28 posters, which can be represented by -28. The absolute value of -28 is 28, the greatest absolute value of any month.
8. The absolute value of -282 is 282, so Death Valley is 282 feet below sea level.
9. a. Let negative numbers represent paying money, and let positive numbers represent receiving money. The amounts on the table can be represented by $-5, 4, -1, 3, -2$.

   b. The spinner landing on red results in a change of $-\$5$ to Lisa's amount of money.
10. Freda's balance of $-\$42$ is greater than Sam's balance of $-\$36$, so Freda has more money credited to her card.
11. Use a negative integer to say that Emily's balance changed by $-\$55$; Use absolute value to say that Emily's balance is \$55 less.

Focus on Higher Order Thinking

12. Yes, it is possible. For example, $|-1| = 1$ and $|1| = 1$.
13. No; $-|-4| = -4$, and $|-(-4)| = |4| = 4$.
14. Angelique's technique only works if the original number is negative. The absolute value of a non-negative number is equal to the number itself, not its opposite.

MODULE 1

Ready to Go On?

1.

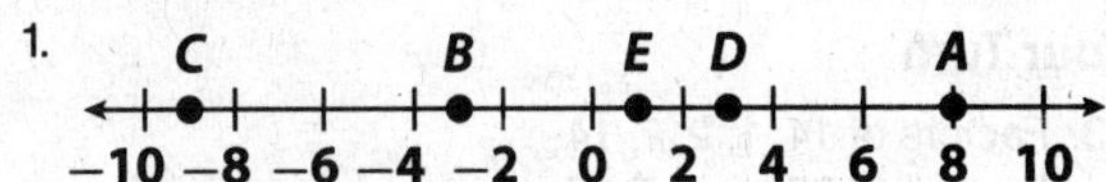

2. 22 is the opposite of -22
3. 0 is the opposite of itself
4. The numbers from left to right on a number line, or from least to greatest, are $-15, -5, -2, 1, 3, 8$.
5. -3 is greater than -15; $-3 > -15$.
6. 9 is greater than -10; $9 > -10$.

7–9.

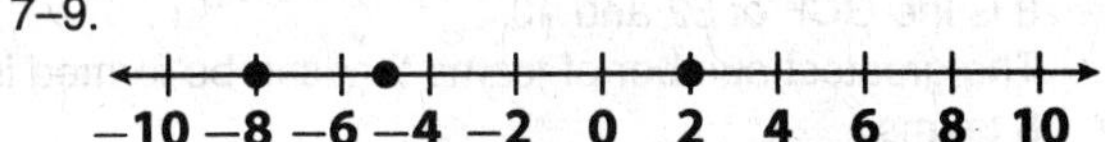

7. 2 is 2 units from 0 on the number line; $|2| = 2$.
8. -8 is 8 units from 0 on the number line; $|-8| = 8$.
9. -5 is 5 units from 0 on the number line; $|-5| = 5$.
10. Sample answer: Sam made a \$20 payment on his credit card. This represents a change of $-\$20$ in the amount he owes.

MODULE 2 *Factors and Multiples*

Are You Ready?

1. 7 × 1   7 × 2   7 × 3   7 × 4   7 × 5
 = 7   = 14   = 21   = 28   = 35
 7, 14, 21, 28, 35
2. 11 × 1   11 × 2   11 × 3   11 × 4   11 × 5
 = 11   = 22   = 33   = 44   = 55
 11, 22, 33, 44, 55
3. 15 × 1   15 × 2   15 × 3   15 × 4   15 × 5
 = 15   = 30   = 45   = 60   = 75
 The first five multiplies are 15, 30, 45, 60, 75.
4. The factors are 1, 2, 3, 4, 6, 8, 12, and 24.
5. The factors are 1, 2, 3, 4, 6, 9, 12, 18, and 36.
6. The factors are 1, 3, 5, 9, 15, and 45.
7. The factors are 1, 2, 4, 8, 16, and 32.
8. $8 \times 15 = 8 \times (10 + 5)$
 $= (8 \times 10) + (8 \times 5)$
 $= 80 + 40$
 $= 120$
9. $6 \times 17 = 6 \times (10 + 7)$
 $= (6 \times 10) + (6 \times 7)$
 $= 60 + 42$
 $= 102$

LESSON 2.1

Your Turn

3. Factors of 14: 1, 2, 7, 14
 Factors of 35: 1, 5, 7, 35
 7 is the GCF of 14 and 35.
4. Factors of 20: 1, 2, 4, 5, 10, 20
 Factors of 28: 1, 2, 4, 7, 14, 28
 4 is the GCF of 20 and 28.
5. Find the greatest common factor of 32 and 40.
 Factors of 32: 1, 2, 4, 8, 16, 32
 Factors of 40: 1, 2, 4, 5, 8, 10, 20, 40
 8 is the GCF of 32 and 40.
 The greatest number of teams that can be formed is 8 teams.
 Find the number of times 8 goes into 32 and into 40.
 $32 \div 8 = 4$
 $40 \div 8 = 5$
 Each team will have 4 girls and 5 boys.

Guided Practice

1.

Factors of 16:	①	②	④	⑧	16			
Factors of 24:	①	②	3	④	6	⑧	12	24

 The common factors of 16 and 24 are 1, 2, 4, and 8.
 The possible numbers of vests that Lee can make are 1, 2, 4, and 8.
 The GCF of 16 and 24 is 8.
 The greatest number of vests Lee can make is 8.

2. Factors of 36: 1, 2, 3, 4, 6, 9, 12, 18, 36
 Factors of 45: 1, 3, 5, 9, 15, 45
 The GCF of 36 and 45 is 9.
 $(9 \times 4) + (9 \times 5) = (9) \times (4 + 5)$
3. Factors of 75: 1, 3, 5, 15, 25, 75
 Factors of 90: 1, 2, 3, 5, 6, 9, 10, 15, 18, 30, 45, 90
 The GCF of 75 and 90 is 15.
 $(15 \times 5) + (15 \times 6) = (15) \times (5 + 6)$
4. 1; if it is not, you did not find the correct GCF of the original numbers.

Independent Practice

5. 1, 2, 3, 4, 6, 12
6. 1, 2, 5, 10, 25, 50
7. 1, 3, 13, 39
8. 1, 2, 4, 8, 16, 32, 64
9. Factors of 40: 1, 2, 4, 5, 8, 10, 20, 40
 Factors of 48: 1, 2, 3, 4, 6, 8, 12, 16, 24, 48
 8 is the GCF of 40 and 48.
10. Factors of 30: 1, 2, 3, 5, 6, 10, 15, 30
 Factors of 45: 1, 3, 5, 9, 15, 45
 15 is the GCF of 30 and 45.
11. Factors of 10: 1, 2, 5, 10
 Factors of 45: 1, 3, 5, 9, 15, 45
 5 is the GCF of 10 and 45.
12. Factors of 25: 1, 5, 25
 Factors of 90: 1, 2, 3, 5, 6, 9, 10, 15, 18, 30, 45, 90
 5 is the GCF of 25 and 90.
13. Factors of 21: 1, 3, 7, 21
 Factors of 40: 1, 2, 4, 5, 8, 10, 20, 40
 1 is the GCF of 21 and 40.
14. Factors of 28: 1, 2, 4, 7, 14, 28
 Factors of 70: 1, 2, 5, 7, 10, 14, 35, 70
 14 is the GCF of 21 and 70.
15. Factors of 60: 1, 2, 3, 4, 5, 6, 10, 12, 15, 20, 30, 60
 Factors of 72: 1, 2, 3, 4, 6, 8, 9, 12, 18, 24, 36, 72
 12 is the GCF of 60 and 72.
16. Factors of 45: 1, 3, 5, 9, 15, 45
 Factors of 81: 1, 3, 9, 27, 81
 9 is the GCF of 45 and 81.
17. Factors of 28: 1, 2, 4, 7, 14, 28
 Factors of 32: 1, 2, 4, 8, 16, 32
 4 is the GCF of 28 and 32.
18. Factors of 55: 1, 5, 11, 55
 Factors of 77: 1, 7, 11, 77
 11 is the GCF of 55 and 77.
19. Factors of 24: 1, 2, 3, 4, 6, 8, 12, 24
 Factors of 32: 1, 2, 4, 8, 16, 32
 1, 2, 4, and 8 are the common factors of 24 and 32.
 The possible numbers of shelves are 1, 2, 4, or 8 shelves.

20. Factors of 56: 1, 2, 4, 7, 8, 14, 28, 56
Factors of 96: 1, 2, 3, 4, 6, 8, 12, 16, 24, 32, 48, 96
8 is the GCF of 56 and 96.
The greatest number of columns in which the two bands can be arranged with the same number of marchers in each column is 8 columns.
$56 \div 8 = 7$
$96 \div 8 = 12$
$7 + 12 = 19$
There will be 19 marchers in each column.

21. Factors of 12: 1, 2, 3, 4, 6, 12
Factors of 42: 1, 2, 3, 6, 7, 14, 21, 42
6 is the GCF of 12 and 42.
The greatest number of groups that can be formed is 6 groups.
$12 \div 6 = 2$
$42 \div 6 = 7$
There will be 2 coaches and 7 players in each of the groups.

22. Factors of 63: 1, 3, 7, 21, 63
Factors of 84: 1, 2, 3, 4, 6, 7, 12, 14, 21, 28, 42, 84
21 is the GCF of 63 and 84.
The greatest number of plates that can be made using all the appetizers is 21 plates.
$63 \div 21 = 3$
$84 \div 21 = 4$
There will be 3 spring rolls and 4 cheese cubes on each of the plates.

23. Factors of 56: 1, 2, 4, 7, 8, 14, 28, 56
Factors of 64: 1, 2, 4, 8, 16, 32, 64
8 is the GCF of 56 and 64.
$56 \div 8 = 7$
$64 \div 8 = 8$
$8 \times (7 + 8) = 8 \times 15$

24. Factors of 48: 1, 2, 3, 4, 6, 8, 12, 16, 24, 48
Factors of 14: 1, 2, 7, 14
2 is the GCF of 48 and 14.
$48 \div 2 = 24$
$14 \div 2 = 7$
$2 \times (24 + 7) = 2 \times 31$

25. Factors of 30: 1, 2, 3, 5, 6, 10, 15, 30
Factors of 54: 1, 2, 3, 6, 9, 18, 27, 54
6 is the GCF of 30 and 54.
$30 \div 6 = 5$
$54 \div 6 = 9$
$6 \times (5 + 9) = 6 \times 14$

26. Factors of 24: 1, 2, 3, 4, 6, 8, 12, 24
Factors of 40: 1, 2, 4, 5, 8, 10, 20, 40
8 is the GCF of 24 and 40.
$24 \div 8 = 3$
$40 \div 8 = 5$
$8 \times (3 + 5) = 8 \times 8$

27. Factors of 55: 1, 5, 11, 55
Factors of 66: 1, 2, 3, 6, 11, 22, 33, 66
11 is the GCF of 55 and 66.
$55 \div 11 = 5$
$66 \div 11 = 6$
$11 \times (5 + 6) = 11 \times 11$

28. Factors of 49: 1, 7, 49
Factors of 63: 1, 3, 7, 9, 21, 63
7 is the GCF of 49 and 63.
$49 \div 7 = 7$
$63 \div 7 = 9$
$7 \times (7 + 9) = 7 \times 16$

29. Factors of 40: 1, 2, 4, 5, 8, 10, 20, 40
Factors of 25: 1, 5, 25
5 is the GCF of 40 and 25.
$40 \div 5 = 8$
$25 \div 5 = 5$
$5 \times (8 + 5) = 5 \times 13$

30. Factors of 63: 1, 3, 7, 9, 21, 63
Factors of 15: 1, 3, 5, 15
3 is the GCF of 63 and 15.
$63 \div 3 = 21$
$15 \div 3 = 5$
$3 \times (21 + 5) = 3 \times 26$

31. The greatest common factor of two numbers is sometimes 1 because 1 is a factor of all whole numbers, and some pairs of whole numbers have no common factors other than 1. For example, 7 and 16 have no common factors other than 1.

Focus on Higher Order Thinking

32. Yes; the GCF of 120 and 36 is 12, so $120 - 36$ can be written as $12 \times 10 - 12 \times 3$, which is $12 \times (10 - 3)$ or 12×7.

33. To find the greatest common factor of three numbers, find the factors of all three numbers and take the greatest factor that is common to all three. For example, for the GCF of 6, 9, and 12, the factors of 6 are 1, 2, 3, and 6; the factors of 9 are 1, 3, and 9; and the factors of 12 are 1, 2, 3, 4, 6, and 12. So, the GCF is 3.

34. Xiao used a common factor that is not the greatest common factor.
Factors of 60: 1, 2, 3, 4, 5, 6, 10, 12, 15, 20, 30, 60
Factors of 90: 1, 3, 5, 6, 9, 10, 15, 18, 30, 90
The GCF of 60 and 90 is 30. He should have written the sum as $30 \times (2 + 3)$.

LESSON 2.2

Your Turn

2. The LCM of 4 and 9 is 36.
Multiples of 4: 4, 8, 12, 16, 20, 24, 28, 32, 36, 40
Multiples of 9: 9, 18, 27, 36, 45, 54, 63, 72, 81, 90

Guided Practice

1. Multiples of 9: 9, 18, 27, 36, 45, 54, 63, 72, 81, 90, 99
   Multiples of 12: 12, 24, 36, 48, 60, 72, 84, 96
   Common multiples of 9 and 12: 36, 72
   The 36th and 72nd visits will have a free beverage and a free appetizer.
   The first visit to have a free beverage and a free appetizer is the 36th visit.
2. Yes; the product of any two numbers is a common multiple of the two. If there are no lesser common multiples, then the product is the LCM.

Independent Practice

3. Multiples of 8: 8, 16, 24, 32, 40, 48, 56, 64, 72, 80
   Multiples of 56: 56, 112
   The LCM of 8 and 56 is 56.
4. Multiples of 25: 25, 50, 75, 100
   Multiples of 50: 50, 100
   The LCM of 25 and 50 is 50.
5. Multiples of 12: 12, 24, 36, 48, 60, 72, 84, 96
   Multiples of 30: 30, 60, 90
   The LCM of 12 and 30 is 60.
6. Multiples of 6: 6, 12, 18, 24, 30, 36, 42, 48
   Multiples of 10: 10, 20, 30, 40, 50, 60, 70
   The LCM of 6 and 10 is 30.
7. Multiples of 16: 16, 32, 48, 64, 80, 96
   Multiples of 24: 24, 48, 72, 96
   The LCM of 16 and 24 is 48.
8. Multiples of 14: 14, 28, 42, 56, 70
   Multiples of 21: 21, 42, 63, 84
   The LCM of 14 and 21 is 42.
9. Multiples of 9: 9, 18, 27, 36, 45, 54, 63
   Multiples of 15: 15, 30, 45, 60
   The LCM of 9 and 15 is 45.
10. Multiples of 5: 5, 10, 15, 20, 25, 30, 35, 40, 45, 50, 55
    Multiples of 11: 11, 22, 33, 44, 55, 66
    The LCM of 5 and 11 is 55.
11. a. Multiples of 3: 3, 6, 9, 12, 15, 18, 21, 24, 27, 30, 33
       Multiples of 5: 5, 10, 15, 20, 25, 30, 35, 40
       The LCM of 3 and 5 is 15
       Kevin will water both plants together on February 15.

    b. No; there are only 28 or 29 days in February, and the next common multiple of 3 and 5 is 30.
12. LCM; the LCM is a multiple of both numbers, so it is greater than or equal to the greater number; the GCF is a factor of both numbers, so it is less than or equal to the lesser number.
13. Multiples of 8: 8, 16, 24, 32, 40, 48, 56, 64, 72, 80
    Multiples of 10: 10, 20, 30, 40, 50, 60, 70
    The LCM of 8 and 10 is 40.
    Both trains will next arrive at the station in 40 minutes.
14. Multiples of 10: 10, 20, 30, 40, 50, 60, 70
    Multiples of 12: 12, 24, 36, 48, 60, 72, 84, 96
    The LCM of 10 and 12 is 60.
    Both trains will next arrive at the station in 60 minutes.
15. Multiples of 8: 8, 16, 24, 32, 40, 48, 56, 64, 72, 80, 88, 96, 104, 112, 120
    Multiples of 10: 10, 20, 30, 40, 50, 60, 70, 80, 90, 100, 110, 120
    Multiples of 12: 12, 24, 36, 48, 60, 72, 84, 96, 108, 120
    The LCM of 8, 10 and 12 is 120.
    All three trains will next arrive at the station in 120 minutes.
16. Multiples of 4: 4, 8, 12, 16, 20, 24, 28, 32
    Multiples of 7: 7, 14, 21, 28, 35, 42, 49
    Both will be watered on day 28; the next days will be multiples of 28, so determine the multiples of 28.
    Multiples of 28: 28, 56, 84, 112
    The plants will be watered together on day 28, day 56, day 84, and so on.

Focus on Higher Order Thinking

17. The LCM is the greater of the two numbers. For example, the LCM of 4 and 8 is 8.
18. The LCM is the product of the two numbers. For example, the LCM of 4 and 9 is 36.
19. Factors of 60: 1, 2, 3, 4, 5, 6, 10, 12, 15, 20, 30, 60
    $12 - 5 = 7$
    Multiples of 12: 12, 24, 36, 48, 60
    Multiples of 5: 5, 10, 15, 20, 25, 30, 35, 40, 45, 50, 55, 60
    5 and 12; 60 is a multiple of each of its factors which are 1, 2, 3, 4, 5, 6, 10, 12, 15, 20, 30, and 60. The factors with a difference of 7 are 5 and 12, and their LCM is 60.
20. To find the LCM of three numbers, list the multiples of each and take the least multiple that is common to all three. For example, find the LCM of 6, 8, and 12. First, list the multiples of each. The multiples of 6 are 6, 12, 18, 24, ... The multiples of 8 are 8, 16, 24, 32, ... The multiples of 12 are 12, 24, 36, ... The LCM of 6, 8, and 12 is 24.

MODULE 2

Ready to Go On?

1. Factors of 20: 1, 2, 4, 5, 10, 20
   Factors of 32: 1, 2, 4, 8, 16, 32
   4 is the GCF of 20 and 32.
2. Factors of 24: 1, 2, 3, 4, 6, 8, 12, 24
   Factors of 56: 1, 2, 4, 7, 8, 14, 28, 56
   8 is the GCF of 24 and 56.
3. Factors of 36: 1, 2, 3, 4, 6, 9, 12, 18, 36
   Factors of 90: 1, 2, 3, 5, 6, 9, 10, 15, 18, 30, 45, 90
   18 is the GCF of 36 and 90.
4. Factors of 45: 1, 3, 5, 9, 15, 45
   Factors of 75: 1, 3, 5, 15, 25, 75
   15 is the GCF of 45 and 75.

5. Factors of 28: 1, 2, 4, 7, 14, 28
   Factors of 32: 1, 2, 4, 8, 16, 32
   4 is the GCF of 28 and 32.
   The greatest number of groups that the principal can make is 4.
6. Factors of 32: 1, 2, 4, 8, 16, 32
   Factors of 20: 1, 2, 4, 5, 10, 20
   4 is the GCF of 32 and 20.
   $32 \div 4 = 8$
   $20 \div 4 = 5$
   $4 \times (8 + 5) = 4 \times 13$
7. Factors of 18: 1, 2, 3, 6, 9, 18
   Factors of 27: 1, 3, 9, 27
   9 is the GCF of 18 and 27.
   $18 \div 9 = 2$
   $27 \div 9 = 3$
   $9 \times (2 + 3) = 9 \times 5$
8. Multiples of 6: 6, 12, 18, 24, 30
   Multiples of 12: 12, 24, 36, 48
   The LCM of 6 and 12 is 12.
9. Multiples of 6: 6, 12, 18, 24, 30, 36, 42
   Multiples of 10: 10, 20, 30, 40, 50
   The LCM of 6 and 10 is 30.
10. Multiples of 8: 8, 16, 24, 32, 40, 48, 56, 64, 72, 80
    Multiples of 9: 9, 18, 27, 36, 45, 54, 63, 72
    The LCM of 8 and 9 is 72.
11. Multiples of 9: 9, 18, 27, 36, 45, 54
    Multiples of 12: 12, 24, 36, 48
    The LCM of 9 and 12 is 36.
12. Multiples of 3: 3, 6, 9, 12, 15, 18, 21
    Multiples of 5: 5, 10, 15, 20, 25, 30
    The LCM of 3 and 5 is 15
    She will run and swim again on the same day in 15 days.
13. Sample answer: Problems in which two different amounts must be split into the same number of groups can be solved using the GCF; problems with events that occur on different schedules can be solved using the LCM.

MODULE 3 *Rational Numbers*

Are You Ready?

1. $\frac{7}{2}$

   $\frac{2}{2}+\frac{2}{2}+\frac{2}{2}+\frac{1}{2}$

   $1+1+1+\frac{1}{2}$

   $3\frac{1}{2}$

2. $\frac{12}{5}$

   $\frac{5}{5}+\frac{5}{5}+\frac{2}{5}$

   $1+1+\frac{2}{5}$

   $2\frac{2}{5}$

3. $\frac{11}{7}$

   $\frac{7}{7}+\frac{4}{7}$

   $1+\frac{4}{7}$

   $1\frac{4}{7}$

4. $\frac{15}{4}$

   $\frac{4}{4}+\frac{4}{4}+\frac{4}{4}+\frac{3}{4}$

   $1+1+1+\frac{3}{4}$

   $3\frac{3}{4}$

5. $2\frac{1}{2}$

   $1+1+\frac{1}{2}$

   $\frac{2}{2}+\frac{2}{2}+\frac{1}{2}$

   $\frac{5}{2}$

6. $4\frac{3}{5}$

   $1+1+1+1+\frac{3}{5}$

   $\frac{5}{5}+\frac{5}{5}+\frac{5}{5}+\frac{5}{5}+\frac{3}{5}$

   $\frac{23}{5}$

7. $3\frac{4}{9}$

   $1+1+1+\frac{4}{9}$

   $\frac{9}{9}+\frac{9}{9}+\frac{9}{9}+\frac{4}{9}$

   $\frac{31}{9}$

8. $2\frac{5}{7}$

   $1+1+\frac{5}{7}$

   $\frac{7}{7}+\frac{7}{7}+\frac{5}{7}$

   $\frac{19}{7}$

9. $8.86 > 8.65$
10. $0.732 < 0.75$
11. $0.22 > 0.022$
12. 0.98, 0.34, 0.27

LESSON 3.1

Your Turn

3. $-15 = -\frac{15}{1}$

4. $0.31 = \frac{31}{100}$

5. $4\frac{5}{9} = \frac{4 \times 9 + 5}{9}$

   $= \frac{36+5}{9}$

   $= \frac{41}{9}$

6. $62 = \frac{62}{1}$

7. All whole numbers and integers are rational numbers. All integers are rational numbers. Some integers are not whole numbers. Some rational numbers are not integers or whole numbers.

8–11.

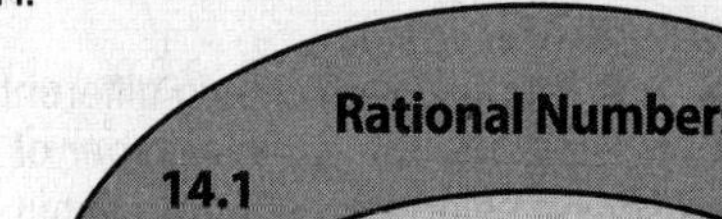
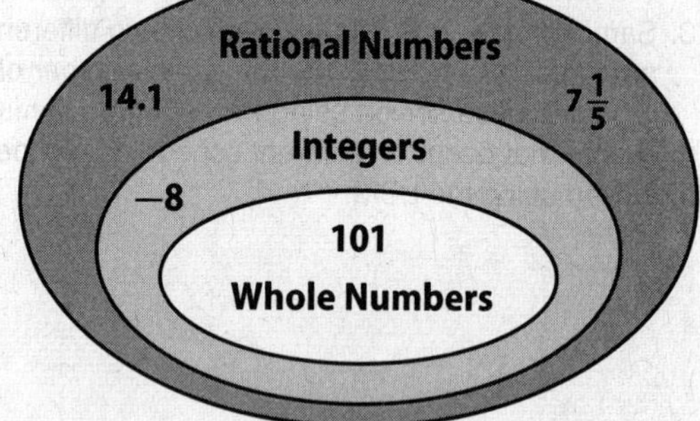

8. 14.1 belongs in the set of rational numbers.
9. $7\frac{1}{5}$ belongs in the set of rational numbers.
10. −8 belongs in the sets of integers and rational numbers.
11. 101 belongs in the sets of whole numbers, integers, and rational numbers.

Guided Practice

1. a. 4 rolls of ribbon divided evenly among the 5 friends. $4 \div 5$.

   b. $\frac{4}{5}$ roll

2. $0.7 = \frac{7}{10}$

3. $-29 = \frac{-29}{1}$

4. $8\frac{1}{3} = \frac{8 \times 3 + 1}{3}$

$= \frac{24 + 1}{3}$

$= \frac{25}{3}$

5–6.

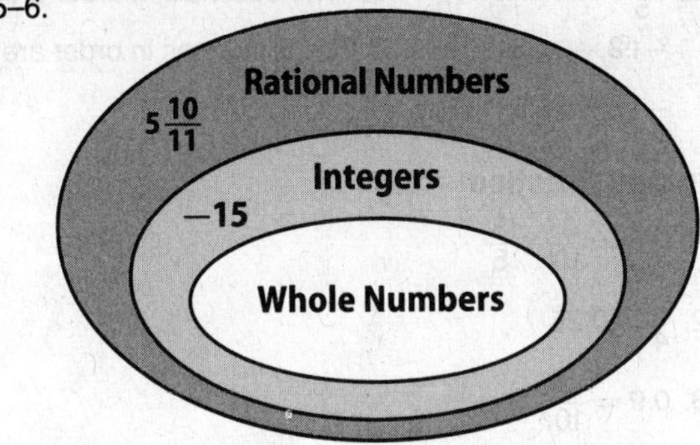

5. −15 belongs to the sets of integers and rational numbers.

6. $5\frac{10}{11}$ belongs to the set of rational numbers.

7. When written in the form $\frac{a}{b}$, noninteger rational numbers have a denominator that does not divide evenly into the numerator.

Independent Practice

8–9. Sample answer:

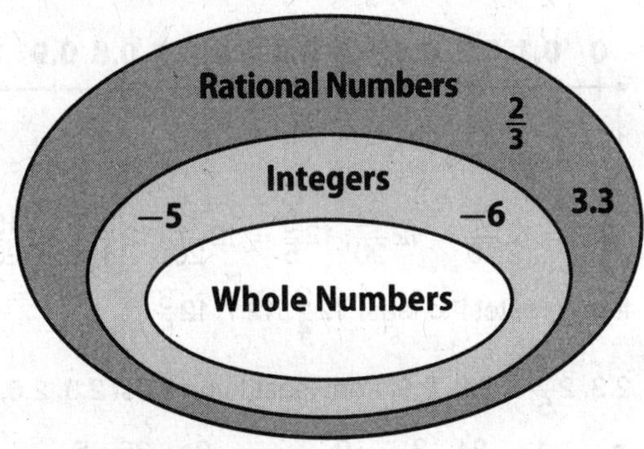

8. Sample answer: −5, −6

9. Sample answer: $\frac{2}{3}$, 3.3

10. a. $\frac{3 + 2 + 4 + 5}{4} = \frac{14}{4}$, or $3\frac{1}{2}$ pieces of fruit

b. Baxter and Hendrick each brought less than $3\frac{1}{2}$ pieces of fruit

c. $\frac{5 + 2 + 3 + 7}{4} = \frac{17}{4}$, or $4\frac{1}{4}$ bottles of water

11. $22 \div 5 = \frac{\$22}{5}$, or \$4.40

12. $2 \div 5$; $\frac{2}{5}$

13. A Venn diagram can represent set relationships visually.

14. $\frac{\$108}{4} = \$27$. 27 belongs in the sets of whole numbers, integers, and rational numbers.

15. $\frac{\$35}{2} = \$17\frac{1}{2}$. $17\frac{1}{2}$ belongs in the set of rational numbers.

16. Jason owes a total of \$29 for water. There are 4 roommates. $\$\frac{29}{4} = \$7\frac{1}{4}$. $7\frac{1}{4}$ belongs to the set of rational numbers.

17. If Lynn fills her 16 cup watering can half full, it'll hold 8 cups of water. She divides the 8 cups between 15 plants. Each plant gets $\frac{8}{15}$ cup.

Focus on Higher Order Thinking

18. $24 \div 6 = 4$, which is a whole number. $\frac{24}{6}$ belongs to the set of whole numbers and the set of integers as well as the set of rational numbers.

19. The oval representing the set of integers and the oval representing the set of whole numbers are inside of the oval representing the set of rational numbers.

20. No; every whole number is an integer.

LESSON 3.2

Your Turn

2. The opposites are −7, 3.5, −2.25, and $-9\frac{1}{3}$.

4–7.

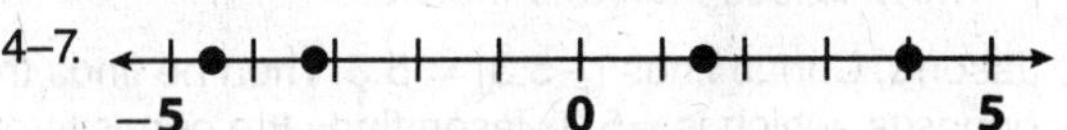

4. −4.5 is 4.5 units from 0; $|-4.5| = 4.5$.

5. $1\frac{1}{2}$ is $1\frac{1}{2}$ units from 0; $\left|1\frac{1}{2}\right| = 1\frac{1}{2}$.

6. 4 is 4 units from 0; $|4| = 4$

7. $-3\frac{1}{4}$ is $3\frac{1}{4}$ units from 0; $\left|-3\frac{1}{4}\right| = 3\frac{1}{4}$

Guided Practice

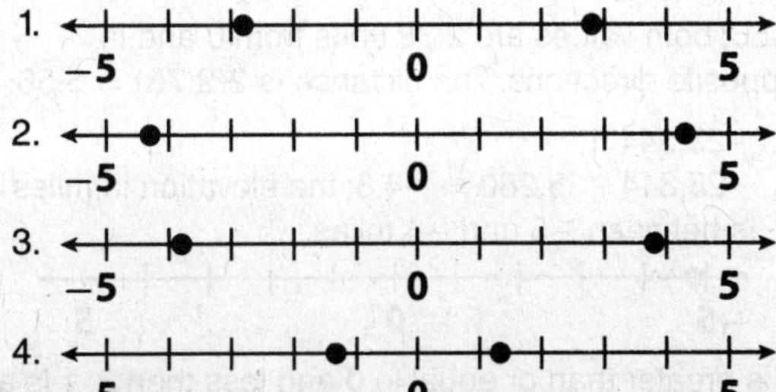

5. The opposite of 3.78 is −3.78.

6. The opposite of $-7\frac{5}{12}$ is $7\frac{5}{12}$.

7. The opposite of 0 is 0.
8. The opposite of 4.2 is −4.2.
9. The opposite of 12.1 is −12.1.
10. The opposite of 2.6 is −2.6.
11. They are the same distance from 0 on the number line.
12. 5.23 is 5.23 units from 0 on a number line; $|5.23| = 5.23$.
13. $-4\frac{2}{11}$ is $4\frac{2}{11}$ units from 0 on a number line; $\left|-4\frac{2}{11}\right| = 4\frac{2}{11}$.
14. 0 is 0 units away from 0; $|0| = 0$
15. $-6\frac{3}{5}$ is $6\frac{3}{5}$ units away from 0; $\left|-6\frac{3}{5}\right| = 6\frac{3}{5}$
16. −2.12 is 2.12 units away from 0; $|-2.12| = 2.12$
17. 8.2 is 8.2 units away from 0; $|8.2| = 8.2$
18. The opposite of a nonzero rational number is a number that has the same absolute value but a different sign. For example, −2.7 is the opposite of 2.7 because both have absolute value 2.7, but opposite signs.

Independent Practice

19. a. Giardi \$85.23, Lewis −\$20.44, Stein \$116.33, Yuan −\$13.50, Wenner \$9.85.
    b. Wenner, because he cannot pay off Girardi or Stein's balance.
    c. Stein; when you find the absolute value of each balance, Stein's is the greatest.
20. a. Trina; $|-85.6|$ is less than $|87.9|$.
    b. No; the opposite of −85.6 meters is 85.6 meters, which is less than 87.9 meters.
21. Jason's; Carlos finds $|-5.3| = 5.3$. Then he finds the opposite, which is −5.3. Jason finds the opposite of −5.3, which is 5.3. Then he finds $|5.3|$, which is 5.3.
22. a. The student made the least negative number that could be formed with the given digits but did not take into account the absolute value symbols.
    b. $|-35.7|$

Focus on Higher Order Thinking

23. To the left; 8.85 is greater than 8.8, so −8.85 is farther from 0 on the number line.
24. 5.56; both values are 2.78 units from 0 and in opposite directions. The distance is 2(2.78) = 5.56.
25. a. −25,344 ft
    b. −25,344 ÷ 5,280 = −4.8; the elevation in miles is between −5 and −4 miles.
    c. 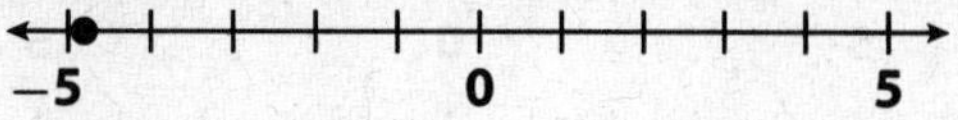

26. It is greater than or equal to 0 and less than 2; 1 is a possible solution.

LESSON 3.3

Your Turn

3. $\frac{3}{5} = 0.6$ and $\frac{7}{10} = 0.7$. The decimals in order are 0.15, 0.6, 0.7, 0.85. The numbers in order are 0.15, $\frac{3}{5}$, $\frac{7}{10}$, 0.85.
5. $1\frac{2}{5} = 1.4$ and $1\frac{9}{10} = 1.9$. The decimals in order are −1.8, −1.25, 1, 1.4, 1.9. The bike times in order are −1.8, −1.25, 1, $1\frac{2}{5}$, $1\frac{9}{10}$.

Guided Practice

1. $0.6 = \frac{6}{10} = \frac{3}{5}$
2. $\frac{1}{4} = 0.25$
3. $0.9 = \frac{9}{10}$
4. $0.1 = \frac{1}{10}$
5. $\frac{3}{10} = 0.3$
6. $1.4 = 1\frac{4}{10} = 1\frac{2}{5}$
7. $\frac{4}{5} = \frac{8}{10} = 0.8$
8. $0.4 = \frac{4}{10} = \frac{2}{5}$
9. $\frac{6}{8} = \frac{3}{4} = 0.75$
10. 0.75, $\frac{1}{2} = 0.5$, 0.4, $\frac{1}{5} = 0.2$

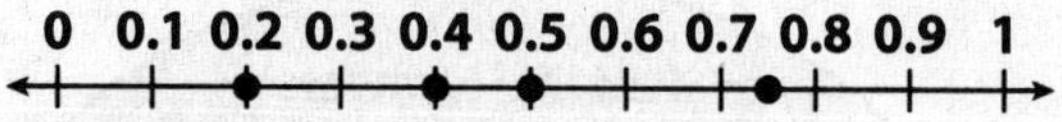

$\frac{1}{5}$, 0.4, $\frac{1}{2}$, 0.75

11. $12.7 = 12\frac{7}{10} = 12\frac{14}{20}$, $12\frac{3}{5} = 12\frac{12}{20}$, $12\frac{3}{4} = 12\frac{15}{20}$; from greatest to least $12\frac{3}{4}$, 12.7, $12\frac{3}{5}$.
12. 2.3, $2\frac{4}{5} = 2.8$, 2.6; from least to greatest 2.3, 2.6, $2\frac{4}{5}$
13. $0.5 = \frac{1}{2} = \frac{24}{48}$, $\frac{3}{16} = \frac{9}{48}$, $0.75 = \frac{3}{4} = \frac{36}{48}$, $\frac{5}{48}$; from least to greatest $\frac{5}{48}$, $\frac{3}{16}$, 0.5, 0.75
14. 0.5, $\frac{1}{5} = 0.2$, 0.35, $\frac{12}{25} = 0.48$, $\frac{4}{5} = 0.8$; from least to greatest $\frac{1}{5}$, 0.35, $\frac{12}{25}$, 0.5, $\frac{4}{5}$
15. $\frac{3}{4} = \frac{15}{20}$, $-\frac{7}{10} = -\frac{14}{20}$, $-\frac{3}{4} = -\frac{15}{20}$, $\frac{8}{10} = \frac{16}{20}$; from least to greatest $-\frac{3}{4}$, $-\frac{7}{10}$, $\frac{3}{4}$, $\frac{8}{10}$

16. $-\frac{3}{8} = -0.375$, $\frac{5}{16} = 0.3125$, -0.65, $\frac{2}{4} = 0.5$; from least to greatest $-0.65, -\frac{3}{8}, \frac{5}{16}, \frac{2}{4}$

17. -2.3, $-2\frac{4}{5} = -2.8$, -2.6; from least to greatest $-2\frac{4}{5}, -2.6, -2.3$

18. -0.6, $-\frac{5}{8} = -0.625$, $-\frac{7}{12} = -.5833\ldots$, -0.72; from least to greatest $-0.72, -\frac{5}{8}, -0.6, -\frac{7}{12}$

19. 1.45, $1\frac{1}{2} = 1.5$, $1\frac{1}{3} = 1.33\ldots$, 1.2; from least to greatest $1.2, 1\frac{1}{3}, 1.45, 1\frac{1}{2}$

20. from least to greatest $-0.35, -0.3, 0.5, 0.55$

21. Sample answer: -7.5 °F; -7.5 °F < -7.2 °F; the graph of -7.5 °F is to the left of the graph of -7.2 °F.

Independent Practice

22. a. Albert; $\frac{1}{2} = 0.5$ and $0.5 > 0.4$, so $\frac{1}{2} > 0.4$ or $0.4 < \frac{1}{2}$.

b. Rosa; $\frac{2}{5} = 0.4$ and $0.4 > 0.25$, so $\frac{2}{5} > 0.25$ or $0.25 < \frac{2}{5}$.

c. Rosa; she spent $0.4 + \frac{2}{5} = 0.4 + 0.4 = 0.8$; Albert spent $0.25 + \frac{1}{2} = 0.25 + 0.5 = 0.75$

23. a. $4.3 = 4\frac{3}{10} = 4\frac{36}{120}$, $5.5 = 5\frac{1}{2} = 5\frac{60}{120}$, $6\frac{1}{6} = 6\frac{20}{120}$, $\frac{15}{4} = 3\frac{3}{4} = 3\frac{90}{120}$, $4\frac{3}{8} = 4\frac{45}{120}$; The weights from greatest to least are $6\frac{1}{6}, 5.5, 4\frac{3}{8}, 4.3, \frac{15}{4}$.

b. Claire, Peter, Brenda, and Jim will receive a free movie ticket; Micah will not receive a free movie ticket.

c. Yes; the smallest donation is is $\frac{15}{4}$ pounds. $\frac{1}{2}$ is equal to $\frac{2}{4}$ pound. $\frac{15}{4} + \frac{2}{4} = \frac{17}{4} = 4\frac{1}{4} = 4.25$ pounds which is enough to win a free movie coupon.

24. a. $1\frac{7}{8} = 1.875$, $-1\frac{1}{8} = -1.125$, $2\frac{1}{2} = 2.5$; from least to greatest $-1\frac{1}{8}, -0.75, 1\frac{7}{8}, 2\frac{1}{2}, 3.1$

b. Kitten D

c. Mean weight

$$= \frac{-0.75 + 1.875 + 3.1 + (-1.125) + 2.5}{5}$$

$$= \frac{5.6}{5} = 1.12$$

Kitten D had the smallest birth weight, $-1\frac{1}{8}$.

$1.12 - (-1.125) = 2.245$

Kitten C had the largest birth weight, 3.1.

$3.1 - 1.12 = 1.98$

Kitten C's birth weight differed most from the mean.

Focus on Higher Order Thinking

25. Negative numbers are less than zero and positive numbers are greater than zero, so the order would be negative, zero, positive.

26. \$11.50; $-$\$11.50 and $-$\$10.75 represent debts of \$11.50 and \$10.75. \$11.50 is a greater amount than \$10.75.

27. The order of the absolute values will be the reverse of the order of the negative rational numbers. The least negative number will be farthest from 0 on a number line. The greatest negative number will be closest to 0 on a number line.

MODULE 3

Ready to Go On?

1. $3 \div 5$ is the same as $\frac{3}{5}$.

2. $5\frac{1}{6} = \frac{5 \times 6 + 1}{6}$

$= \frac{30 + 1}{6}$

$= \frac{31}{6}$

3. $-12 = -\frac{12}{1}$

4. -12 belongs to the sets of integers and rational numbers.

5. $\frac{7}{8}$ belongs to the set of rational numbers.

6. 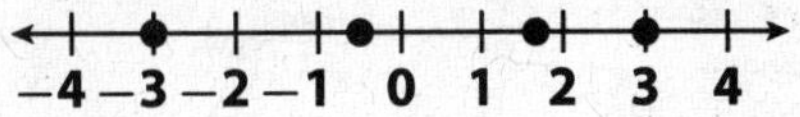

7. $-\frac{1}{3}, \frac{7}{12}$

8. $|9.8| = 9.8$; $\left|-\frac{10}{3}\right| = \frac{10}{3}$

9. $18\frac{1}{2} = 18.5$, $-\frac{1}{4} = -0.25$; from greatest to least: $21, 18\frac{1}{2}, 6.2, 1.75, -\frac{1}{4}, -4, -5.9$

10. Convert so that all numbers are in the same form, either as all decimals or all fractions with the same denominator. Order them as they appear on the number line: left to right for least to greatest.

Solutions Key

Number Operations

MODULE 4 *Operations with Fractions*

Are You Ready?

1. $\frac{9}{4} = \frac{4}{4} + \frac{4}{4} + \frac{1}{4}$

$= 1 + 1 + \frac{1}{4}$

$= 2 + \frac{1}{4}$

$= 2\frac{1}{4}$

2. $\frac{8}{3} = \frac{3}{3} + \frac{3}{3} + \frac{2}{3}$

$= 1 + 1 + \frac{2}{3}$

$= 2 + \frac{2}{3}$

$= 2\frac{2}{3}$

3. $\frac{23}{6} = \frac{6}{6} + \frac{6}{6} + \frac{6}{6} + \frac{5}{6}$

$= 1 + 1 + 1 + \frac{5}{6}$

$= 3 + \frac{5}{6}$

$= 3\frac{5}{6}$

4. $\frac{11}{2} = \frac{2}{2} + \frac{2}{2} + \frac{2}{2} + \frac{2}{2} + \frac{2}{2} + \frac{1}{2}$

$= 1 + 1 + 1 + 1 + 1 + \frac{1}{2}$

$= 5 + \frac{1}{2}$

$= 5\frac{1}{2}$

5. $\frac{17}{5} = \frac{5}{5} + \frac{5}{5} + \frac{5}{5} + \frac{2}{5}$

$= 1 + 1 + 1 + \frac{2}{5}$

$= 3 + \frac{2}{5}$

$= 3\frac{2}{5}$

6. $\frac{15}{8} = \frac{8}{8} + \frac{7}{8}$

$= 1 + \frac{7}{8}$

$= 1\frac{7}{8}$

7. $\frac{33}{10} = \frac{10}{10} + \frac{10}{10} + \frac{10}{10} + \frac{3}{10}$

$= 1 + 1 + 1 + \frac{3}{10}$

$= 3 + \frac{3}{10}$

$= 3\frac{3}{10}$

8. $\frac{29}{12} = 2 + \frac{5}{12}$

$= 2\frac{5}{12}$

9. $6 \times 5 = 30$
10. $8 \times 9 = 72$
11. $10 \times 11 = 110$
12. $7 \times 8 = 56$
13. $9 \times 7 = 63$
14. $8 \times 6 = 48$
15. $9 \times 11 = 99$
16. $11 \times 12 = 132$
17. $35 \div 7 = 5$
18. $56 \div 8 = 7$
19. $28 \div 7 = 4$
20. $48 \div 8 = 6$
21. $36 \div 4 = 9$
22. $45 \div 9 = 5$
23. $72 \div 8 = 9$
24. $40 \div 5 = 8$

LESSON 4.1

Your Turn

1. $\frac{1}{6} \times \frac{3}{5} = \frac{1 \times 3}{6 \times 5}$

$= \frac{1 \times \cancel{3}^{1}}{{}_{2}\cancel{6} \times 5}$

$= \frac{1 \times 1}{2 \times 5}$

$= \frac{1}{10}$

2. $\frac{3}{4} \times \frac{7}{9} = \frac{3 \times 7}{4 \times 9}$

$= \frac{{}^{1}\cancel{3} \times 7}{4 \times \cancel{9}_{3}}$

$= \frac{1 \times 7}{4 \times 3}$

$= \frac{7}{12}$

3. $\frac{3}{7} \times \frac{2}{3} = \frac{3 \times 2}{7 \times 3}$

$= \frac{{}^{1}\cancel{3} \times 2}{7 \times \cancel{3}_{1}}$

$= \frac{1 \times 2}{7 \times 1}$

$= \frac{2}{7}$

4. $\frac{4}{5} \times \frac{2}{7} = \frac{4 \times 2}{5 \times 7}$

$= \frac{8}{35}$

5. $\frac{7}{10} \times \frac{8}{21} = \frac{7 \times 8}{10 \times 21}$

$= \frac{{}^{1}\cancel{7} \times \cancel{8}^{4}}{{}_{5}\cancel{10} \times \cancel{21}_{3}}$

$= \frac{1 \times 4}{5 \times 3}$

$= \frac{4}{15}$

6. $\frac{6}{7} \times \frac{1}{6} = \frac{6 \times 1}{7 \times 6}$

$= \frac{{}^{1}\cancel{6} \times 1}{7 \times \cancel{6}_{1}}$

$= \frac{1 \times 1}{7 \times 1}$

$= \frac{1}{7}$

8. $\frac{5}{8} \times 24 = \frac{5}{8} \times \frac{24}{1}$

$= \frac{5 \times \cancel{24}^{3}}{{}_{1}\cancel{8} \times 1}$

$= \frac{5 \times 3}{1 \times 1}$

$= \frac{15}{1} = 15$

9. $\frac{3}{5} \times 20 = \frac{3}{5} \times \frac{20}{1}$

$= \frac{3 \times \cancel{20}^{4}}{{}_{1}\cancel{5} \times 1}$

$= \frac{3 \times 4}{1 \times 1}$

$= \frac{12}{1} = 12$

10. $\frac{1}{3} \times 8 = \frac{1}{3} \times \frac{8}{1}$

$= \frac{1 \times 8}{3 \times 1}$

$= \frac{8}{3}$

11. $\frac{1}{4} \times 14 = \frac{1 \times 14}{4 \times 1}$

$= \frac{1 \times \cancel{14}^{7}}{{}_{2}\cancel{4} \times 1}$

$= \frac{1 \times 7}{2 \times 1}$

$= \frac{7}{2}$

12. $3\frac{7}{10} \times 7 = \frac{37}{10} \times \frac{7}{1}$

$= \frac{37 \times 7}{10 \times 1}$

$= \frac{37 \times 7}{10 \times 1}$

$= \frac{259}{10}$

$= 25\frac{9}{10}$

13. $2\frac{3}{10} \times 10 = \frac{23}{10} \times \frac{10}{1}$

$= \frac{23 \times \cancel{10}^{1}}{{}_{1}\cancel{10} \times 1}$

$= \frac{23 \times 1}{1 \times 1}$

$= 23$

15. $\frac{5}{14} + \frac{1}{6} = \frac{5^{\times 3}}{14^{\times 3}} + \frac{1^{\times 7}}{6^{\times 7}}$

$= \frac{15}{42} + \frac{7}{42}$

$= \frac{22}{42}$

$= \frac{11}{21}$

16. $\frac{5}{12} - \frac{3}{20} = \frac{5^{\times 5}}{12^{\times 5}} - \frac{3^{\times 3}}{20^{\times 3}}$

$= \frac{25}{60} - \frac{9}{60}$

$= \frac{16}{60}$

$= \frac{4}{15}$

17. $\frac{5}{12} - \frac{3}{8} = \frac{5^{\times 2}}{12^{\times 2}} - \frac{3^{\times 3}}{8^{\times 3}}$

$= \frac{10}{24} - \frac{9}{24}$

$= \frac{1}{24}$

18. $1\frac{3}{10} + \frac{1}{4} = \frac{13}{10} + \frac{1}{4}$

$= \frac{13^{\times 2}}{10^{\times 2}} + \frac{1^{\times 5}}{4^{\times 5}}$

$= \frac{26}{20} + \frac{5}{20}$

$= \frac{31}{20} = 1\frac{11}{20}$

19. $\frac{2}{3} + 6\frac{1}{5} = \frac{2}{3} + \frac{31}{5}$

$= \frac{2^{\times 5}}{3^{\times 5}} + \frac{31^{\times 3}}{5^{\times 3}}$

$= \frac{10}{15} + \frac{93}{15}$

$= \frac{103}{15}$, or $6\frac{13}{15}$

20. $3\frac{1}{6} - \frac{1}{7} = \frac{19}{6} - \frac{1}{7}$

$= \frac{19^{\times 7}}{6^{\times 7}} - \frac{1^{\times 6}}{7^{\times 6}}$

$= \frac{133}{42} - \frac{6}{42}$

$= \frac{127}{42}$

$= 3\frac{1}{42}$

Guided Practice

1. $\frac{1}{2} \times \frac{5}{8} = \frac{1 \times 5}{2 \times 8}$

$= \frac{5}{16}$

2. $\frac{3}{5} \times \frac{5}{9} = \frac{3 \times 5}{5 \times 9}$

$= \frac{3 \times \cancel{5}^1}{_1\cancel{5} \times 9}$

$= \frac{3 \times 1}{1 \times 9}$

$= \frac{1}{3}$

3. $\frac{3}{8} \times \frac{2}{5} = \frac{3 \times 2}{8 \times 5}$

$= \frac{3 \times \cancel{2}^1}{_4\cancel{8} \times 5}$

$= \frac{3 \times 1}{4 \times 5}$

$= \frac{3}{20}$

4. $2\frac{2}{3} \times 16 = \frac{19}{8} \times \frac{16}{1}$

$= \frac{19 \times 16}{8 \times 1}$

$= \frac{19 \times \cancel{16}^2}{_1\cancel{8} \times 1}$

$= \frac{19 \times 2}{1 \times 1}$

$= \frac{38}{1} = 38$

5. $1\frac{4}{5} \times \frac{5}{12} = \frac{9}{5} \times \frac{5}{12}$

$= \frac{9 \times 5}{5 \times 12}$

$= \frac{^3\cancel{9} \times \cancel{5}^1}{_1\cancel{5} \times \cancel{12}_4}$

$= \frac{3 \times 1}{1 \times 4}$

$= \frac{3}{4}$

6. $1\frac{2}{10} \times 5 = \frac{12}{10} \times \frac{5}{1}$

$= \frac{12 \times 5}{10 \times 1}$

$= \frac{12 \times \cancel{5}^1}{_2\cancel{10} \times 1}$

$= \frac{12 \times 1}{2 \times 1}$

$= 6$

7. $\frac{1}{4} \times 12 = \frac{1}{4} \times \frac{12}{1}$

$= \frac{1 \times \cancel{12}^3}{_1\cancel{4} \times 1}$

$= \frac{1 \times 3}{1 \times 1}$

$= \frac{3}{1} = 3$

$\frac{1}{4}$ of 12 bottles of water = 3 bottles

8. $\frac{2}{3} \times 24 = \frac{2}{3} \times \frac{24}{1}$

$= \frac{2 \times \cancel{24}^8}{_1\cancel{3} \times 1}$

$= \frac{2 \times 8}{1}$

$= \frac{16}{1} = 16$

$\frac{2}{3}$ of 24 bananas = 16 bananas

9. $\frac{3}{5} \times 40 = \frac{3}{5} \times \frac{40}{1}$

$= \frac{3 \times \cancel{40}^8}{_1\cancel{5} \times 1}$

$= \frac{3 \times 8}{1 \times 1}$

$= \frac{24}{1} = 24$

$\frac{3}{5}$ of \$40 restaurant bill = \$24

10. $\frac{5}{6} \times 18 = \frac{5}{6} \times \frac{18}{1}$

$= \frac{5 \times \cancel{18}^3}{_1\cancel{6} \times 1}$

$= \frac{5 \times 3}{1 \times 1}$

$= \frac{15}{1} = 15$

$\frac{5}{6}$ of 18 pencils = 15 pencils

11. $\frac{3}{8} + \frac{5}{24} = \frac{3^{\times 3}}{8^{\times 3}} + \frac{5}{24}$

$= \frac{9}{24} + \frac{5}{24}$

$= \frac{14}{24}$, or $\frac{7}{12}$

12. $\frac{1}{20} + \frac{5}{12} = \frac{1^{\times 3}}{20^{\times 3}} + \frac{5^{\times 5}}{12^{\times 5}}$

$= \frac{3}{60} + \frac{25}{60}$

$= \frac{28}{60}$

$= \frac{7}{15}$

13. $\frac{9}{20} - \frac{1}{4} = \frac{9}{20} - \frac{1^{\times 5}}{4^{\times 5}}$

$= \frac{9}{20} - \frac{5}{20}$

$= \frac{4}{20}$, or $\frac{1}{5}$

14. $\frac{9}{10} - \frac{3}{14} = \frac{9^{\times 7}}{10^{\times 7}} - \frac{3^{\times 5}}{14^{\times 5}}$

$= \frac{63}{70} - \frac{15}{70}$

$= \frac{48}{70}$, or $\frac{24}{35}$

15. $3\frac{3}{8} + \frac{5}{12} = \frac{27^{\times 3}}{8^{\times 3}} - \frac{5^{\times 2}}{12^{\times 2}}$

$= \frac{81}{24} + \frac{10}{24}$

$= \frac{91}{24}$, or $3\frac{19}{24}$

16. $5\frac{7}{10} - \frac{5}{18} = \frac{57}{10} - \frac{5}{18}$

$= \frac{57^{\times 9}}{10^{\times 9}} - \frac{5^{\times 5}}{18^{\times 5}}$

$= \frac{513}{90} - \frac{25}{90}$

$= \frac{488}{90}$

$= \frac{244}{45}$, or $5\frac{19}{45}$

17. You can use the GCF to simplify fractions when you find sums, differences, and products of fractions. You can use the LCM of the denominators of fractions to add and subtract fractions.

Independent Practice

18. $\frac{2}{3} \times \frac{3}{4} = \frac{2 \times 3}{3 \times 4}$

$= \frac{6}{12}$

$= \frac{6 \div 6}{12 \div 6}$

$= \frac{1}{2}$

The bag weighs $\frac{1}{2}$ pound.

19. a. $\frac{5}{8} \times 16 = \frac{5}{8} \times \frac{16}{1}$

$= \frac{5 \times \not{16}^{2}}{{}_{1}\not{8} \times 1}$

$= \frac{10}{1} = 10$

She buys 10 pounds.

b. Marianne needs to buy 13 − 10 = 3 more pounds of soil.

$\frac{5}{8} \times 4 = \frac{5}{8} \times \frac{4}{1}$

$= \frac{5 \times \not{4}^{1}}{{}_{2}\not{8} \times 1}$

$= \frac{5}{2} = 2\frac{1}{2}$

$\frac{5}{8} \times 5 = \frac{5}{8} \times \frac{4}{1}$

$= \frac{5 \times 5}{8 \times 1}$

$= \frac{25}{2} = 3\frac{1}{8}$

She will need to buy 5 more bags.

20. a. First, add the fraction of brass and percussion instruments.

$\frac{2}{5} + \frac{1}{3} = \frac{2^{\times 3}}{5^{\times 3}} + \frac{1^{\times 5}}{3^{\times 5}}$

$= \frac{6}{15} + \frac{5}{15}$

$= \frac{11}{15}$

Then subtract the sum from the whole band.

$= \frac{1^{\times 15}}{1^{\times 15}} - \frac{11}{15}$

$= \frac{15}{15} - \frac{11}{15}$

$= \frac{4}{15}$

The fraction of woodwinds in the band is $\frac{4}{15}$.

b. Multiply the fraction of woodwinds by one half.

$\frac{4}{15} \times \frac{1}{2} = \frac{4 \times 1}{15 \times 2}$

$= \frac{4}{30}$

$= \frac{2}{15}$

$\frac{2}{15}$ of the band is clarinets.

c. Multiply the fraction of brass instruments by the fraction of tubas to find the fraction of tubas in the band.

$\frac{2}{5} \times \frac{1}{8} = \frac{2 \times 1}{5 \times 8}$

$= \frac{2}{40}$

$= \frac{1}{20}$

Then multiply the fraction of tubas in the band by the number of members in the band.

$\frac{1}{20} \times 240 = \frac{1}{20} \times \frac{240}{1}$

$= \frac{1 \times 240}{20 \times 1}$

$= \frac{240}{20}$

$= 12$

Of the 240 instruments in the band, 12 are tubas.

21. a. oranges $\frac{1}{2} \times \frac{3}{1} = \frac{3}{2} = 1\frac{1}{2}$;

apples $\frac{3}{5} \times \frac{3}{1} = \frac{9}{5} = 1\frac{4}{5}$;

blueberries $\frac{1}{4} \times \frac{3}{1} = \frac{3}{4}$ cup;

peaches $\frac{2}{3} \times \frac{3}{1} = 2$

b. Sample answer: If you triple 3, it becomes 9. If you triple $\frac{1}{2}$, it becomes $1\frac{1}{2}$. Add $9 + 1\frac{1}{2}$ to get $10\frac{1}{2}$.

22. $5\frac{3}{4} - 1\frac{7}{8} = \frac{23}{4} - \frac{15}{8}$

$= \frac{23^{\times 2}}{4^{\times 2}} - \frac{15}{8}$

$= \frac{46}{8} - \frac{15}{8}$

$= \frac{31}{8}$, or $3\frac{7}{8}$

The second container holds $3\frac{7}{8}$ more quarts.

23. a. $15 \times 1\frac{1}{2} = \frac{15}{1} \times 1\frac{1}{2}$

$= \frac{15}{1} \times \frac{3}{2}$

$= \frac{15 \times 3}{1 \times 2}$

$= \frac{45}{2}$

$= 22\frac{1}{2}$

It will take $22\frac{1}{2}$ minutes.

b. 15 min for the teacher's introduction + a total of 15 min for each of the students to get ready $+ 22\frac{1}{2}$ min for speeches $= 15 + 15 + 22\frac{1}{2}$ min $= 52\frac{1}{2}$ min. Since there is an hour available, there is enough time.

c. There will be a total of 60 min $- 52\frac{1}{2} = 7\frac{1}{2}$ minutes left on the camera.

Focus on Higher Order Thinking

24. $\frac{5}{6} \times 360 = \frac{5}{6} \times \frac{360}{1}$

$= \frac{5 \times \cancel{360}^{60}}{{}_1\cancel{6} \times 1}$

$= \frac{300}{1} = 300$

The sale price is $300.00.

25. Cameron divided the numerator of $\frac{3}{7}$ by the GCF of 3 and 9, but forgot to divide the denominator of $\frac{4}{9}$ by the GCF. He should have multiplied $\frac{1 \times 4}{7 \times 3}$.

26. Writing a whole number as a fraction with a denominator of 1 is the same as dividing the whole number by 1 does not change its value, so the product is the same.

LESSON 4.2

Your Turn

5. The reciprocal of $\frac{7}{8}$ is $\frac{8}{7}$.

6. The reciprocal of 9, or $\frac{9}{1}$, is $\frac{1}{9}$.

7. The reciprocal of $\frac{1}{11}$ is $\frac{11}{1} = 11$.

10. $\frac{9}{10} \div \frac{2}{5} = \frac{9}{10} \times \frac{5}{2}$

$= \frac{9 \times \cancel{5}^1}{{}_2\cancel{10} \times 2}$

$= \frac{9}{4}$, or $2\frac{1}{4}$

11. $\frac{9}{10} \div \frac{3}{5} = \frac{9}{10} \times \frac{5}{3}$

$= \frac{{}^3\cancel{9} \times \cancel{5}^1}{{}_2\cancel{10} \times \cancel{3}_1}$

$= \frac{3}{2}$, or $1\frac{1}{2}$

Guided Practice

1. The reciprocal of $\frac{2}{5}$ is $\frac{5}{2}$.

2. The reciprocal of 9 is $\frac{1}{9}$.

3. The reciprocal of $\frac{10}{3}$ is $\frac{3}{10}$.

4. $\frac{4}{3} \div \frac{5}{3} = \frac{4}{3} \times \frac{3}{5}$

$= \frac{4 \times \cancel{3}^1}{{}_1\cancel{3} \times 5}$

$= \frac{4}{5}$

5. $\frac{3}{10} \div \frac{4}{5} = \frac{3}{10} \times \frac{5}{4}$

$= \frac{3 \times \cancel{5}^1}{{}_2\cancel{10} \times 4}$

$= \frac{3}{8}$

6. $\frac{1}{2} \div \frac{2}{5} = \frac{1}{2} \times \frac{5}{2}$

$= \frac{1 \times 5}{2 \times 2}$

$= \frac{5}{4}$, or $1\frac{1}{4}$

7. Multiply the dividend by the reciprocal of the divisor.

Independent Practice

8. $8 \div \frac{2}{3} = \frac{8}{1} \times \frac{3}{2}$

$= \frac{{}^4\cancel{8} \times 3}{1 \times \cancel{2}_1}$

$= \frac{12}{1} = 12$

9. $7 \div \frac{3}{4} = \frac{7}{1} \times \frac{4}{3}$

$= \frac{7 \times 4}{1 \times 3}$

$= \frac{28}{3}$, or $9\frac{1}{3}$

10. $\frac{4}{15} \div \frac{2}{5} = \frac{4}{15} \times \frac{5}{2}$

$= \frac{{}^2\cancel{4} \times \cancel{5}^1}{{}_3\cancel{15} \times \cancel{2}_1}$

$= \frac{2}{3}$

11. $\frac{5}{8} \div \frac{7}{8} = \frac{5}{8} \times \frac{8}{7}$

$= \frac{5 \times \cancel{8}^1}{_1\cancel{8} \times 7}$

$= \frac{5}{7}$

12. $\frac{7}{16} \div \frac{3}{8} = \frac{7}{16} \times \frac{8}{3}$

$= \frac{7 \times \cancel{8}^1}{_2\cancel{16} \times 3}$

$= \frac{7}{6}$, or $1\frac{1}{6}$

13. $\frac{4}{5} \div \frac{7}{10} = \frac{4}{5} \times \frac{10}{7}$

$= \frac{4 \times \cancel{10}^2}{_1\cancel{5} \times 7}$

$= \frac{8}{7}$, or $1\frac{1}{7}$

14. $\frac{1}{2} \div \frac{1}{8} = \frac{1}{2} \times \frac{8}{1}$

$= \frac{1 \times \cancel{8}^4}{_1\cancel{2} \times 1}$

$= \frac{4}{1}$

4 parfaits

15. $\frac{4}{5} \div \frac{1}{10} = \frac{4}{5} \times \frac{10}{1}$

$= \frac{4 \times \cancel{10}^2}{_1\cancel{5} \times 1}$

$= \frac{8}{1} = 8$

There are 8 tenths in $\frac{4}{5}$.

16. $\frac{1}{2} \div \frac{1}{12} = \frac{1}{2} \times \frac{12}{1}$

$= \frac{1 \times \cancel{12}^6}{_1\cancel{2} \times 1}$

$= \frac{6}{1}$

6 honeybees

17. $\frac{1}{4} \div \frac{1}{16} = \frac{1}{4} \times \frac{16}{1}$

$= \frac{1 \times \cancel{16}^4}{_1\cancel{4} \times 1}$

$= \frac{4}{1} = 4$

4 runners will be needed.

18. $\frac{2}{3} \div 6 = \frac{2}{3} \div \frac{6}{1}$

$= \frac{2}{3} \times \frac{1}{6}$

$= \frac{^1\cancel{2} \times 1}{3 \times \cancel{6}_3}$

$= \frac{1}{9}$

$\frac{1}{9}$ quart

19. $\frac{3}{4} \div \frac{1}{12} = \frac{3}{4} \times \frac{12}{1}$

$= \frac{3 \times \cancel{12}^3}{_1\cancel{4} \times 1}$

$= \frac{9}{1}$

9 bags

20. a. $\frac{2}{3} \div 6$, if the sister ate $\frac{1}{3}$ of the salad, $\frac{2}{3}$ of the salad is left to divide among 6 friends.

b. $\frac{2}{3} \div 6 = \frac{2}{3} \div \frac{6}{1}$

$= \frac{2}{3} \times \frac{1}{6}$

$= \frac{^1\cancel{2} \times 1}{3 \times \cancel{6}_3}$

$= \frac{1}{9}$

Each friend receives $\frac{1}{9}$ of the original salad.

21. $\frac{3}{5} \div \frac{6}{1} = \frac{3}{5} \times \frac{1}{6}$

$= \frac{^1\cancel{3} \times 1}{5 \times \cancel{6}_2}$

$= \frac{1}{10}$

$\frac{1}{10}$ pound

Focus on Higher Order Thinking

22. $\frac{9}{10} \div \frac{1}{20} = \frac{9}{10} \times \frac{20}{1}$;

$= \frac{9 \times \cancel{20}^2}{_1\cancel{10} \times 1}$

$= \frac{18}{1} = 18$

18 birdhouses

23. 2;

$\frac{3}{4} \div \frac{1}{3} = \frac{3}{4} \times \frac{3}{1}$

$= \frac{3 \times 3}{4 \times 1}$

$= \frac{9}{4}$, or $2\frac{1}{4}$

So, a maximum of 2 pieces will measure $\frac{1}{3}$ meter.

$\frac{1}{4} \times \frac{1}{3} = \frac{1}{12}$

Sun Yi will have $\frac{1}{12}$ meter left over.

24. Sample answer: You paint $\frac{1}{6}$ of a fence each hour. How many hours will it take to paint $\frac{3}{4}$ of the fence?

$\frac{3}{4} \div \frac{1}{6} = \frac{3}{4} \times \frac{6}{1}$

$= \frac{3 \times \cancel{6}^3}{_2\cancel{4} \times 1}$

$= \frac{9}{2}$

$= 4\frac{1}{2}$

It would take $4\frac{1}{2}$ hours.

25. Greater than $\frac{1}{2}$; since the quotient was a mixed number, the original fraction contained more than 1 unit of $\frac{1}{2}$.

26. In a fraction less than 1, the numerator is less than the denominator. In its reciprocal, the numerator is greater than the denominator, making it a fraction greater than 1.

27. Robyn; Robyn is dividing $\frac{5}{8}$ into smaller groups than Susan; there are more thirty-seconds in $\frac{5}{8}$ than there are sixteenths.

$\frac{5}{8} \div \frac{1}{16} = \frac{5}{8} \times \frac{16}{1}$; $\quad \frac{5}{8} \div \frac{1}{32} = \frac{5}{8} \times \frac{32}{1}$

$= \frac{5 \times \cancel{16}^{2}}{{}_{1}\cancel{8} \times 1} \quad = \frac{5 \times \cancel{32}^{4}}{{}_{1}\cancel{8} \times 1}$

$= \frac{10}{1} = 10 \quad = \frac{20}{1} = 20$

LESSON 4.3

Your Turn

6. $10\frac{1}{2} \div 1\frac{1}{4} = \frac{21}{2} \div \frac{5}{4}$

$= \frac{21}{2} \times \frac{4}{5}$

$= \frac{21 \times \cancel{4}^{2}}{{}_{1}\cancel{2} \times 5}$

$= \frac{42}{5}$, or $8\frac{2}{5}$

She will need 9 containers.

8. $12\frac{3}{8} \div 2\frac{2}{3} = \frac{99}{8} \div \frac{11}{4}$

$= \frac{99}{8} \times \frac{4}{11}$

$= \frac{{}^{9}\cancel{99} \times \cancel{4}^{1}}{{}_{2}\cancel{8} \times \cancel{11}_{1}}$

$= \frac{9}{2}$, or $4\frac{1}{2}$ meters

9. $14\frac{1}{12} \div 4\frac{1}{3} = \frac{169}{12} \div \frac{13}{3}$

$= \frac{169}{12} \times \frac{3}{13}$

$= \frac{{}^{13}\cancel{169} \times \cancel{3}^{1}}{{}_{4}\cancel{12} \times \cancel{13}_{1}}$

$= \frac{13}{4}$, or $3\frac{1}{4}$ yards

Guided Practice

1. $4\frac{1}{4} \div \frac{3}{4}$

$\frac{17}{4} \div \frac{3}{4}$

$\frac{17}{4} \times \frac{4}{3} =$

$\frac{17}{3} = 5\frac{2}{3}$

2. $1\frac{1}{2} \div 2\frac{1}{4}$

$\frac{3}{2} \div \frac{9}{4}$

$\frac{3}{2} \times \frac{4}{9} =$

$\frac{12}{18} = \frac{2}{3}$

3. $4 \div 1\frac{1}{8} = \frac{4}{1} \div \frac{9}{8}$

$= \frac{4}{1} \times \frac{8}{9}$

$= \frac{4 \times 8}{1 \times 9}$

$= \frac{32}{9}$, or $3\frac{5}{9}$

4. $3\frac{1}{5} \div 1\frac{1}{7} = \frac{16}{5} \div \frac{8}{7}$

$= \frac{16}{5} \times \frac{7}{8}$

$= \frac{{}^{2}\cancel{16} \times 7}{5 \times \cancel{8}_{1}}$

$= \frac{14}{5}$, or $2\frac{4}{5}$

5. $8\frac{1}{3} \div 2\frac{1}{2} = \frac{25}{3} \div \frac{5}{2}$

$= \frac{25}{3} \times \frac{2}{5}$

$= \frac{{}^{5}\cancel{25} \times 2}{3 \times \cancel{5}_{1}}$

$= \frac{10}{3}$, or $3\frac{1}{3}$

6. $15\frac{1}{3} \div 3\frac{5}{6} = \frac{46}{3} \div \frac{23}{6}$

$= \frac{46}{3} \times \frac{6}{23}$

$= \frac{{}^{2}\cancel{46} \times \cancel{6}^{2}}{{}_{1}\cancel{3} \times \cancel{23}_{1}}$

$= \frac{4}{1} = 4$

7. $26 \div 5\frac{1}{2} = \frac{26}{1} \div \frac{11}{2}$;

$= \frac{26}{1} \times \frac{2}{11}$

$= \frac{52}{11}$, or $4\frac{8}{11}$

The width is $4\frac{8}{11}$ feet.

8. $230 \div 12\frac{1}{2} = \frac{230}{1} \div \frac{25}{2}$;

$= \frac{230}{1} \times \frac{2}{25}$

$= \frac{{}^{46}\cancel{230} \times 2}{1 \times \cancel{25}_{5}}$

$= \frac{92}{5}$, or $18\frac{2}{5}$

The width is $18\frac{2}{5}$ feet.

9. Once you change any mixed numbers to fractions, the process for dividing is the same.

Independent Practice

10.

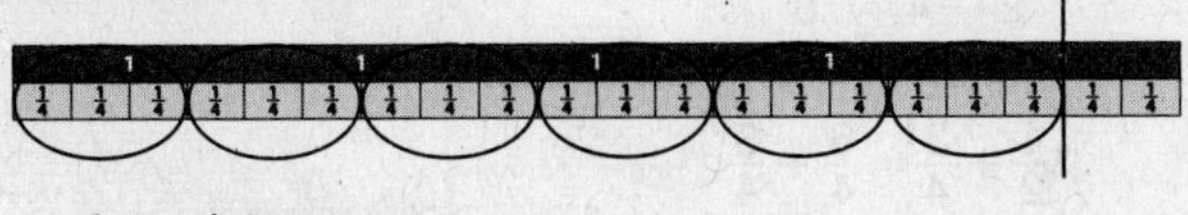

6 servings

11.

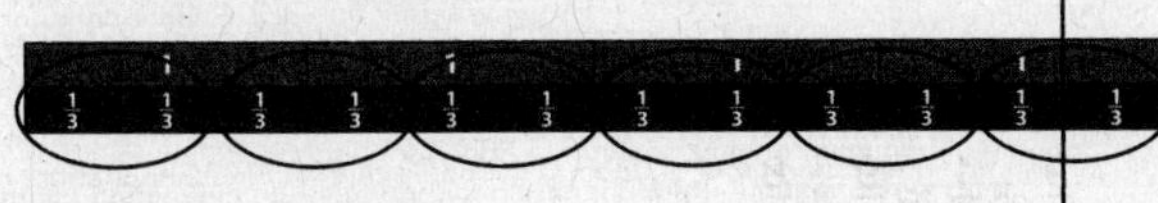

5 pieces; $\frac{1}{3}$ yard

12. $2\frac{3}{8} \div \frac{1}{4} = \frac{19}{8} \div \frac{1}{4}$

$= \frac{19}{8} \times \frac{4}{1}$

$= \frac{76}{8}$, or $9\frac{1}{2}$

No; he has only enough meat to make $9\frac{1}{2}$ quarter pound hamburgers.

13. a. $5\frac{1}{2} \div \frac{3}{4} = \frac{11}{2} \div \frac{3}{4}$

$= \frac{11}{2} \times \frac{4}{3}$

$= \frac{44}{6}$, or $7\frac{1}{3}$

No, it only makes $7\frac{1}{3}$ servings.

b. $\frac{11}{20}$ of a cup; $5\frac{1}{2} \div 10 = \frac{11}{2} \div \frac{10}{1}$

$= \frac{11}{2} \times \frac{1}{10}$

$= \frac{11}{20}$

c. She would need $\frac{3}{4} \times 10 = 7\frac{1}{2}$ cups total, so she would need $7\frac{1}{2} - 5\frac{1}{2} = 2$ more cups of trail mix.

14. $30\frac{1}{2} \div 6\frac{1}{2} = \frac{91}{3} \div \frac{13}{2}$

$= \frac{91}{3} \times \frac{2}{13}$

$= \frac{{}^{7}\cancel{91} \times 2}{3 \times \cancel{13}_{1}}$

$= \frac{14}{3}$, or $4\frac{2}{3}$

$4\frac{2}{3}$ in.

15. $11\frac{11}{16} \div 2\frac{3}{4} = \frac{187}{16} \div \frac{11}{4}$

$= \frac{187}{16} \times \frac{4}{11}$

$= \frac{{}^{17}\cancel{187} \times \cancel{4}^{1}}{{}_{4}\cancel{16} \times \cancel{11}_{1}}$

$= \frac{17}{4}$, or $4\frac{1}{4}$

Yes, because the height of the mirror is $4\frac{1}{4}$ feet, and 5 feet is more than $4\frac{1}{4}$ feet.

16. $25\frac{1}{2} \div 6 = \frac{51}{2} \div \frac{6}{1}$

$= \frac{51}{2} \times \frac{1}{6}$

$= \frac{{}^{17}\cancel{51} \times 1}{2 \times \cancel{6}_{2}}$

$= \frac{17}{4}$, or $4\frac{1}{4}$

$4\frac{1}{4}$ feet

17. $60\frac{3}{8} \div 11\frac{1}{2} = \frac{483}{8} \div \frac{23}{2}$

$= \frac{483}{2} \times \frac{2}{23}$

$= \frac{{}^{21}\cancel{483} \times \cancel{2}^{1}}{{}_{4}\cancel{8} \times \cancel{23}_{1}}$

$= \frac{21}{4}$, or $5\frac{1}{4}$

$5\frac{1}{4}$ feet

Focus on Higher Order Thinking

18. Sample answer: The answer seems reasonable because $11\frac{2}{3}$ can be rounded to 12, and $2\frac{5}{6}$ can be rounded to 3, and $12 \div 3 = 4$, which is close to $4\frac{2}{17}$. $4\frac{2}{17} \times 2\frac{5}{6} = 11\frac{2}{3}$, so Micah's answer is correct.

19. He used the reciprocal of $\frac{3}{4}$ instead of the reciprocal of $2\frac{3}{4}$, which is $\frac{4}{11}$.

20. Divide $3\frac{4}{5}$ by $2\frac{5}{7}$, since $3\frac{4}{5}$ is the product of $2\frac{5}{7}$ and the missing number.

$3\frac{4}{5} \div 2\frac{5}{7} = \frac{19}{5} \div \frac{19}{7}$

$= \frac{{}^{1}\cancel{19} \times 7}{5 \times \cancel{19}_{1}}$

$= \frac{7}{5}$, or $1\frac{2}{5}$

The missing number is $1\frac{2}{5}$.

LESSON 4.4

Your Turn

1. Write the expression.

$\left(\frac{1}{2} + \frac{3}{4}\right) \div \frac{1}{8}$

Find the total amount of soup made.

$\left(\frac{1}{2} + \frac{3}{4}\right) = \frac{1^{\times 2}}{2^{\times 2}} + \frac{3}{4}$

$= \frac{2}{4} + \frac{3}{4}$

$= \frac{5}{4}$

Find how many times $\frac{1}{8}$ of the soup can be used.

$\frac{5}{4} \div \frac{1}{8} = \frac{5}{4} \times \frac{8}{1}$

$$= \frac{5 \times \cancel{8}^{2}}{{}_{1}\cancel{4} \times 1}$$

$$= \frac{5 \times 2}{1 \times 1}$$

$$= 10$$

The chef can make 10 batches of soup.

Guided Practice

1. Write the expression.

$$\left(1\frac{1}{3} + \frac{5}{6}\right) \div \frac{1}{6}$$

Find the total amount of paper needed.

$$1\frac{1}{3} + \frac{5}{6} = 1\frac{2}{6} + \frac{5}{6}$$

$$= 1\frac{7}{6}$$

$$= 2\frac{1}{6}$$

Find the number of pieces of paper that are $\frac{1}{6}$ yard long.

$$2\frac{1}{6} \div \frac{1}{6} = \frac{13}{6} \times \frac{6}{1}$$

$$= 13$$

The student will cut 13 pieces.

Independent Practice

2. Sample answer: You have 5 $\frac{3}{4}$ pizzas and give $\frac{1}{2}$ of a pizza to a friend. You want to cut the remaining pizzas into slices that are $\frac{1}{8}$ the size of a whole pizza. How many of these slices will you have?

$$\left(5\frac{3}{4} - \frac{1}{2}\right) \div \frac{1}{8}$$

Find the amount of pizza left.

$$5\frac{3}{4} - \frac{1}{2} = 5\frac{3}{4} - \frac{2}{4}$$

$$= 5\frac{1}{4}$$

Find the number of slices you will have.

$$5\frac{1}{4} \div \frac{1}{8} = \frac{21}{4} \times \frac{8}{1}$$

$$= \frac{21 \times \cancel{8}^{2}}{{}_{1}\cancel{4} \times 1}$$

$$= \frac{42}{1}$$

$$= 42$$

You will have 42 slices.

3. $175 \div \left(3\frac{1}{4} + 5\frac{1}{2}\right)$

Find the total number of miles walked.

$$3\frac{1}{4} + 5\frac{1}{2} = 3\frac{1}{4} + 5\frac{2}{4}$$

$$= 8\frac{3}{4}$$

Find the amount spent per mile.

$$175 \div 8\frac{3}{4} = \frac{175}{1} \times \frac{4}{35}$$

$$= \frac{{}^{5}\cancel{175} \times 4}{1 \times \cancel{35}_{1}}$$

$$= \frac{20}{1}$$

$$= 20$$

His parents pay $20 per mile.

4. Write the expression.

$$\left(1\frac{1}{2} + \frac{3}{4}\right) \div \frac{1}{8}$$

Find the total amount of clay.

$$1\frac{1}{2} + \frac{3}{4} = \frac{6}{4} + \frac{3}{4}$$

$$= \frac{9}{4}$$

Find the number of $\frac{1}{8}$ -pound portions of clay.

$$\frac{9}{4} \div \frac{1}{8} = \frac{9}{4} \times \frac{8}{1}$$

$$= 18$$

18 students can get enough clay to finish the project.

5. Write the expression.

$$3\frac{1}{3} \div \left(\frac{1}{4} + \frac{1}{6}\right) \times 5$$

Find the amount of time needed to time and style.

$$\frac{1}{4} + \frac{1}{6} = \frac{3}{12} + \frac{2}{12}$$

$$= \frac{5}{12}$$

Find the number of appointments in 1 day.

$$3\frac{1}{3} \div \frac{5}{12} = \frac{10}{3} \times \frac{12}{5}$$

$$= 8$$

Find the number of appointments in 5 days.

$5 \times 8 = 40$

The hairstylist can schedule 40 appointments each week.

6. Write the expression.

$$\left(10\frac{1}{12} - 2\frac{3}{8}\right) \div 1\frac{2}{3}$$

Find the amount of the board that can be used.

$$10\frac{1}{12} - 2\frac{3}{8} = 10\frac{2}{24} - 2\frac{9}{24}$$

$$= 7\frac{17}{24}$$

Find number of picture frames that can be made.

$$7\frac{17}{24} \div 1\frac{2}{3} = \frac{185}{24} \div \frac{5}{3}$$

$$= \frac{185}{24} \times \frac{3}{5}$$

$$= \frac{37}{8}$$

$$= 4\frac{5}{8}$$

The number of completed picture frames that can be made is 4 picture frames.

7. Write the expression.

$$\left(15\frac{5}{6} \times 10\frac{2}{5}\right) \div \left(1\frac{1}{3} \times 1\frac{1}{3}\right)$$

Find the area of the backyard.

$$15\frac{5}{6} \times 10\frac{2}{5} = \frac{95}{6} \times \frac{52}{5}$$

$$= \frac{494}{3}$$

Find the area of a piece of sod.

$$1\frac{1}{3} \times 1\frac{1}{3} = \frac{4}{3} \times \frac{4}{3}$$

$= \frac{16}{9}$

Find the number of pieces of sod to cover the backyard.

$\frac{494}{3} \div \frac{16}{9} = \frac{494}{3} \times \frac{9}{16}$

$= \frac{741}{8}$

$= 92\frac{5}{8}$

Jim will need to buy 93 pieces of sod to cover his backyard.

8. Write the expression to find the number of bags of clay needed to make both pieces.

$\left(\frac{3}{5} + \frac{7}{10}\right) \div \frac{4}{5}$

Find the amount of clay needed for the 2 pieces.

$\frac{3}{5} + \frac{7}{10} = \frac{6}{10} + \frac{7}{10}$

$= \frac{13}{10}$

Find the number of bags.

$\frac{13}{10} \div \frac{4}{5} = \frac{13}{10} \times \frac{5}{4}$

$= \frac{13}{8}$

$= 1\frac{5}{8}$

Eva will need $1\frac{5}{8}$ bags of clay.

Write the expression to find the number of bags of clay that will be left over.

$\left(3 - 1\frac{5}{8}\right) \times \frac{4}{5}$

Find the number of bags of clay left over.

$3 - 1\frac{5}{8} = 2\frac{8}{8} - 1\frac{5}{8}$

$= 1\frac{3}{8}$

Find the weight of the left over bags.

$1\frac{3}{8} \times \frac{4}{5} = \frac{11}{8} \times \frac{4}{5}$

$= \frac{11}{10}$

$= 1\frac{1}{10}$

There will be $1\frac{1}{10}$ pounds left over.

9. Write the expression.

$\left(1\frac{1}{3} + 1\frac{1}{4} + \frac{7}{8}\right) - 3\left(\frac{3}{4}\right)$

Find the amount Mark has.

$1\frac{1}{3} + 1\frac{1}{4} + \frac{7}{8} = 1\frac{8}{24} + 1\frac{6}{24} + \frac{21}{24}$

$= 2\frac{35}{24}$

$= 3\frac{11}{24}$

Find the amount of paint used.

$3\left(\frac{3}{4}\right) = \frac{9}{4}$

$= 2\frac{1}{4}$

Find the amount of paint left.

$3\frac{11}{24} - 2\frac{1}{4} = 3\frac{11}{24} - 2\frac{6}{24}$

$= 1\frac{5}{24}$

There are $1\frac{5}{24}$ gallons of paint left.

10. Write the expression.

$\left(2\frac{3}{4} + 3\frac{3}{5} + 5\frac{1}{2}\right) \div 3$

Find the total number of hours worked.

$2\frac{3}{4} + 3\frac{3}{5} + 5\frac{1}{2} = 2\frac{15}{20} + 3\frac{12}{20} + 5\frac{10}{20}$

$= 10\frac{37}{20}$

$= 11\frac{17}{20}$

Find the number of hours worked each day.

$11\frac{17}{20} \div 3 = \frac{237}{20} \div 3$

$= \frac{237}{20} \times \frac{1}{3}$

$= \frac{79}{20}$

$= 3\frac{19}{20}$

Trina will work $3\frac{57}{60}$ hr or 3 hours 57 minutes each day.

Focus on Higher Order Thinking

11. Sample answer: A person taking a test averages $\frac{3}{8}$ minute to read a question and $\frac{5}{6}$ minute to answer the question. It takes the person 29 minutes to answer all of the questions. How many questions are on the test?

Find the total time to read and answer 1 question.

$\frac{3}{8} + \frac{5}{6} = \frac{9}{24} + \frac{20}{24}$

$= \frac{29}{24}$

Find the number of questions that can be answered in 29 minutes.

$29 \div \frac{29}{24} = 29 \times \frac{24}{29}$

$= 24$

24 questions can be answered in 29 minutes.

12. Yes; they will hike a distance of $8\frac{1}{10} - 2\frac{2}{5} = 5\frac{7}{10}$ miles. At an average speed of 3 miles per hour, they will hike this distance in $5\frac{7}{10} \div 3 = 1\frac{9}{10}$ hours. Noon is 2 hours from 10 A.M., so they will reach the $8\frac{1}{10}$-mile marker before noon.

13. Sample answer:

1) Add $\frac{3}{8} + \frac{3}{4} = 1\frac{1}{8}$ to find the total amount of walnuts needed. Then divide $1\frac{1}{8} \div \frac{1}{4} = 4\frac{1}{2}$ to find how many scoops.

2) Divide $\frac{3}{8} \div \frac{1}{4} = 1\frac{1}{2}$ scoops for the oatmeal and divide $\frac{3}{4} \div \frac{1}{4} = 3$ scoops for the salad. Then add $1\frac{1}{2} + 3 = 4\frac{1}{2}$.

MODULE 4

Ready to Go On?

1. $\frac{4}{5} \times \frac{3}{4} = \frac{4 \times 3}{5 \times 4}$

$= \frac{{}^{1}\cancel{4} \times 3}{5 \times \cancel{4}_{1}}$

$= \frac{3}{5}$

2. $\frac{5}{7} \times \frac{9}{10} = \frac{5 \times 9}{7 \times 10}$

$= \frac{{}^{1}\cancel{5} \times 9}{7 \times \cancel{10}_{2}}$

$= \frac{1 \times 9}{7 \times 2}$

$= \frac{9}{14}$

3. $\frac{3}{8} + 2\frac{1}{2} = \frac{3}{8} + \frac{5}{2}$

$= \frac{3}{8} + \frac{5^{\times 4}}{2^{\times 4}}$

$= \frac{3}{8} + \frac{20}{8}$

$= \frac{23}{8}$, or $2\frac{7}{8}$

4. $1\frac{3}{5} - \frac{5}{6} = \frac{8}{5} - \frac{5}{6}$

$= \frac{8^{\times 6}}{5^{\times 6}} - \frac{5^{\times 5}}{6^{\times 5}}$

$= \frac{48}{30} - \frac{25}{30}$

$= \frac{23}{30}$

5. $\frac{1}{3} \div \frac{7}{9} = \frac{1}{3} \times \frac{9}{7}$

$= \frac{1 \times \cancel{9}^{3}}{{}_{1}\cancel{3} \times 7}$

$= \frac{3}{7}$

6. $\frac{1}{3} \div \frac{5}{8} = \frac{1}{3} \times \frac{8}{5}$

$= \frac{1 \times 8}{3 \times 5}$

$= \frac{8}{15}$

7. $\frac{3}{4} \div \frac{3}{8} = \frac{3}{4} \times \frac{8}{3}$

$= \frac{24}{12}$

$= 2$

She cut 2 pieces.

8. $3\frac{1}{3} \div \frac{2}{3} = \frac{10}{3} \div \frac{2}{3}$

$= \frac{10}{3} \times \frac{3}{2}$

$= \frac{{}^{5}\cancel{10} \times \cancel{3}^{1}}{{}_{1}\cancel{3} \times \cancel{2}_{1}}$

$= \frac{5}{1} = 5$

9. $1\frac{7}{8} \div 2\frac{2}{5} = \frac{15}{8} \div \frac{12}{5}$

$= \frac{{}^{5}\cancel{15} \times 5}{8 \times \cancel{12}_{4}}$

$= \frac{25}{32}$

10. $4\frac{1}{4} \div 4\frac{1}{2} = \frac{17}{4} \div \frac{9}{2}$

$= \frac{17}{4} \times \frac{2}{9}$

$= \frac{17 \times \cancel{2}^{1}}{{}_{2}\cancel{4} \times 9}$

$= \frac{17}{18}$

11. $8\frac{1}{3} \div 4\frac{2}{7} = \frac{25}{3} \div \frac{30}{7}$

$= \frac{25}{3} \times \frac{7}{30}$

$= \frac{{}^{5}\cancel{25} \times 7}{3 \times \cancel{30}_{6}}$

$= \frac{35}{18}$, or $1\frac{17}{18}$

12. Write an expression to find the total number of miles walked on both trails.

$5\frac{1}{3} + 5\frac{1}{3}\left(1\frac{3}{4}\right) = \frac{16}{3} + \frac{16}{3}\left(\frac{7}{4}\right)$

Multiply the second half of the expression first to find the length of the second trail.

$\frac{16}{3} \times \frac{7}{4} = \frac{112}{12}$

Add the length of both trails together.

$\frac{16}{3} + \frac{112}{12}$

$= \frac{16^{\times 4}}{3^{\times 4}} + \frac{112}{12}$

$= \frac{64}{12} + \frac{112}{12}$

$= \frac{176}{12} = \frac{44}{3}$, or $14\frac{2}{3}$

13. Sample answer: You want to divide $3\frac{3}{4}$ pounds of grapes into bags that hold $\frac{3}{4}$ pound each. Divide $3\frac{3}{4}$ by $\frac{3}{4}$ to find that you can fill 5 bags.

MODULE 5 *Operations with Decimals*

Are You Ready?

1. $\frac{70}{100} = 0.7$
2. $\frac{40}{100} = 0.4$
3. $\frac{53}{100} = 0.53$
4. $\frac{100}{100} = 1.0$
5. $0.49 \times 10 = 4.9$
6. $25.34 \times 1{,}000 = 25{,}340$
7. $87 \times 100 = 8{,}700$
8. 20 decreased by 8: $20 - 8$
9. the quotient of 14 and 7: $14 \div 7$
10. the difference between 72 and 16: $72 - 16$
11. the sum of 19 and 3: $19 + 3$

LESSON 5.1

Your Turn

3.
```
      109
321)34,989
   -32 1
     2 889
   - 2 889
         0
```
$34{,}989 \div 321 = 109$

4.
```
      587
125)73,375
   -62 5
    10 87
   -10 00
       875
       875
         0
```
$73{,}375 \div 125 = 587$

6.
```
    231 R21
25)5,796
  -50
    79
  - 75
     46
   - 25
     21
```
$5{,}796 \div 25 = 231 \text{ R}21$

7.
```
    46 R16
67)3,098
  -2 68
    418
  - 402
     16
```
$3{,}098 \div 67 = 46 \text{ R}16$

8.
```
   105 R3
15)1578
  -15
    78
   -75
     3
```
105 bags can be filled. There will be 3 rocks left over.

Guided Practice

1. $31{,}969 \div 488 = 30{,}000 \div 500 = 60$

2.
```
     96
32)3,072
  -288
    192
   -192
      0
```
$3{,}072 \div 32 = 96$

3.
```
     89
51)4,539
  -408
    459
   -459
      0
```
$4{,}539 \div 51 = 89$

4.
```
    98 R7
95)9,317
  -855
    767
   -760
      7
```
$9{,}317 \div 95 = 98 \text{ R}7$

5.
```
     42
53)2,226
  -212
    106
   -106
      0
```
$2{,}226 \div 53 = 42$

6.
```
     61
74)4,514
  -444
     74
    -74
      0
```
$4{,}514 \div 74 = 61$

7.
```
    94 R15
37)3,493
  -333
    163
   -148
     15
```
$3{,}493 \div 37 = 94 \text{ R}15$

24 R9
8. 83)2,001
−166
341
−332
9
2,001 ÷ 83 = 24 R9

127
9. 313)39,751
−313
845
−626
2191
−2191
0
39,751 ÷ 313 = 127

81 R28
10. 438)35,506
−35 04
466
− 438
28
35,506 ÷ 438 = 81 R28

11. Write the division expression.
8,982 ÷ 28
Round the dividend, the number of items.
8,982 rounds to 9,000.
Round the divisor, the number of classrooms.
28 rounds to 30.
Estimate the quotient.
9,000 ÷ 30 = 300
The number of items each classroom donated is about 300 items.

12. Write the division expression.
1,120 ÷ 35
32
35)1,120
−105
70
−70
0
Each row has 32 seats.

84
13. 12)1,012
−96
52
−48
4
84 full boxes with 4 paperweights left over, so another box will be needed. 85 boxes will be needed.

14. Start from left to right in the dividend, and divide the divisor into the dividend to get the first digit in the quotient. Multiply this digit by the divisor and subtract the resulting product from the dividend. Then bring down the next number and repeat the process.

Independent Practice

268
15. 167)44,756
−334
1135
−1002
1336
−1336
0
44,756 ÷ 167 = 268

94 R114
16. 931)87,628
−8379
3838
−3724
114
87,628 ÷ 931 = 94 R114

209
17. 317)66,253
−634
2853
−2853
0
66,253 ÷ 317 = 209

246 R241
18. 309)76,255
−618
1445
−1236
2095
−1854
241
76,255 ÷ 309 = 246 R241

86 R39
19. 590)50,779
−4720
3579
−3540
39
50,779 ÷ 590 = 86 R39

908
20. 107)97,156
−963
856
−856
0
97,156 ÷ 107 = 908

587
21. 368)216,016
−1840
3201
−2944
2576
−2576
0
216,016 ÷ 368 = 587

22. $$\begin{array}{r} 1{,}494 \text{ R}41 \\ 72\overline{)107{,}609} \\ \underline{-72} \\ 356 \\ \underline{-288} \\ 680 \\ \underline{-648} \\ 329 \\ \underline{-288} \\ 41 \end{array}$$
107,609 ÷ 72 = 1,494 R41

23. Write the division expression.
8,450 ÷ 125
$$\begin{array}{r} 67 \text{ R}75 \\ 125\overline{)8450} \\ \underline{-750} \\ 950 \\ \underline{-875} \\ 75 \end{array}$$
8,450 ÷ 125 = 67 R75
67 full rows; 75 extra trees; $\frac{75}{125} = \frac{3}{5}$

24. Find the number of necklaces that can be made with the silver beads.
8,160 ÷ 85
$$\begin{array}{r} 96 \\ 85\overline{)8160} \\ \underline{-765} \\ 510 \\ \underline{-510} \\ 0 \end{array}$$
Find the number of necklaces that can be made with the black beads.
2,880 ÷ 30
$$\begin{array}{r} 96 \\ 30\overline{)2880} \\ \underline{-270} \\ 180 \\ \underline{-180} \\ 0 \end{array}$$
She has enough beads of each type for 96 necklaces.

25. Find the number of free admissions given on Saturday.
6,742 ÷ 175
$$\begin{array}{r} 38 \\ 175\overline{)6742} \\ \underline{-525} \\ 1492 \\ \underline{-1400} \\ 92 \end{array}$$
38 people were given free admission on Saturday.
Find the number of free admissions given on Sunday.
5,487 ÷ 175
$$\begin{array}{r} 31 \\ 175\overline{)5487} \\ \underline{-525} \\ 237 \\ \underline{-175} \\ 62 \end{array}$$
31 people were given free admission on Sunday.
Find the total for the two days.
38 + 31 = 69
69 people were given free admission.

26. Find the number of tickets sold last year.
19,950 ÷ 15
$$\begin{array}{r} 1330 \\ 15\overline{)19{,}950} \\ \underline{-15} \\ 49 \\ \underline{-45} \\ 45 \\ \underline{-45} \\ 0 \end{array}$$
Multiply the number of tickets sold last year by this year's ticket price. 1,330 × 20 = 26,600
The school will raise $26,600.

27. The quotient is 10 times greater because the dividend is 10 times greater; 95,540 ÷ 562 = 170.

28. Find the number of times the diameter of the moon goes into the distance from the earth to the moon.
384,400 ÷ 3,476
$$\begin{array}{r} 110 \text{ R}2040 \\ 3476\overline{)384{,}400} \\ \underline{-3476} \\ 3680 \\ \underline{-3476} \\ 2040 \end{array}$$
384,400 ÷ 3,476 = 110 R2040
110 moon diameters and more than half of another moon diameter, so round up to 111.
About 111 moons could be lined up in a row.

29. Multiply the quotient and the divisor, then add the remainder to the product. If the division was done correctly, the result will equal the dividend.

30. No; the total cost of the car is $16,750 + $2,295 = $19,045. If she pays $395 per month it will take 19,045 ÷ 395 = 48 R 85 or 49 months to pay off the car, more than the car dealership will allow.

Focus on Higher Order Thinking

31. No; 78,114 is about 80,000 and 192 is about 200; 80,000 ÷ 200 = 400, and 40 isn't close to 400.

32. Yes; the dividend increased by more than 2,000 when rounded, and a greater dividend results in a smaller quotient. The divisor decreased from 305 to 300, which also results in a larger quotient.

33. More; the whole amount is divided into smaller portions, so there will be more bags; since 25 is half of 50, they will have twice as many bags.

LESSON 5.2

Your Turn

5. $$\begin{array}{r} 0.42 \\ \underline{+0.27} \\ 0.69 \end{array}$$

6. $$\begin{array}{r} 0.610 \\ \underline{+0.329} \\ 0.939 \end{array}$$

7. 3.25
 +4.60
 7.85

8. 17.27
 +3.88
 21.15

Guided Practice

1.

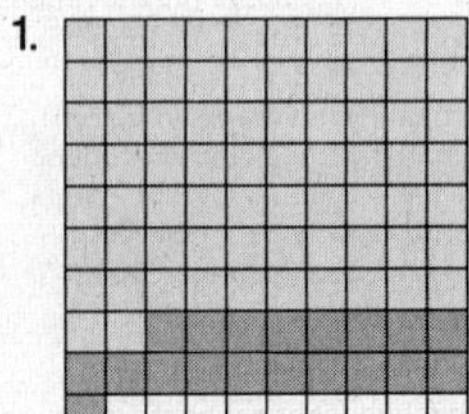

0.72 + 0.19 = 0.91

2.

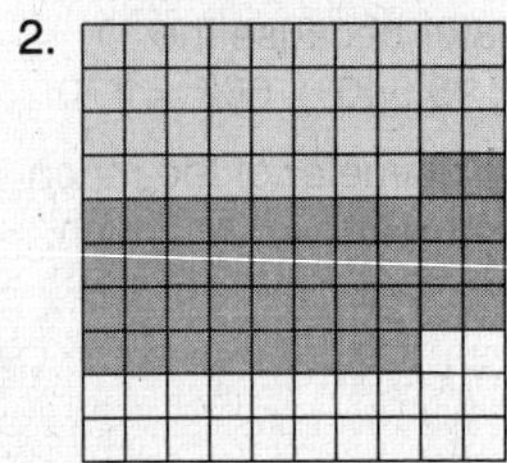

0.38 + 0.4 = 0.78

3. 54.87 → 55
 + 7.48 → + 7
 62.35 → 62

4. 2.19 → 2
 +34.92 → +35
 37.11 → 37

5. 0.215 → 0
 +3.74 → +4
 3.955 → 4

6. 9.73 → 10
 −7.16 → − 7
 2.57 → 3

7. 18.419 → 18
 −6.47 → −6
 11.949 → 12

8. 5.006 → 5
 −3.2 → −3
 1.806 → 2

9. 17.2
 +12.9
 30.1

10. 28.341
 +37.500
 65.841

11. 25.360
 −2.004
 23.356

12. 15.52
 − 8.17
 7.35

13. 25.68
 +12.00
 37.68

14. 150.25
 −78.00
 72.25

15. 16.50
 +14.75
 31.25

The hose is 31.25 feet long.

16. 20.08
 −8.72
 11.36

She has $11.36 left.

17. You align the digits by place value when you add or subtract decimals, just as you align digits for whole numbers.

Independent Practice

18. 28.600
 −0.975
 27.625

19. 5.600
 −0.105
 5.495

20. 7.030
 +33.006
 40.036

21. 57.420
 4.000
 +1.602
 63.022

22. 2.250
 65.470
 +2.333
 70.053

23. 18.419
 −6.470
 11.949

24. 83.00
 −12.76
 70.24

25. 102.010
 −95.602
 6.408

26. a. $5\frac{815}{1,000} + 6\frac{21}{1,000}$

b. $11\frac{836}{1,000} = 11.836$

27. Find the cost of Stephen's lunch.
 2.29
 4.75
 +1.29
 8.33

Find the cost of Jahmya's lunch.

```
  2.89
  4.59
+1.39
  8.87
```

Find the difference in cost between the two lunches.

```
  8.87
−8.33
  0.54
```

Jahmya's lunch cost more. It cost $0.54 more.

28. Find the total cost of the lunch and the tip.

```
  8.87
+1.75
 10.62
```

Find the amount of change from a $20 bill.

```
  20.00
−10.62
   9.38
```

She should receive $9.38 in change.

29. Find the cost of Stephen's lunch, the take-out fruit salad and the tip.

```
  8.33
  2.25
+2.89
 13.47
```

Find the amount of change from a $10 bill and a $5 bill.

```
  15.00
−13.47
   1.53
```

He should receive $1.53 in change.

30. Find the width of the three shims.

```
  0.750
  0.125
+0.090
  0.965
```

Find the difference between the gap and the sum of the three shims.

```
  1.200
−0.965
  0.235
```

The width of the fourth shim is 0.235 centimeter.

31. a. Find the sum of the lengths of the 5 songs.

```
  6.50
  8.00
  3.93
  4.10
+5.05
 27.58
```

Find the amount of break time between songs.

```
  0.05
  0.05
  0.05
+0.05
  0.20
```

Find the sum of the length of the songs and the breaks.

```
  27.58
+ 0.20
  27.78
```

It takes 27.78 minutes to listen to the CD.

b. Find the difference between the time on the disc and the length of the CD.

```
  60.00
−27.78
  32.22
```

He can buy 32.22 minutes of music.

Focus on Higher Order Thinking

32. $2.47 + 7.1 = 9.57$; $7.1 + 2.47 = 9.57$; $9.57 - 2.47 = 7.1$; $9.57 - 7.1 = 2.47$

33. Sample answer: The sum of $2.55 + (3.72 + 1.45) = 2.55 + 5.17 = 7.72$. Using the Commutative Property, the sum can be written as $2.55 + (1.45 + 3.72) = 7.72$, and using the Associative Property, the sum can be written as $(2.55 + 1.45) + 3.72 = 7.72$.

34. Yes. The number being subtracted is rounded up. Subtracting a greater number results in a smaller difference than the actual difference.

LESSON 5.3

Your Turn

3.

```
      12.6 ←   1 decimal places
    × 15.3 ← +1 decimal places
       378
      6300
   + 12600
    192.78 ← 2 decimal places
```

4.

```
      9.76 ←   2 decimal places
    × 0.46 ← +2 decimal places
      5856
    +39040
    4.4896 ← 4 decimal places
```

5.

```
      7.14 ←   2 decimal places
    × 6.78 ← +2 decimal places
      5712
     49980
   +428400
   48.4092 ← 4 decimal places
```

6.

```
     11.49 ←   2 decimal places
    × 8.27 ← +2 decimal places
      8043
     22980
   +919200
   95.0223 ← 4 decimal places
```

7.

```
   15.5
 ×  2.5
    775
 + 3100
  38.75;
  38.75 miles
```

8. Round 15.5 to 15 and 2.5 to 3; $15 \times 3 = 45$, and 45 is close to 38.75.

Guided Practice

1. 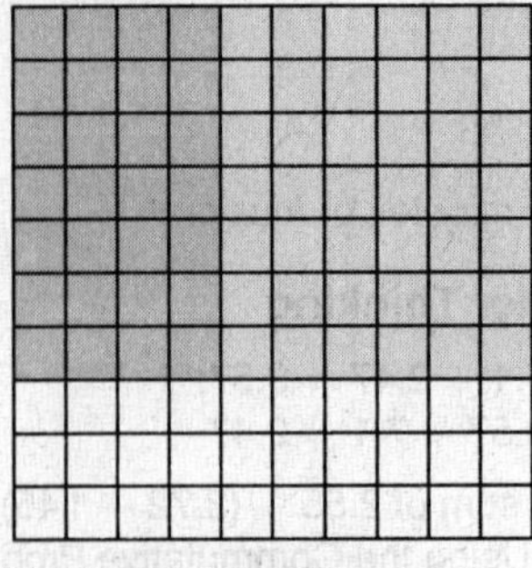

$0.4 \times 0.7 = 0.28$

2. 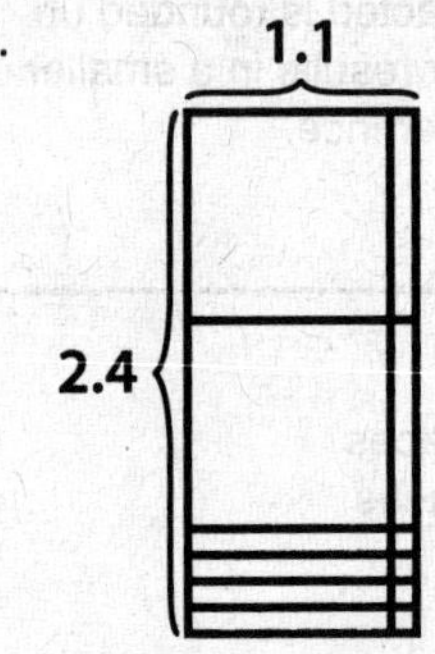

$1.1 \times 2.4 = 2.64$

3.
```
  0.18
 ×0.06
0.0108
```

4.
```
   35.15
 ×   3.7
   24605
+ 105450
 130.055
```

5.
```
  0.96
 ×0.12
   192
  +960
0.1152
```

6.
```
      62.19
    × 32.5
      31095
     124380
  + 1865700
  2,021.175
```

7.
```
  4.37
 × 3.4
  1748
+13110
14.858
```

8.
```
   3.762
 ×  0.66
   22572
+ 225720
 2.48292
```

9.
```
    6.95
 ×   3.4
    2780
 + 20850
 $23.630
```

10.
```
     18.5
   ×9.40
     7400
 + 166500
 $173.900
```

11.
```
    11.5
   ×2.54
     460
    5750
 + 23000
 $29.210
```

12.

Week 1	Week 4
10.4	10.6
×2.65	×2.70
520	7420
6240	+21200
+20800	28.620
27.560	

Catherine spent $28.62 − $27.56 = $1.06 more in week 4 than in week 1.

13. Divide the product by one of the decimals. The quotient should be the other decimal value.

Independent Practice

14. Round 8.354 to 8, and round 11.81 to 12. Simon used about $8 \times 12 = 96$ pounds of water.

15. Round 2.394 to 2, and round 7.489 to 7. The snail will travel about $2 \times 7 = 14$ inches.

16. Round 9.87 to 10, and round 1.09 to 1. The area of the garden is about $10 \times 1 = 10$ square meters.

17. Round 8.75 to 9, and round 37.5 to 38. Kaylynn earns about $342 in a week.

18. Round 10.25 to 10, and round 30.5 to 31. Amanda earns about $310 in a week.

19.

Kaylynn	Amanda
8.75	10.25
× 37.5	× 30.5
4375	5125
61250	+307500
+262500	312.625
328.125	

The difference in salaries is $328.125 − $312.625 = $15.50.

20. Round 8.804 to 9, and round 0.903 to 1. The printer will print about $9 \times 1 = 9$ pages.

21.
```
    2.25
 ×   8.7
    1575
 + 18000
  19.575
```

It will cost $19.58 + $4.00 = $23.58.

22. $35.23; Sample answer: Multiply each distance driven by 2.25, add 4 to each product, and then add the two sums.

23.
```
   10.75
 ×   1.9
    9675
 + 10750
  20.425 miles
```

24. 8.8 × 3.75 = 33 miles; Friday

25. On Monday, Kay took her longest bike ride of 8.2 × 4.25 = 34.85 miles. On Thursday she took her shortest bike ride of 10.75 × 1.9 = 20.425 miles. The difference is 34.85 − 20.425 = 14.425 miles.

26. Yes; on Wednesday she rode about 11 miles per hour for about 3 hours, and 11 × 3 = 33. On Tuesday she rode about 10 miles per hour for about 3 hours, and 10 × 3 = 30. 33 − 30 = 3.

Focus on Higher Order Thinking

27. 3.48 is closer to 3, and 7.33 is closer to 7; 7 × 3 = 21.

28. The jeweler makes $2,376.44 − $1,376.44 = $140.89 per ounce he resells. Buying and reselling 73.5 ounces, he makes 140.89 × 73.5 = 10,355.415, or $10,355.42 rounded to the nearest hundredth.

29.
```
  22 karat        18 karat
      73.5            73.5
   × 0.916         × 0.585
      4410            3675
      7350           58800
  + 661500        + 367500
   67.3260         42.9975
```

A 22 karat statue that weighs 73.5 ounces contains 67.3995 ounces of gold. An 18 karat gold statue that weighs 73.5 ounces contains 42.8505 ounces of gold. The 22 karat statue contains 67.3995 − 42.8505 = 24.549 ounces more gold.

LESSON 5.4

Your Turn

3.
```
   1.95
 5)9.75
  −5
   47
  −45
    25
   −25
     0
```
1.95

4.
```
   0.92
 7)6.44
  −63
    14
   −14
     0
```
0.92

5.
```
  29.2
 3)87.6
  −6
   27
  −27
     6
    −6
     0
```
29.2

6.
```
    7.13
 14)99.82
   −98
     18
    −14
      42
     −42
       0
```
7.13

7. The divisor, 0.5, has 1 decimal place, so multiply the dividend and divisor by 10 before dividing; 0.5 × 10 = 5, and 4.25 × 10 = 42.5.
```
   8.5
 5)42.5
  −40
    25
   −25
     0
```
8.5

8. The divisor, 0.84, has 2 decimal places, so multiply the dividend and divisor by 100 before dividing; 0.84 × 100 = 84, and 15.12 × 100 = 1,512.
```
      18
 84)1,512
   −84
    672
   −672
      0
```
18

Guided Practice

1.
```
   7.25
 4)29.00
  −28
    10
    −8
    20
   −20
     0
```
7.25

2.
```
   6.125
 8)49.000
  −48
    10
    −8
    20
   −16
    40
   −40
     0
```
6.125

```
     3.4
3. 2)6.8
    −6
      8
     −8
      0
```
3.4

```
          0.15
4. 096)014.40
        −96
         480
        −480
           0
```
0.15

```
      77
5. 5)385
    −35
      35
     −35
       0
```
77

```
     2.15
6. 3)6.45
    −6
      4
     −3
      15
     −15
       0
```
2.15

```
       33.16
7. 17)563.72
     −51
       53
      −51
        27
       −17
        102
       −102
          0
```
33.16

```
       1.95
8. 42)81.90
     −42
      399
     −378
       210
      −210
         0
```
1.95

```
       19
9. 35)665
     −35
      315
     −315
        0
```
19

```
        0.3
10. 78)23.4
      −234
         0
```
0.3

```
          6.2
11. 127)787.4
        −762
         254
        −254
           0
```
6.2

```
       405
12. 9)3645
     −36
       04
       −0
        45
       −45
         0
```
405

```
        250
13. 36)9000
      −72
       180
      −180
        00
        −0
         0
```
250

```
        11.8
14. 16)188.8
      −16
        28
       −16
        128
       −128
          0
```
11.8

```
        1.25
15. 8)10.00
      −8
       20
      −16
        40
       −40
         0
```
1.25 pounds

```
            3.5
16. 328)1148.0
        −984
        1640
       −1640
           0
```
3.5 pounds

18.25
17. 4)73.00
−4
33
−32
10
−8
20
−20
0
18.25 seconds

18
18. 25)450
−25
200
−200
0
18

2.729
19. 161)439.500
−322
1175
−1127
480
−322
1580
−1449
131...
$2.73 per gallon

20
20. 254)5080
−508
00
−0
0
20 inches

21. You multiply both numbers by the same power of 10 so that the divisor becomes a whole number. Then you can divide as if you were dividing by a whole number, making sure to correctly place the decimal point in the quotient.

Independent Practice

4.29
22. 25)107.25
−100
72
−50
225
−225
0
$4.29

8.50
23. 75)637.50
−600
375
−375
0
$8.50

24. Andrew's fee minus the monthly membership rate is $16.25 − $5.00 = $11.25. Each movie rental is $1.25.
9
125)1125
−1125
0
Andrew rented 9 movies.

25. a. Marissa will pay $5.00 for the monthly membership. That leaves her $18.50 − $5.00 = $13.50 to spend on movies. Each movie rental costs $1.25.
10.8
125)13500
−125
1000
−1000
0
She can rent 10 movies.

b. She could be rounding 10.8 up to 11, but she doesn't have enough money for 11 movies.

0.5
26. 25)12.5
−125
0
$0.50

27. Potatoes cost $1.20 per pound. Carrots cost $1.80 per pound. Beef costs $2.39 per pound. Bell peppers cost $0.50 per pound. Beef costs the most per pound.

28. If carrots cost $0.50 less per pound, they would cost $1.80 − $0.50 = $1.30 per pound. 8.5 × $1.30 = $11.05.

29. a. Brenda plans to have 10.92 liters of punch, and there will be 26 people at the party.
0.42
26)10.92
−104
52
−52
0
Each guest will drink 0.42 liters of punch.

b. She plans to have 6.5 gallons of frozen yogurt and there will be 26 people eating the frozen yogurt.
0.25
26)6.50
−52
130
−130
0
Each guest will eat 0.25 gallons of frozen yogurt.

c. Brenda plans to have 3.9 pounds of cheese, and there will be 26 people eating the cheese.
0.15
26)3.90
−26
130
−130
0
Each guest will eat 0.15 pounds of cheese.

30. Yellow fabric

$$\begin{array}{r} 6.75 \\ 128\overline{)864.00} \\ -768 \\ \hline 960 \\ -896 \\ \hline 640 \\ -640 \\ \hline 0 \end{array}$$

White fabric

$$\begin{array}{r} 4.8 \\ 95\overline{)456.0} \\ -380 \\ \hline 760 \\ -760 \\ \hline 0 \\ -640 \\ \hline 0 \end{array}$$

The yellow fabric costs $6.75 per yard. The white fabric costs $4.80 per yard. The yellow fabric costs more per yard.

31.

$$\begin{array}{r} 42 \\ 3\overline{)128} \\ -12 \\ \hline 08 \\ -6 \\ \hline 2 \end{array}$$

She can make 42 strips.

Focus on Higher Order Thinking

32. The eight friends spent a total of $85.43 + $32.75 + $239.66 = $357.84.

$$\begin{array}{r} 44.73 \\ 8\overline{)357.84} \\ -32 \\ \hline 37 \\ -32 \\ \hline 58 \\ -56 \\ \hline 24 \\ -24 \\ \hline 0 \end{array}$$

Each person will owe $44.73.

33. Constance has already saved $40, so she still needs $195.75 − $40 = $155.75.

$$\begin{array}{r} 19.46875 \\ 8\overline{)155.75000} \\ -8 \\ \hline 75 \\ -72 \\ \hline 37 \\ -32 \\ \hline 55 \\ -48 \\ \hline 70 \\ -64 \\ \hline 60 \\ -56 \\ \hline 40 \\ -40 \\ \hline 0 \end{array}$$

She needs to save for 20 weeks.

34. Grocery store

$$\begin{array}{r} 1.15 \\ 12\overline{)13.80} \\ -12 \\ \hline 18 \\ -12 \\ \hline 60 \\ -60 \\ \hline 0 \end{array}$$

Convenience store

$$\begin{array}{r} 1.18 \\ 10\overline{)11.80} \\ -10 \\ \hline 18 \\ -10 \\ \hline 80 \\ -80 \\ \hline 0 \end{array}$$

The grocery store; at the grocery store each bottle costs $1.15, while at the convenience store each bottle costs $1.18.

LESSON 5.5

Your Turn

1. $58 \div (6.2 + 5.4)$
$= 58 \div 11.6$
$= 5$
Casey paid $5 per yard of fabric.

2. He paid $\frac{29}{2} \times \frac{3}{5} = \frac{87}{10} = 8\frac{7}{10}$ dollars or $14.5 × 0.6 = $8.70.

Guided Practice

1. $188.3 \times \frac{5}{7} = 188\frac{3}{10} \times \frac{5}{7}$;
$188\frac{3}{10} \times \frac{5}{7} = 134\frac{1}{2}$
$134\frac{1}{2}$ miles

2. $\frac{3}{4} \times 530.40 = 0.75 \times 530.4$
$= 397.8$
$397.80

Independent Practice

3. $8.75 \times \frac{2}{5} = 8\frac{3}{4} \times \frac{2}{5}$
$8\frac{3}{4} \times \frac{2}{5} = 3\frac{1}{2}$
$3\frac{1}{2}$ gallons

4. $(3 + 4.2) \times 1.75$
$= 7.2 \times 1.75$
$= 12.6$
$12.60

5. $(16.2 + 11.8) \times 0.4$
$= 28 \times 0.4$
$= 11.2$
$11.2 \div 5.6 = 2$
2 batteries

6. $(11.5 + 10.7) \times 0.4$;
$= 22.2 \times 0.4$
$= 8.88$
$8.88 \div 2.96 = 3$
3 movies

7. They earned $7.84 on Wednesday, and spent $7.84 × 0.75 = $5.88 on the gift; No. After buying the gift, they have $7.84 − $5.88 = $1.96 left which is not enough money for the card.

8. Sample answer: Nestor charged \$9.50 an hour to rake leaves. He worked 8 hours one week and 12.5 hours the next. How much did Nestor earn raking leaves? He earned \$194.75.

9. $(35.4 + 18.2) \times 2.5 = 134$;
   $134 \div 35.75 = 3.748...$
   3 games

10. $(21.8 + 26.6) \times 2.5 = 121$
    $121 \div 17.5 = 6.9...$
    Alice can afford 6 tickets.

Focus on Higher Order Thinking

11. The expression can be written as $(5 \times 3) \div \frac{1}{3}$;
    $5 \times 3 \div \frac{1}{3}$
    $= 15 \div \frac{1}{3}$
    $= \frac{15}{1} \div \frac{1}{3}$
    $= \frac{15}{1} \times \frac{3}{1}$
    $= 45$
    The pizzas will serve 45 party guests.

12. She should have used parentheses to group the addition to find the total number of hours before multiplying.
    $7.5 \times (18.5 + 20) = 7.5 \times 38.5 = \$288.75$

13. 35; \$7.50 + \$0.75 = \$8.25; \$288.75 ÷ \$8.25 = 35

MODULE 5

Ready to Go On?

1.
```
     37
34)1265
  -102
   245
  -238
     7
```
Because there is a remainder of 7, Landon will need to build a total of 38 shelves.

2. $3.218 - 2.41 = 0.808$
   She ran 0.808 more kilometers on Saturday than on Sunday.

3.
```
    3.9
 × 0.72
     78
 +2730
  2.808
```
2.808 miles

4.
```
   1.22
 × 0.07
 0.0854
```

5.
```
    2.65
  ×  4.7
    1855
 +10600
  12.455
```

6.
```
  160
4)640
 -4
  24
 -24
   00
  -00
    0
```
160

7.
```
   18.23
26)473.98
  -26
   213
  -208
     59
    -52
     78
    -78
      0
```
18.23

8.
```
  2.97
9)26.73
 -18
   87
  -81
   63
  -63
    0
```
2.97

9.
```
   1.25
32)40.00
  -32
    80
   -64
   160
  -160
     0
```
1.25

10. $126 \div (11.5 \times 2.3)$
    $= 126 \div 26.45$
    $= 4.7...$
    4 doors

11. Sample answer: Finding how many $\frac{1}{4}$ cup servings of rice are in a 4.75 cup container.

UNIT 3

Solutions Key

Proportionality: Ratios and Rates

MODULE 6 *Representing Ratios and Rates*

Are You Ready?

1. $\frac{6}{9} = \frac{6 \div 3}{9 \div 3}$
   $= \frac{2}{3}$
2. $\frac{4}{10} = \frac{4 \div 2}{10 \div 2}$
   $= \frac{2}{5}$
3. $\frac{15}{20} = \frac{15 \div 5}{10 \div 2}$
   $= \frac{3}{4}$
4. $\frac{20}{24} = \frac{20 \div 4}{24 \div 4}$
   $= \frac{5}{6}$
5. $\frac{16}{56} = \frac{16 \div 8}{56 \div 8}$
   $= \frac{2}{7}$
6. $\frac{45}{72} = \frac{45 \div 9}{72 \div 9}$
   $= \frac{5}{8}$
7. $\frac{18}{60} = \frac{18 \div 6}{60 \div 6}$
   $= \frac{3}{10}$
8. $\frac{32}{72} = \frac{32 \div 8}{72 \div 8}$
   $= \frac{4}{9}$
9. $\frac{12}{15} = \frac{12 \div 3}{15 \div 3}$
   $= \frac{4}{5}$
10. $\frac{5}{6} = \frac{5 \times 5}{6 \times 5}$
    $= \frac{25}{30}$
11. $\frac{16}{24} = \frac{16 \div 4}{24 \div 4}$
    $= \frac{4}{6}$
12. $\frac{3}{9} = \frac{3 \times 7}{9 \times 7}$
    $= \frac{21}{63}$
13. $\frac{15}{40} = \frac{15 \div 5}{40 \div 5}$
    $= \frac{3}{8}$
14. $\frac{18}{30} = \frac{18 \div 3}{30 \div 3}$
    $= \frac{6}{10}$
15. $\frac{48}{64} = \frac{48 \div 4}{64 \div 4}$
    $= \frac{12}{16}$
16. $\frac{2}{7} = \frac{2 \times 9}{7 \times 9}$
    $= \frac{18}{63}$

LESSON 6.1

Your Turn

5. 3:1; 3 to 1; $\frac{3}{1}$
6. 8:3; 8 to 3; $\frac{8}{3}$
7. 1:1; 1 to 1; $\frac{1}{1}$
8. Sample answer:
   $\frac{8}{10} \div \frac{2}{2} = \frac{4}{5}$,
   $\frac{8}{10} \times \frac{2}{2} = \frac{16}{20}$,
   $\frac{8}{10} \times \frac{1.5}{1.5} = \frac{12}{15}$
9. Sample answer:
   $\frac{5}{2} \times \frac{2}{2} = \frac{10}{4}$,
   $\frac{5}{2} \times \frac{3}{3} = \frac{15}{6}$,
   $\frac{5}{4} \times \frac{4}{4} = \frac{20}{8}$

Guided Practice

1. 1 to 5
2. In the apartment complex, there are 5 cats per dog.
3. $15 \div 5 = 3$ dogs
4. $5 \times 5 = 25$ cats
5. Sample answer: 2 to 5; 2:5; $\frac{2}{5}$
6. Sample answer: 5 to 12; 5:12; $\frac{5}{12}$
7. Sample answer:
   $\frac{10 \div 2}{12 \div 2} = \frac{5}{6}$,
   $\frac{10}{12} \times \frac{2}{2} = \frac{20}{24}$,
   $\frac{10}{12} \times \frac{1.5}{1.5} = \frac{25}{30}$

8. Sample answer:
$\frac{14}{2} = \frac{14 \div 2}{2 \div 2} = \frac{7}{1}$,
$\frac{14}{2} \times \frac{1.5}{1.5} = \frac{21}{3}$,
$\frac{14}{2} \times \frac{2}{2} = \frac{28}{4}$

9. Sample answer:
$\frac{4}{7} \times \frac{2}{2} = \frac{8}{14}$,
$\frac{4}{7} \times \frac{3}{3} = \frac{12}{21}$,
$\frac{4}{7} \times \frac{4}{4} = \frac{16}{28}$

10. Sample answer: The ratios 2:5 and 4:10 are equivalent. Each term of 4:10 is 2 times the corresponding term in of 2:5.

Independent Practice

11. Sample answer: There is 1 cup of water for every 3 cups of milk; multiplying each quantity by 2 gives 2 to 6, multiplying each quantity by 3 gives 3 to 9, and multiplying each quantity by 4 gives 4 to 12.

12. Sample answer: There are 20 peppers for every 15 tomatoes;
$\frac{20}{15} = \frac{20 \div 5}{15 \div 5} = \frac{4}{3}$,
$\frac{20}{15} \times \frac{2}{2} = \frac{40}{30}$,
$\frac{20}{15} \times \frac{5}{5} = \frac{100}{75}$

13.

Roses	4	8	12	16	20
Carnations	6	12	18	24	30

16 roses and 24 carnations

14. To use 30 strawberries, Ed should make $30 \div 10 = 3$ servings of the fruit salad. 4 bananas $\times$ 3 = 12 bananas, 3 apples $\times$ 3 = 9 apples, and 6 pears $\times$ 3 = 18 pears.

15. No. The current ratio is $\frac{120}{100}$ or $\frac{6}{5}$. The ratio after the sale will be $\frac{96}{76}$, or $\frac{24}{19}$. Because $\frac{6}{5} = \frac{24}{20}$, the two ratios are not equivalent.

16. Since the orange juice concentrate and cups of water are being combined, they should be added to create the total, $2 + 3.5 = 5.5$.

$\frac{2}{5.5} \times \frac{3}{3} = \frac{6 \text{ cups of orange juice concentrate}}{16.5 \text{ cups of water}}$

16.5 cups

17. a. $\frac{5}{3} \times \frac{6}{6} = \frac{30 \text{ North American butterflies}}{18 \text{ South American butterflies}}$

18 South American butterflies

b. $\frac{3}{2} \times \frac{6}{6} = \frac{18 \text{ South American butterflies}}{12 \text{ European butterflies}}$

12 European butterflies

18. a. Sinea spent \$8 on games on her last trip and \$12 on souvenirs, so the ratio of games to souvenirs is 8 to 12, or 2 to 3. 2 to 3 is equivalent to 24 to 36, so she'll spend \$36 on souvenirs.

b. Ren's ratio of souvenirs to snacks is 20 to 10. 20 to 10 is equivalent to 2 to 1, so he'll spend \$24 on snacks.

c. Based on past data, Ren will spend twice as much as Sinea on snacks, or \$30, and twice as much on souvenirs as on snacks, or \$60.

Focus on Higher Order Thinking

19. Since the diagram shows 3 boxes for girls and 2 for boys, the ratio is 3:2. If there are 50 students in the chorus, each box must represent 10 students, so there are 30 girls and 20 boys.

20. In both processes you multiply or divide the terms, or numerator and denominator, by the same number.

21. Tina did not multiply both terms by the same number.

LESSON 6.2

Your Turn

4. 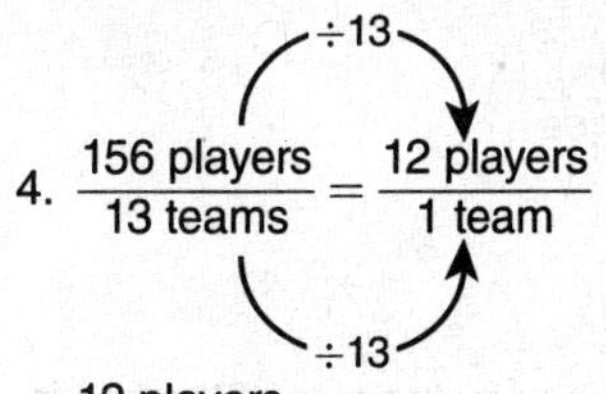

$\frac{156 \text{ players}}{13 \text{ teams}} = \frac{12 \text{ players}}{1 \text{ team}}$

12 players

5. 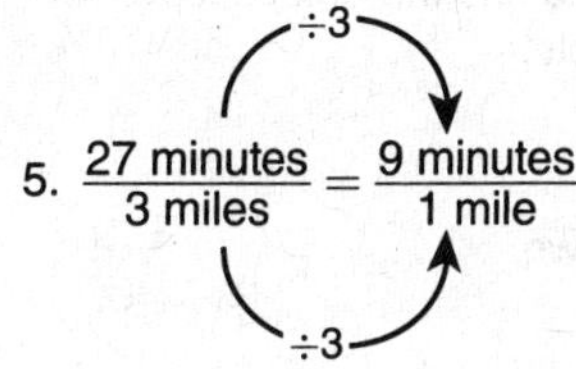

$\frac{27 \text{ minutes}}{3 \text{ miles}} = \frac{9 \text{ minutes}}{1 \text{ mile}}$

The unit rate is 9 minutes per mile.

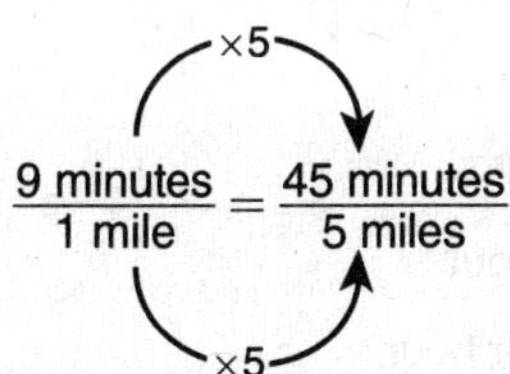

$\frac{9 \text{ minutes}}{1 \text{ mile}} = \frac{45 \text{ minutes}}{5 \text{ miles}}$.

It will take her 45 minutes to jog 5 miles.

Guided Practice

1. Regular: $\frac{\$3.36}{16 \text{ oz}} = \$0.21$ per oz

Family size: $\frac{\$7.60}{40 \text{ oz}} = \$0.19$ per oz

2. The family size costs less per ounce, so it is the better buy.

3. $\frac{\$10}{5 \text{ bags}} = \$2$ per bag

$\frac{\$2}{1 \text{ bag}} = \frac{\$48}{24 \text{ bags}}$

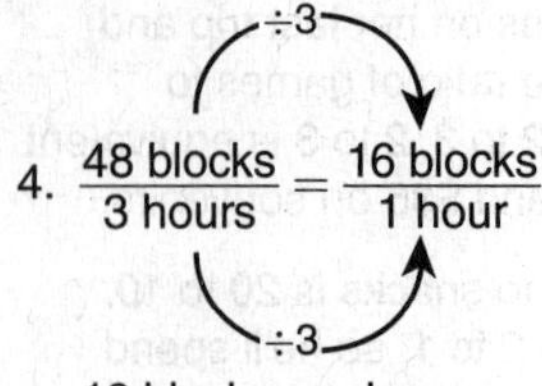

4. $\frac{48 \text{ blocks}}{3 \text{ hours}} = \frac{16 \text{ blocks}}{1 \text{ hour}}$

16 blocks per hour

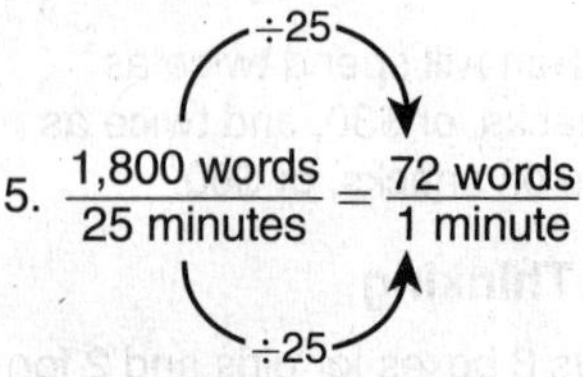

5. $\frac{1{,}800 \text{ words}}{25 \text{ minutes}} = \frac{72 \text{ words}}{1 \text{ minute}}$

72 words per minute

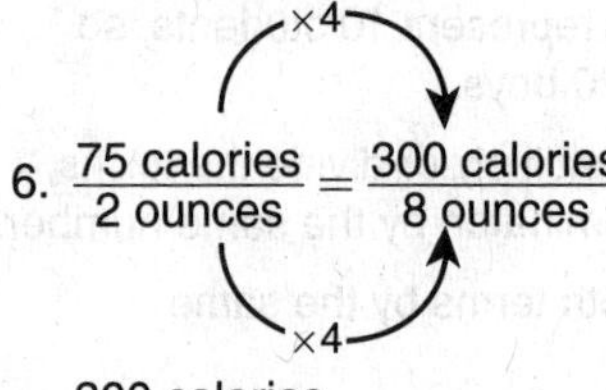

6. $\frac{75 \text{ calories}}{2 \text{ ounces}} = \frac{300 \text{ calories}}{8 \text{ ounces}}$

300 calories

7. 5 dozen oranges $= 5 \times 12 = 60$ oranges

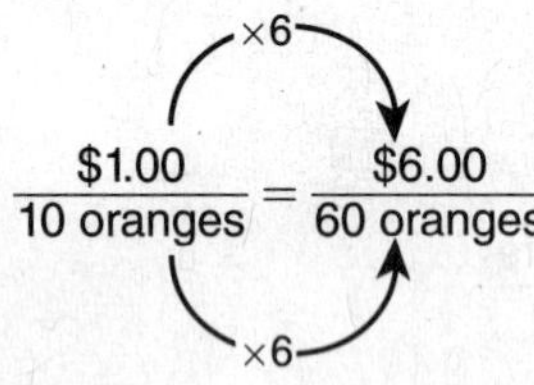

$\frac{\$1.00}{10 \text{ oranges}} = \frac{\$6.00}{60 \text{ oranges}}$

$6.00

8. Divide the cost of each box by the size of the box in ounces, or another unit, to find the unit cost per ounce. Compare unit costs.

Independent Practice

9. $\frac{\$112.50}{9 \text{ lawns}} = \$12.50$ per lawn

10. $\frac{\$122.50}{7 \text{ lawns}} = \$17.50$ per lawn

11. $\frac{\$112.50}{7.5 \text{ hours}} = \$15$ per hour

Taryn earns $15 per hour

$\frac{\$122.50}{5 \text{ hours}} = \$24.50$ per hour

Alastair earns $24.50 per hour.
Alastair earns more per hour.

12. Taryn will spend 49 hours, and Alastair will spend 30 hours. Taryn earns $15 per hour, and $735 \div 15 = 49$. Alastair earns $24.50 per hour, and $735 \div 24.50 = 30$.

13. a. $\frac{180 \text{ minutes}}{36 \text{ sculptures}} = \frac{5 \text{ minutes}}{1 \text{ sculpture}}$

5 minutes

$\frac{252 \text{ balloons}}{36 \text{ sculptures}} = \frac{7 \text{ balloons}}{1 \text{ sculpture}}$

7 balloons

b. $\frac{252 \text{ balloons}}{180 \text{ minutes}} = \frac{1.4 \text{ balloons}}{1 \text{ minute}}$

$1\frac{2}{5}$ balloons per minute

c. $1\frac{2}{5}$ balloons per minute $\times$ 10 minutes $= 14$ balloons

14. $\frac{\$7.40}{8 \text{ pounds}} = \$0.925$ per pound

$\frac{\$5.38}{4 \text{ pounds}} = \$1.345$ per pound

The 8-pound bag costs less per pound.

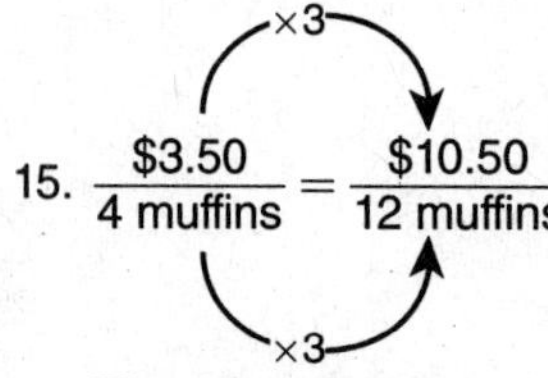

15. $\frac{\$3.50}{4 \text{ muffins}} = \frac{\$10.50}{12 \text{ muffins}}$

The price per dozen is $10.50.

16. a. $\frac{\$21.25}{25 \text{ whistles}} = \$0.85$ per whistle

$\frac{\$36.00}{50 \text{ whistles}} = \$0.72$ per whistle

$\frac{\$60.00}{80 \text{ whistles}} = \$0.75$ per whistle

The difference between the highest unit price and the lowest unit price is $\$0.85 - \$0.72 = \$0.13$ per whistle.

b. $\frac{\$10.00}{25 \text{ kazoos}} = \$0.40$ per kazoo

$\frac{\$18.50}{50 \text{ kazoos}} = \$0.37$ per kazoo

$\frac{\$27.20}{80 \text{ kazoos}} = \$0.34$ per kazoo

The highest unit price per kazoo is $0.40 per kazoo.

c. She should order 80 kazoos, which only cost $0.34 per kazoo.

Focus on Higher Order Thinking

17. There are 12 inches in 1 foot, and $2.54 \times 12 = 30.48$ centimeters per foot. There are 3 feet per yard, and $30.48 \text{ cm} \times 3 = 91.44$ centimeters per yard.

18. Philip compared pounds to dollars and found the weight per dollar. The correct unit cost is $\frac{\$2.50}{2 \text{ pounds}} = \$1.25$ per pound.

19. The unit costs are $1.10 per pound for a 1-pound bag, $0.99 per pound for a 2-pound bag, and $0.88 per pound for a 3-pound bag. The unit cost decreases by $0.11 per pound as the quantity increases.

LESSON 6.3

Your Turn

2. No, the ratios are not equivalent.

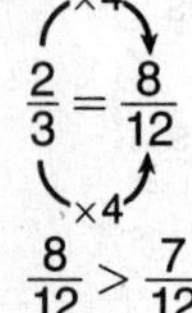

$\frac{2}{3} = \frac{8}{12}$

$\frac{8}{12} > \frac{7}{12}$

Guided Practice

1. a.

Apples	5	10	15	20
Oranges	6	12	18	24

Apples	2	4	6	8
Oranges	3	6	9	12

b. No; $\frac{5}{6} > \frac{4}{6}$; Celeste is using too few apples, 4 for every 6 oranges instead of 5 for every 6 oranges.

2. No; Neha; Sample answer: Neha used 72 bananas for every 90 oranges compared with Daniel's 70 bananas for every 90 oranges.

$\frac{4}{5} > \frac{7}{9}$

Neha used the greater ratio of bananas to oranges in her fruit salad.

3. Sample answer:

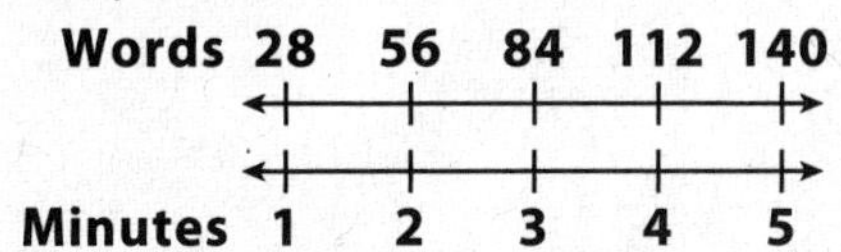

No, Tim can read only 140 words in 5 minutes.

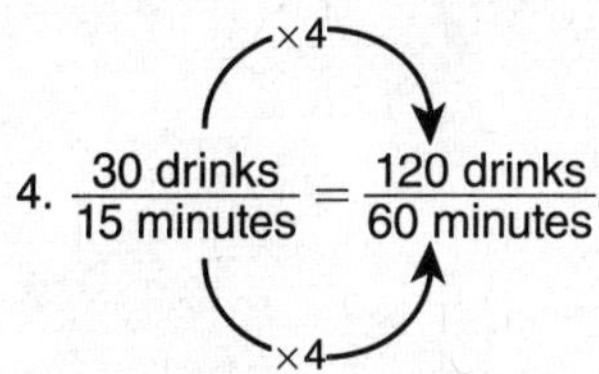

4. $\frac{30 \text{ drinks}}{15 \text{ minutes}} = \frac{120 \text{ drinks}}{60 \text{ minutes}}$. (×4)

Yes, the cafeteria sells 120 drinks per hour.

5. You must assume that the rate does not change.

Independent Practice

6. No, Gina did not use the same ratio as her teacher. 9 to 6 is not equivalent to 4 to 3.

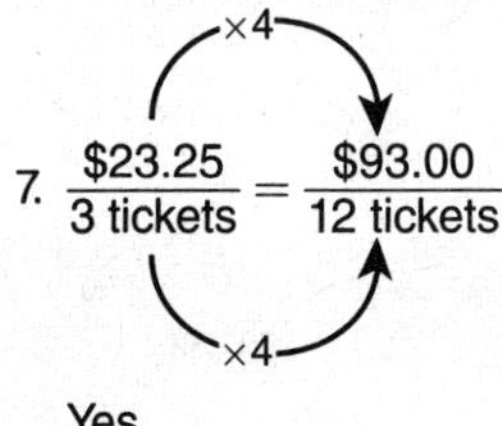

7. $\frac{\$23.25}{3 \text{ tickets}} = \frac{\$93.00}{12 \text{ tickets}}$ (×4)

Yes

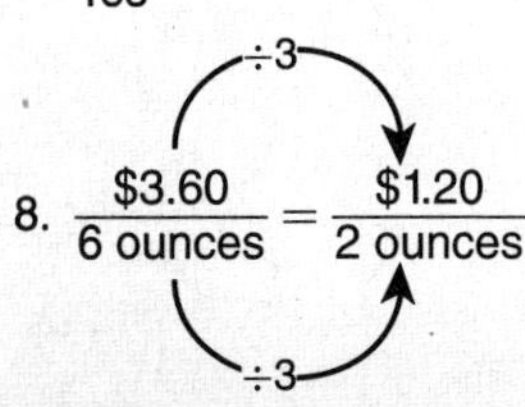

8. $\frac{\$3.60}{6 \text{ ounces}} = \frac{\$1.20}{2 \text{ ounces}}$ (÷3)

Less than

9. Sue: $\frac{300 \text{ miles}}{12 \text{ gallons}} = \frac{25 \text{ miles}}{1 \text{ gallon}}$ (÷12)

Jen: $\frac{140 \text{ miles}}{5 \text{ gallons}} = \frac{28 \text{ miles}}{1 \text{ gallon}}$ (÷5)

Jen's car

10. a. $\frac{2 \text{ free}}{10 \text{ paid}} = \frac{1}{5}$

b. $\frac{8 \text{ free}}{25 \text{ paid}} = \frac{8}{25}$

c. No. $\frac{1}{5} = \frac{5}{25}$. Since $\frac{8}{25} > \frac{5}{25}$, Sam's ratio is greater than Pablo's.

11. a. $\frac{\$3.00}{2 \text{ pounds}} = \frac{\$9.00}{6 \text{ pounds}}$. (×3) You can buy 6 pounds of apples.

b. No; 1 pound = 16 ounces, so 6 pounds × 16 ounces per pound = 96 ounces. Since each apple weighs about 5 ounces, you can buy

96 ounces × $\frac{1 \text{ apple}}{5 \text{ ounces}} \approx$ 19 apples.

12. California fan palm tree: $\frac{85 \text{ inches}}{5 \text{ years}}$ = 17 inches per year

Queen palm tree: $\frac{96 \text{ inches}}{8 \text{ years}}$ = 12 inches per year

The California fan palm tree grew faster than the queen palm tree.

13. Theo: $\frac{228 \text{ miles}}{4 \text{ hours}}$ = 57 miles per hour

57 miles × 2 hours = 114 miles

Lex: $\frac{186 \text{ miles}}{3 \text{ hours}}$ = 62 miles per hour

62 miles × 2 hours = 124 miles

Yes, they could have both driven 112 miles in 2 hours.

14. $\frac{\$15.00}{2 \text{ yards}}$ = $7.50 per yard

$\frac{\$37.50}{5 \text{ yards}}$ = $7.50 per yard

Yes, they both cost $7.50 per yard.

Focus on Higher Order Thinking

15.

6	12	18	24
4.5	9	13.5	18

808	40.4	20.2	10.1
1,024	512	256	128

16. Sample answer: In Tim's snack mix, the ratio of raisins to nuts is 5 to 9. In Sharon's, the ratio of raisins to nuts is 12 to 15. Which mix has the greater ratio of raisins to nuts?
17. Sample answer: Be sure the rates are equivalent by dividing the top term in each ratio by the bottom term.
18. Sample answer: If he thinks the job will take at least 4 hours; if it takes 4 hours, he will earn $50, and if it takes more than 4 hours, he will earn more than $50.

MODULE 6

Ready to Go On?

1. $\frac{8}{5}$
2. $\frac{4}{19}$
3. $\frac{6}{23}$
4. $\frac{8}{5} = \frac{16}{10}, \frac{8}{5} = \frac{24}{15}$ (×2, ×2; ×3, ×3)
5. $\frac{75 \text{ meters}}{30 \text{ seconds}} = \frac{2.5 \text{ meters}}{1 \text{ second}}$; 2.5 meters (÷30, ÷30)

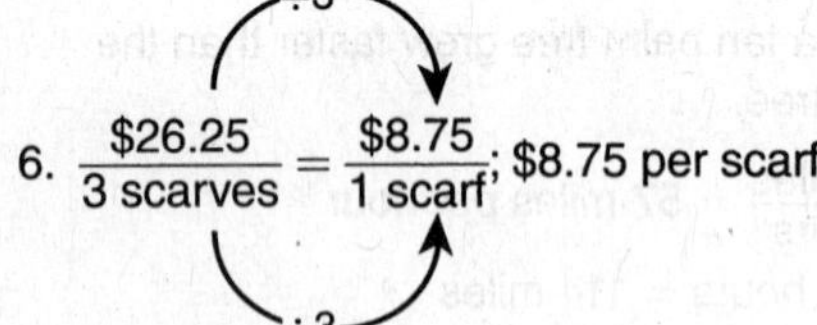

6. $\frac{\$26.25}{3 \text{ scarves}} = \frac{\$8.75}{1 \text{ scarf}}$; $8.75 per scarf (÷3, ÷3)
7. Danny: $\frac{\$35.00}{3 \text{ hours}} \approx \$11.67$ per hour

   Martin: $\frac{\$24.00}{2 \text{ hours}} = \$12.00$ per hour

   Danny offers a better deal.
8. $\frac{3 \text{ men}}{8 \text{ women}} = \frac{12 \text{ men}}{32 \text{ women}}$; 12 men (×4, ×4)
9. Compare ratios and rates by finding equivalent ratios and rates with a common second term. Make predictions by finding a unit rate and multiplying by the unit rate.

MODULE 7 *Applying Ratios and Rates*

Are You Ready?

1–4.

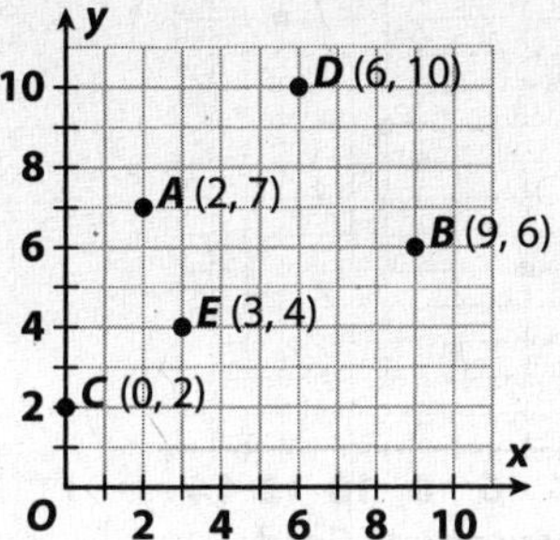

5. $\frac{6}{8} = \frac{24}{32}$ (×4)

6. $\frac{4}{6} = \frac{8}{12}$ (×2)

7. $\frac{1}{8} = \frac{7}{56}$ (×7)

8. $\frac{9}{12} = \frac{3}{4}$ (÷3)

9. $\frac{5}{9} = \frac{25}{45}$ (×5)

10. $\frac{5}{6} = \frac{20}{24}$ (×4)

11. $\frac{36}{45} = \frac{12}{15}$ (÷3)

12. $\frac{20}{36} = \frac{10}{18}$ (÷2)

13. $3 \times 1 = 3$
$3 \times 2 = 6$
$3 \times 3 = 9$
$3 \times 4 = 12$
$3 \times 5 = 15$
3, 6, 9, 12, 15

14. $7 \times 1 = 7$
$7 \times 2 = 14$
$7 \times 3 = 21$
$7 \times 4 = 28$
$7 \times 5 = 35$
7, 14, 21, 28, 35

15. $8 \times 1 = 8$
$8 \times 2 = 16$
$8 \times 3 = 24$
$8 \times 4 = 32$
$8 \times 5 = 40$
8, 16, 24, 32, 40

LESSON 7.1

Your Turn

3.

Time (min)	2	3	4	5	6
Water used (gal)	8	12	16	20	24

Graph the ordered pairs (2, 8), (3, 12), (4, 16), (5, 20), (6, 24).

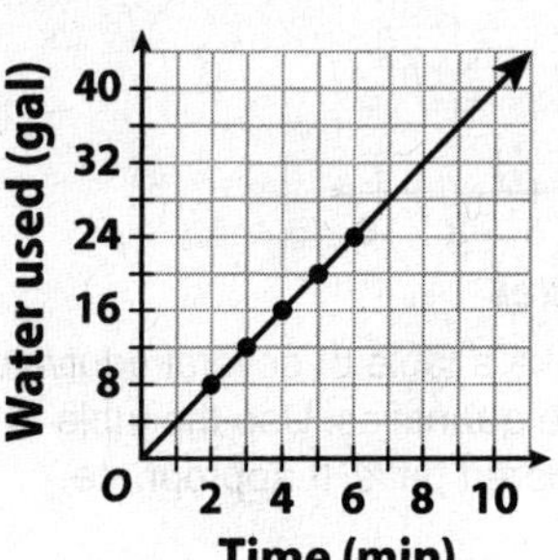

It took 8 minutes.

Guided Practice

1.

Sulfur atoms	6	9	21	27
Oxygen atoms	12	18	42	54

$\frac{12}{6} = \frac{18}{9} = \frac{42}{21} = \frac{54}{27}$

2. Graph the ordered pairs (6, 12), (9, 18), (21, 42), and (27, 54).

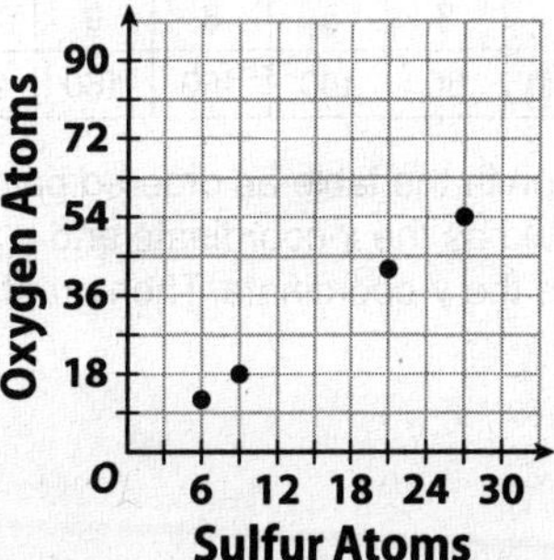

3.

Width (in.)	2	4	7	8
Length (in.)	4	8	14	16

$\frac{4}{2} = \frac{8}{4} = \frac{14}{7} = \frac{16}{8}$

4. Graph the ordered pairs (2, 4), (4, 8), (7, 14), (8, 16).

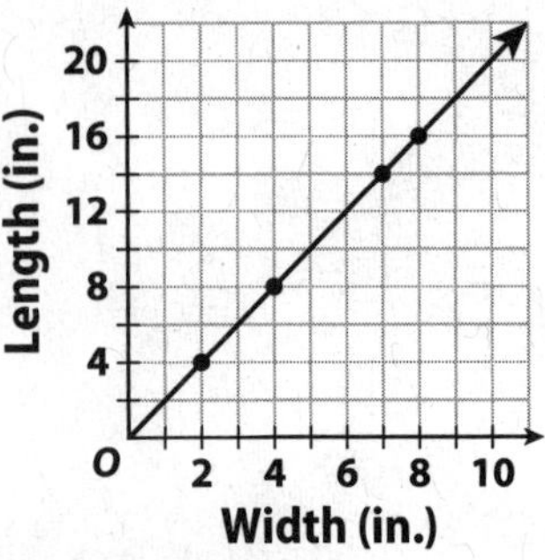

5.

Boxes	5	8	10
Candles	60	96	120

Graph the ordered pairs (5, 60), (8, 96), (10, 120).

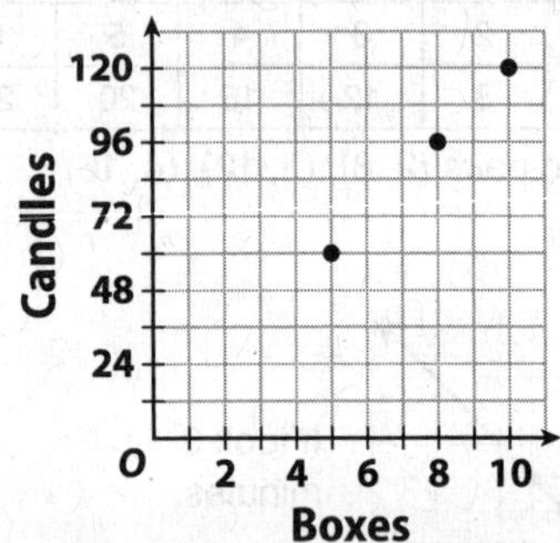

7 boxes

6. Sample answer: Make a table of several equivalent ratios or rates for the quantities. Use the table to make and graph ordered pairs. If appropriate, connect the points.

Independent Practice

7. $\frac{\text{money collected}}{\text{sweatshirts sold}}$

$= \frac{\$60}{3 \text{ sweatshirts}}$

$= \frac{\$20}{1 \text{ sweatshirt}}$

= \$20 per sweatshirt sold

8.

Sweatshirts sold	3	5	8	9	12
Money collected ($)	60	100	160	180	240

9. Write the information in the table as ordered pairs with Sweatshirts sold as the *x*-coordinate and Money collected as the *y*-coordinate. Then graph the ordered pairs.

10. (3, 60), (5, 100), (8, 160), (9, 180), (12, 240)

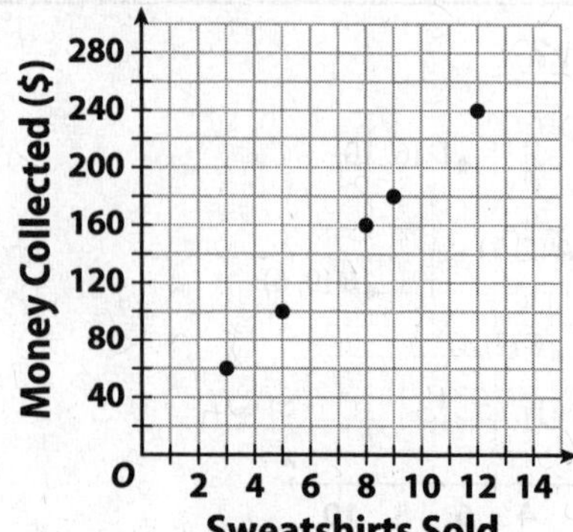

11. The rate is \$20 per sweatshirt sold, so multiply the number of sweatshirts by $\frac{20}{1}$ or 20. 24 × \$20 = \$480.
12. The point does not make sense. The *x*-coordinate of 5.5 means that 5.5 sweatshirts were sold, but it does not make sense to sell half of a sweatshirt.
13. I found the unit rate, or 55 miles per hour. Then, I multiplied the unit rate by 6 hours. 6 × 55 = 330 miles.
14. 8 weeks; Sample answer: (8, 56) is on the graph.
15. Sample answer: the number of days that are in any number of weeks.

Focus on Higher Order Thinking

16.

Time (min)	1	2	5	20
Distance (m)	5	10	25	100

$\frac{\text{distance}}{\text{time}} = \frac{5}{1}, \frac{10}{2}, \frac{25}{5}, \frac{100}{20}$

$\frac{\text{time}}{\text{distance}} = \frac{1}{5}, \frac{2}{10}, \frac{5}{25}, \frac{20}{100}$

a. Yes; each rate is equal to $\frac{1}{5}$ min/m.

b. Sample answer: My graph would have time on the horizontal axis and distance on the vertical axis. My friend's would have the axes reversed.

17. Sample answer: For each quantity, choose a scale for the corresponding axis that includes the maximum value from the table.

LESSON 7.2

Your Turn

1. $\frac{\text{cheese pizzas}}{\text{total pizzas}} = \frac{2 \times 5}{5 \times 5} = \frac{10}{25}$

10 cheese pizzas

2. $\frac{50 \text{ minutes}}{4 \text{ sprinklers}} = \frac{12.5 \text{ minutes}}{1 \text{ sprinkler}}$

$\frac{12.5 \times 10}{1 \times 10} = \frac{125 \text{ minutes}}{10 \text{ sprinklers}}$

It will take 125 minutes to water the entire lawn with 10 sprinklers.

3. $\frac{20 \text{ miles}}{1 \text{ inch}} = \frac{50 \text{ miles}}{2.5 \text{ inches}}$

50 miles

Guided Practice

1. $\frac{3 \times 6}{5 \times 6} = \frac{18}{30}$

2. $\frac{4 \div 2}{10 \div 2} = \frac{2}{5}$

3. $\frac{\text{Leila's profit}}{\text{Jo's profit}} = \frac{3 \times 15}{4 \times 15} = \frac{45}{60}$
   $45

4. $\frac{\text{width}}{\text{length}} = \frac{4 \times 3}{6 \times 3} = \frac{12}{18}$
   18 inches

5. $\frac{24 \times 7.5}{7 \times 7.5} = \frac{180 \text{ feet}}{52.5 \text{ seconds}}$
   It will take 52.5 seconds to move 180 feet.

6. $\frac{27 \text{ minutes}}{6 \text{ hours}} = \frac{4.5 \text{ minutes}}{1 \text{ hour}}$
   $\frac{4.5 \times 8}{1 \times 8} = \frac{36 \text{ minutes}}{8 \text{ hours}}$
   The couple will rest 36 minutes in 8 hours.

7. $\frac{16 \text{ kilometers}}{1 \text{ centimeter}} = \frac{24 \text{ kilometers}}{1.5 \text{ centimeters}}$
   24 kilometers

8. Sample answer: A chili recipe calls for 3 cans of beans for every 2 pounds of turkey. How many cans of beans are needed for 6 pounds of turkey?

Independent Practice

9. a. $\frac{72 \text{ miles}}{6 \text{ inches}} = \frac{12 \text{ miles}}{1 \text{ inch}}$
   1 inch = 12 miles
   b. 24 miles; the distance from Liberty to Foston on the map is 4 in., so the distance from Foston to West Quall is 2 in.
   $\frac{12 \text{ mi}}{1 \text{ in.}} = \frac{24 \text{ mi}}{2 \text{ in.}}$

10. a. $\frac{\text{cups of pineapple juice}}{\text{total cups of punch}} = \frac{4 \times 4.5}{24 \times 4.5} = \frac{18}{108}$
   18 cups pineapple juice
   $\frac{\text{cups of orange juice}}{\text{total cups of punch}} = \frac{8 \times 4.5}{24 \times 4.5} = \frac{36}{108}$
   36 cups orange juice
   $\frac{\text{cups of seltzer}}{\text{total cups of punch}} = \frac{12 \times 4.5}{24 \times 4.5} = \frac{54}{108}$
   54 cups seltzer
   b. $\frac{\text{servings of punch}}{\text{cups of punch}} = \frac{18 \times 4.5}{24 \times 4.5} = \frac{81}{108}$
   81 servings of punch
   c. For every cup of seltzer you use, how much orange juice do you use?
   $\frac{36}{54} = \frac{2}{3}$ cup

11. a. $\frac{\text{left side seats}}{\text{right side seats}} = \frac{2 \times 30}{3 \times 30} = \frac{60}{90}$
   60 seats
   b. There are 90 seats on the left side.

12. a. $\frac{20 \text{ miles}}{1 \text{ inch}} = \frac{90 \text{ miles}}{4.5 \text{ inches}}$
   90 miles
   b. $\frac{18 \text{ miles}}{1 \text{ inch}} = \frac{90 \text{ miles}}{5 \text{ inches}}$
   5 inches

13. There are 60 minutes in an hour, so $\frac{27 \text{ in.} \times 20}{3 \text{ min} \times 20} = \frac{540 \text{ in.}}{60 \text{ min}}$. To find the number of feet in 540 inches, divide by 12.
   $540 \div 12 = 45$ feet

14. $\frac{8 \text{ mi}}{80 \text{ min}} = 0.1$ mi/min

15. Marta's unit rate is 0.1 mi/min.
   Loribeth's unit rate is $\frac{9 \text{ mi}}{60 \text{ min}} = 0.15$ mi/min.
   Ira's unit rate is $\frac{15 \text{ mi}}{75 \text{ min}} = 0.2$ mi/min.
   Ira has the fastest rate.

16. 93 miles; 3.5 hours is equal to 210 minutes.
   In 210 minutes, Marta travels 21 miles.
   (0.1 mi/min)(210 min) = 21 mi
   Loribeth travels 30 miles.
   (0.15 mi/min)(210 min) = 31.5 mi
   Ira travels 42 miles
   (0.2 mi/min)(210 min) = 42 mi
   The total distance is 21 + 31.5 + 42 = 94.5 miles.

17. No. The caterpillar's unit rate should be 5 feet per minute.

Focus on Higher Order Thinking

18. The numerator and the denominator will have the same numbers. For example, $\frac{1 \text{ mi}}{1 \text{ sec}} = \frac{17 \text{ mi}}{17 \text{ sec}}$.

19. a.

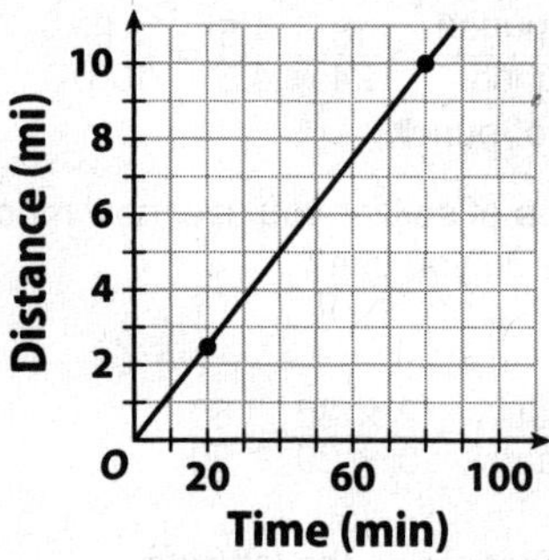

b. Sample answer: I drew a line through the points (0, 0) and (20, 2.5). 80 is the x-coordinate of the point on the line with a y-coordinate of 10. So 80 minutes is the answer.

LESSON 7.3

Your Turn

4. There are 12 inches in a foot.

$\frac{12 \text{ inches}}{1 \text{ foot}}$

$\frac{6 \times 12}{1 \times 12} = \frac{72}{12}$

The doorway is 72 inches tall.

5. There are 8 fluid ounces in 1 cup.

$\frac{8 \text{ fluid ounces}}{1 \text{ cup}}$

$\frac{40 \div 8}{8 \div 8} = \frac{5}{1}$

There are 5 cups of milk.

6. There are 1,000 milliliters in 1 liter.

$\frac{1{,}000 \text{ milliliters}}{1 \text{liter}}$

$\frac{2 \times 1{,}000}{1 \times 1{,}000} = \frac{2{,}000}{2}$

Josie's water bottle has a capacity of 2,000 milliliters.

7. There are 100 centimeters in 1 meter.

$\frac{100 \text{ centimeters}}{1 \text{ meter}}$

$\frac{350 \div 100}{100 \div 100} = \frac{3.5}{1}$

The ribbon is 3.5 meters long.

8. $250 \cancel{\text{centimeters}} \cdot \frac{1 \text{ meter}}{100 \cancel{\text{centimeters}}}$

$= \frac{250}{100} \text{ m} = 2.5 \text{ meters}$

9. $1\frac{3}{4} \text{ quarts} \cdot \frac{32 \text{ fluid ounces}}{1 \text{ quart}} = 56 \text{ fluid ounces}$

Guided Practice

1. $\frac{4}{1} = \frac{12}{3}$, so 12 cups = 3 quarts

2. $\frac{4}{1} = \frac{48}{12}$, so 48 cups = 12 quarts

3. $\frac{16 \text{ cups}}{1 \text{ gallon}}$

$\frac{16 \times 2}{1 \times 2} = \frac{32}{2}$

2 gallons equal 32 cups.

4. $\frac{1{,}000 \text{ grams}}{1 \text{ kilogram}}$

$\frac{1{,}000 \times 3.5}{1 \times 3.5} = \frac{3{,}500}{3.5}$

3.5 kilograms equal 3,500 grams.

5. $1{,}750 \text{ milligrams} \cdot \frac{1 \text{ gram}}{1{,}000 \text{ milligrams}} = 1.75 \text{ grams}$

6. $42 \text{ inches} \cdot \frac{1 \text{ ft}}{12 \text{ in.}}$

$\frac{42}{12} \text{ ft}$

$3\frac{1}{2} \text{ ft}$

7. Sample answer: Use a model, proportion, or a conversion factor to convert rates.

Independent Practice

8. Sample answer: 1 gallon = 4 quarts and 1 quart = 2 pints. $4 \times 2 = 8$, so $\frac{1 \text{ gallon}}{8 \text{ pints}}$.

9. Carol: $42 \cancel{\text{inches}} \cdot \frac{1 \text{ ft}}{12 \cancel{\text{in.}}} = 3.5 \text{ ft}$

$42 \text{ inches} \cdot \frac{1 \text{ yd}}{36 \cancel{\text{in.}}} = 1\frac{1}{6} \text{ yd}$

Tino: $2.5 \cancel{\text{feet}} \cdot \frac{12 \text{ in.}}{1 \cancel{\text{ft}}} = 30 \text{ in.}$

$2.5 \cancel{\text{feet}} \cdot \frac{1 \text{ yd}}{3 \cancel{\text{ft}}} = \frac{5}{6} \text{ yd}$

Baxtor: $1.5 \cancel{\text{yards}} \cdot \frac{36 \text{ in.}}{1 \cancel{\text{yd}}} = 54 \text{ in.}$

$1.5 \cancel{\text{yards}} \cdot \frac{3 \text{ ft}}{1 \cancel{\text{yd}}} = 4.5 \text{ ft}$

The total length in inches is $42 + 30 + 54 =$ 126 inches.

In feet, the total length is $3.5 + 2.5 + 4.5 =$ 10.5 feet.

In yards, the total length is $1\frac{1}{6} + \frac{5}{6} + 1\frac{3}{6} = 3\frac{1}{2}$ yards.

10. a. $21 \cancel{\text{books}} \cdot \frac{17 \text{ cm}}{1 \cancel{\text{book}}} = 357 \text{ centimeters}$

b. Yes; $357 \cancel{\text{centimeters}} \cdot \frac{1 \text{ m}}{100 \cancel{\text{cm}}} = 3.57 \text{ meters.}$

$3.57 > 3.5$, so Suzanna's board is long enough.

11. The larger size; 64 pints of Brand A cost $\$2.50 \times 64 = \$160$, and 32 quarts of Brand B cost $\$4.50 \times 32 = \$144$.

12. The gallon size of Brand B is the best deal. The prices for each size are as follows: Brand A small size $\$2.50 \times 8 = \$20.00$ per gallon, Brand A large size $\$4.50 \times 4 = \$18.00$ per gallon, Brand B small size $\$4.25 \times 4 = \$17.00$ per gallon, and Brand B large size \$9.50 per gallon.

13. $3{,}000 \cancel{\text{meters}} \cdot \frac{1 \text{ km}}{1{,}000 \cancel{\text{m}}} = 3 \text{ kilometers}$

14. Convert 5 feet to 60 inches. Then add 6 inches.

15. $\frac{1}{4}\ \cancel{\text{mile}} \cdot \frac{5,280\text{ ft}}{1\ \cancel{\text{mi}}} = 1,320\text{ ft}$

The distance is 1,320 feet.

16. $9\frac{1}{2}\ \cancel{\text{feet}} \cdot \frac{12\text{ in.}}{1\ \cancel{\text{ft}}} = 114\text{ in.}$

$114 - 2\frac{1}{2} = 111\frac{1}{2}$

$111\frac{1}{2}\ \cancel{\text{inches}} \cdot \frac{1\text{ ft}}{12\ \cancel{\text{in.}}} = 9\frac{7}{24}\text{ ft}$

The California condor's wingspan is $111\frac{1}{2}$ inches, or $9\frac{7}{24}$ feet, longer than the bee hummingbird's wingspan.

17. $13\ \cancel{\text{kilograms}} \cdot \frac{1,000\text{ g}}{1\ \cancel{\text{kg}}} = 13,000\text{ g}$

$\frac{13,000}{1.6} = 8,125$

The California condor's mass is 8,125 times the mass of the hummingbird.

18. a. Clark: $1\frac{3}{4}\ \cancel{\text{miles}} \cdot \frac{5,280\text{ ft}}{1\ \cancel{\text{mi}}} = 9,240\text{ ft}$

Julio: $2,640\ \cancel{\text{yards}} \cdot \frac{3\text{ ft}}{1\ \cancel{\text{yd}}} = 7,920\text{ ft}$

Jim: 17,160 ft

Julio lives closest to the park. Jim lives farthest from the park.

b. $\frac{17,160}{2} = 8,580$

No; Clark lives $1\frac{3}{4}$ miles, or 9,240 feet, from the park. Jim lives 17,160 feet from the park, and $\frac{1}{2} \times 17,160 = 8,580$ feet, and $9,240 > 8,580$.

Focus on Higher Order Thinking

19. $50\ \cancel{\text{fluid ounces}} \cdot \frac{1\text{ c}}{8\ \cancel{\text{fl oz}}} = 6\frac{1}{4}\text{ c}$

$4\text{ jars} = 4\ \cancel{\text{pints}} \cdot \frac{2\text{ c}}{1\ \cancel{\text{pt}}} = 8\text{ c}$

$8 - 6\frac{1}{4} = 1\frac{3}{4}$

She will need to fill the jar 4 times, and will have $1\frac{3}{4}$ cups left in the jar.

20. a. $120\ \cancel{\text{yd}} \cdot \frac{3\text{ ft}}{1\ \cancel{\text{yd}}} = 360\text{ ft}$

$53\frac{1}{3}\ \cancel{\text{yd}} \cdot \frac{3\text{ ft}}{1\ \cancel{\text{yd}}} = 160\text{ ft}$

The dimensions are 360 feet by 160 feet.

b. The perimeter is $2(360) + 2(160) = 1,040$ feet.

c. 5 laps; 1 mile is 1,760 yards, and 1,760 yards is 5,280 feet. 5 laps is $5 \times 1,040$ feet $= 5,200$ feet.

21. You get the original number of cups. Example:

$2\ \cancel{\text{cups}} \cdot \frac{8\text{ fluid ounces}}{1\ \cancel{\text{cup}}} = 16\text{ fluid ounces},$

$16\ \cancel{\text{fluid ounces}} \cdot \frac{1\text{ cup}}{8\ \cancel{\text{fluid ounces}}} = 2\text{ cups}$

22. Convert 15 miles to 79,200 feet, then use 1 hour per 3,600 seconds to convert 1 hour to 3,600 seconds. Finally, divide to simplify to 22 feet per second.

LESSON 7.4

Your Turn

2. $6\ \cancel{\text{qt}} \times \frac{0.946\text{ L}}{1\ \cancel{\text{qt}}} \approx 5.676\text{ L}$

3. $14\ \cancel{\text{ft}} \times \frac{0.305\text{ m}}{1\ \cancel{\text{ft}}} \approx 4.27\text{ m}$

4. $255.6\ \cancel{\text{g}} \times \frac{1\text{ oz}}{28.4\ \cancel{\text{g}}} = 9\text{ oz}$

5. $7\ \cancel{\text{L}} \times \frac{1\text{ qt}}{0.946\ \cancel{\text{L}}} = 7.42\text{ qt}$

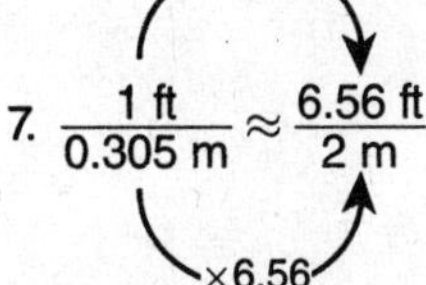

7. $\frac{1\text{ ft}}{0.305\text{ m}} \approx \frac{6.56\text{ ft}}{2\text{ m}}$ (×6.56)

$2\text{ m} \approx 6.56\text{ ft}$

$\frac{1\text{ ft}}{0.305\text{ m}} \approx \frac{9.84\text{ ft}}{3\text{ m}}$ (×9.84)

$3\text{ m} \approx 9.84\text{ ft}$

$A = lw$

$= 9.84 \cdot 6.56$

$= 64.55\text{ ft}^2$

Guided Practice

1. $5\ \cancel{\text{mi}} \times \frac{1.61\text{ km}}{1\ \cancel{\text{mi}}} \approx 8.05\text{ km}$

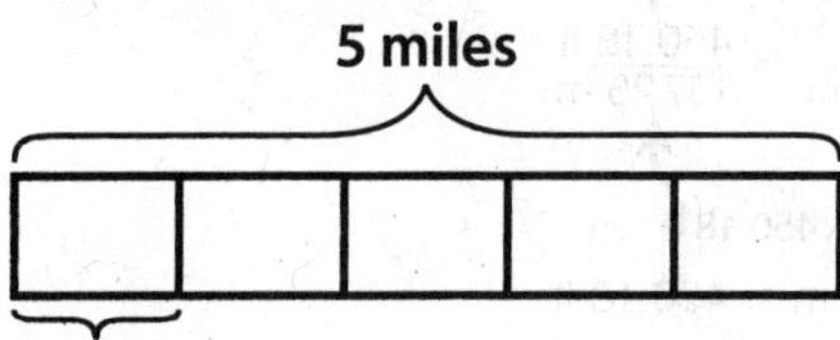

2. $5\ \cancel{\text{gal}} \times \frac{3.79\text{ L}}{1\ \cancel{\text{gal}}} = 18.95\text{ L}$

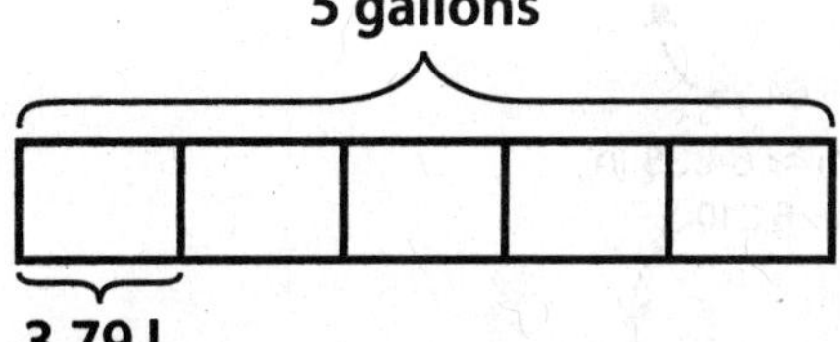

3. $12\ \cancel{\text{in.}} \times \frac{2.54\text{ cm}}{1\ \cancel{\text{in.}}} = 30.48\text{ cm}$

4. $4\ \cancel{\text{lb}} \times \frac{0.454\text{ kg}}{1\ \cancel{\text{lb}}} = 1.816\text{ kg}$

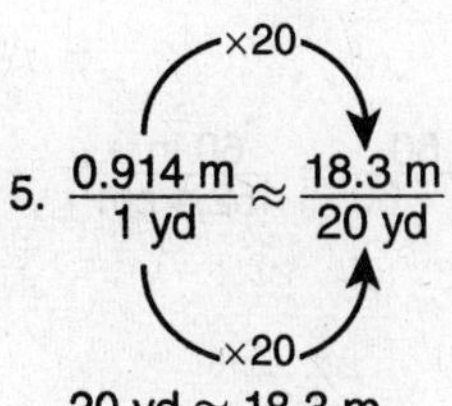

5. $\frac{0.914\text{ m}}{1\text{ yd}} \approx \frac{18.3\text{ m}}{20\text{ yd}}$ (×20)

$20\text{ yd} \approx 18.3\text{ m}$

×12

6. $\frac{1\text{ oz}}{28.3\text{ g}} \approx \frac{12\text{ oz}}{339.6\text{ g}}$

×12

12 oz ≈ 339.6 g

×5

7. $\frac{1\text{ qt}}{0.946\text{ L}} \approx \frac{5\text{ qt}}{4.73\text{ L}}$

×5

5 qt ≈ 4.73 L

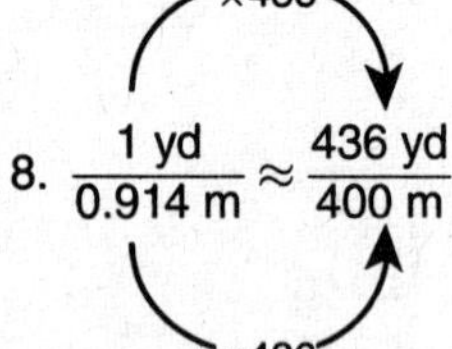

×436

8. $\frac{1\text{ yd}}{0.914\text{ m}} \approx \frac{436\text{ yd}}{400\text{ m}}$

×436

400 m ≈ 436 yd

×2.64

9. $\frac{1\text{ gal}}{3.79\text{ L}} \approx \frac{1\text{ gal}}{10\text{ L}}$

×2.64

10 L ≈ 2.64 gal

×450.18

10. $\frac{1\text{ ft}}{0.305\text{ m}} \approx \frac{450.18\text{ ft}}{137.25\text{ m}}$

×450.18

137.25 m ≈ 450.18 ft

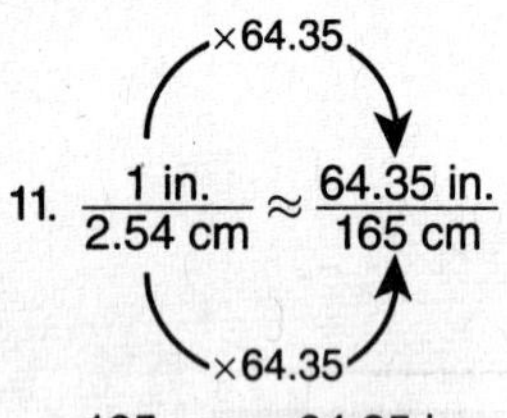

×64.35

11. $\frac{1\text{ in.}}{2.54\text{ cm}} \approx \frac{64.35\text{ in.}}{165\text{ cm}}$

×64.35

165 cm ≈ 64.35 in.

×6,210

12. $\frac{1\text{ mi}}{1.61\text{ km}} \approx \frac{6{,}210\text{ mi}}{10{,}000\text{ km}}$

×6,210

10,000 km ≈ 6,210 mi

13. $\frac{1\text{ in.}}{2.54\text{ cm}} = \frac{60\text{ in.}}{?\text{ cm}} \rightarrow \frac{1\text{ in.} \times 60}{2.54\text{ cm} \times 60} = \frac{60\text{ in.}}{152.4\text{ cm}},$

$60\,\cancel{\text{in.}} \times \frac{2.54\text{ cm}}{1\,\cancel{\text{in.}}} = 152.4\text{ cm}$

Independent Practice

14. 2 meters. 6 ft is equal to 2 yards, and a meter is longer than a yard.
15. 1 inch
16. 1 meter
17. 1 mile
18. 1 ounce
19. 1 liter
20. 10 kilograms
21. 4 liters

×2

22. $\frac{1\text{ mi}}{1.61\text{ km}} \approx \frac{2\text{ mi}}{3.22\text{ km}}$

×2

2 mi ≈ 3.22 km
2 miles is greater 3 km.

23. $50\,\cancel{\text{lbs}} \times \frac{0.454\text{ kg}}{1\,\cancel{\text{lb}}} = 22.7\text{ kg}$

24. $55\frac{\cancel{\text{km}}}{\text{h}} \times \frac{1\text{ mi}}{1.61\,\cancel{\text{km}}}$

$\frac{55\text{ mi}}{1.61\text{ h}} \approx 34\text{ mi/h}$

25. $\frac{1}{2}\cancel{\text{gal}} \times \frac{3.79\text{ L}}{1\,\cancel{\text{gal}}}$

$\frac{3.79\text{ L}}{2} \approx 1.9\text{ L}$

Therefore, the 2-liter bottle holds more.

26. $12\,\cancel{\text{fl oz}} \times \frac{29.6\text{ mL}}{1\,\cancel{\text{fl oz}}} = 355.2\text{ mL} \approx 355\text{ mL}$

27. $1.25\,\cancel{\text{kg}} \times \frac{1\text{ lb}}{0.454\,\cancel{\text{kg}}} \approx 2.75$ pounds

28. No; $8\,\cancel{\text{kg}} \times \frac{1\text{ lb}}{0.454\,\cancel{\text{kg}}} = 17.6$ pounds. Michael probably does not weigh only 17.6 pounds.

29. a. Yes; 1 gal ≈ 3.79 L and therefore two half-gallon jugs can hold the 3 liters of liquid.

b. No; if 1 liter of water leaks out there will still be 2 liters left, and a half-gallon jug can only hold 1.895 liters because 1 gal = $3.79\text{ L} \times \frac{1}{2} = 1.895\text{ L}$.

30. $1.25\,\cancel{\text{mi}} \times \frac{1.61\text{ km}}{1\,\cancel{\text{mi}}} = 2.0125\text{ km}$

31. a. $\left(16\,\cancel{\text{ft}} \times \frac{0.305\text{ m}}{1\,\cancel{\text{ft}}}\right)\left(3\,\cancel{\text{ft}} \times \frac{0.305\text{ m}}{1\,\cancel{\text{ft}}}\right)$

$= (16 \times 3 \times 0.305 \times 0.305)\text{ m}^2$

$= 4.4652\text{ m}^2$

b. $\frac{\$28}{\text{m}^2} \times 4.47\text{ m}^2 = \$125.03$

32. $10\,\cancel{\text{yd}} \times \frac{0.914\text{ m}}{1\,\cancel{\text{yd}}} \approx$ every 9.14 m, or 9 m and 14 cm

33. Use either a proportion, or a conversion factor, to multiply the number of pounds by 0.454 kg/lb.

$8.4\ \cancel{lb} \times \frac{0.454\ kg}{1\ \cancel{lb}} \approx 3.8136\ kg$

Focus on Higher Order Thinking

34. Annalisa's height in inches and centimeters is: 64 in.

$64\ \cancel{in.} \times \frac{2.54\ cm}{1\ \cancel{in.}} \approx 162.5\ cm$

Stefan's height in inches and centimeters is:

$7.5\ \cancel{cm} \times \frac{1\ in.}{2.54\ \cancel{cm}} \approx 3\ in.$

3 in. + 64 in. = 67.0 in.

162.5 cm + 7.5 cm = 170.0 cm

Keiko's height in inches and centimeters is:

67 in. − 1.5 in. = 65.5 in.

$65.5\ \cancel{in.} \times \frac{2.54\ cm}{1\ \cancel{in.}} \approx 166.5\ cm$

35. Sample answer: Use the conversion factor for converting yards to meters twice in order to convert square yards to square meters.

$\frac{\$20}{1\ \cancel{yd^2}} \times \frac{1\ \cancel{yd}}{0.914\ m} \times \frac{1\ \cancel{yd}}{0.914\ m} = \frac{\$20}{0.835396\ m^2}$

$\approx \$23.94\ /\ m^2$

MODULE 7

Ready to Go On?

1. $\frac{\text{time}}{\text{number of laps}} = \frac{10\ \text{minutes}}{2\ \text{laps}} = \frac{5\ \text{minutes}}{1\ \text{lap}}$

5 laps will take Charlie 5 × 5 min. = 25 minutes.

2. $\frac{\text{pledge}}{\text{distance}} = \frac{\$0.40 \times 60}{0.25\ \text{mile} \times 60} = \frac{\$24.00}{15\ \text{miles}}$

$24.00

3. $\frac{\text{earnings}}{\text{savings}} = \frac{\$15 \times 5}{\$6 \times 5} = \frac{\$75}{\$30}$

$30

4. $\frac{1\ \text{meter}}{100\ \text{centimeters}}$

$\frac{1 \times 18}{100 \times 18} = \frac{18}{1{,}800}$

18 meters equal 1,800 centimeters.

5. $5\ \cancel{\text{pounds}} \cdot \frac{16\ oz}{1\ \cancel{lb}} = 80\ \text{ounces}$

6. 1 quart = 2 pints, 1 pint = 2 cups, and 1 cup = 8 ounces

$\frac{1\ \text{quart}}{32\ \text{ounces}}$

$\frac{1 \times 6}{32 \times 6} = \frac{6}{192}$

6 quarts equal 192 fluid ounces.

7. $9\ \cancel{\text{liters}} \cdot \frac{1{,}000\ mL}{1\ \cancel{L}} = 9{,}000\ \text{milliliters}$

8. $5\ \cancel{\text{inches}} \cdot \frac{2.54\ cm}{1\ \cancel{in.}} = 12.7\ cm$

9. $198.9\ \cancel{\text{grams}} \cdot \frac{1\ oz}{28.4\ \cancel{g}} \approx 6.9615\ oz$

10. $8\ \cancel{\text{gallons}} \cdot \frac{3.79\ L}{1\ \cancel{gal}} = 30.32\ L$

11. $12\ \cancel{\text{feet}} \cdot \frac{0.305\ m}{1\ \cancel{ft}} = 3.66\ m$

12. Sample answer: Shelia travels 110 miles in 2 hours. At this rate, how far will she travel in 6 hours?

MODULE 8 *Percents*

Are You Ready?

1. $\frac{9}{18} = \frac{3}{6}$ (÷3 numerator and denominator)

2. $\frac{4}{6} = \frac{12}{18}$ (×3 numerator and denominator)

3. $\frac{25}{30} = \frac{5}{6}$ (÷5 numerator and denominator)

4. $\frac{12}{15} = \frac{36}{45}$ (×3 numerator and denominator)

5. $\frac{15}{24} = \frac{5}{8}$ (÷3 numerator and denominator)

6. $\frac{24}{32} = \frac{6}{8}$ (÷4 numerator and denominator)

7. $\frac{50}{60} = \frac{10}{12}$ (÷5 numerator and denominator)

8. $\frac{5}{9} = \frac{20}{36}$ (×4 numerator and denominator)

9. $\frac{3}{8} \times \frac{4}{11} = \frac{3}{{}_2\cancel{8}} \times \frac{\cancel{4}^1}{11}$
 $= \frac{3}{22}$

10. $\frac{8}{15} \times \frac{5}{6} = \frac{{}^4\cancel{8}}{{}_3\cancel{15}} \times \frac{\cancel{5}^1}{\cancel{6}_3}$
 $= \frac{4}{9}$

11. $\frac{7}{12} \times \frac{3}{14} = \frac{{}^1\cancel{7}}{{}_4\cancel{12}} \times \frac{\cancel{3}^1}{\cancel{14}_2}$
 $= \frac{1}{8}$

12. $\frac{9}{20} \times \frac{4}{5} = \frac{9}{{}_5\cancel{20}} \times \frac{\cancel{4}^1}{5}$
 $= \frac{9}{25}$

13. $\frac{7}{10} \times \frac{20}{21} = \frac{{}^1\cancel{7}}{{}_1\cancel{10}} \times \frac{\cancel{20}^2}{\cancel{21}_3}$
 $= \frac{2}{3}$

14. $\frac{8}{18} \times \frac{9}{20} = \frac{{}^{1}\cancel{{}^2\cancel{8}}}{{}_2\cancel{18}} \times \frac{\cancel{9}^1}{\cancel{20}_5}$
 $= \frac{1}{5}$

15.
```
   20
×0.25
  100
  400
 5.00 or 5
```

16.
```
16.99
 ×0.3
5.097
```

17.
```
  75
×0.2
15.0 or 15
```

18.
```
 5.5
×1.1
  55
 550
6.05
```

19.
```
11.99
 ×0.8
9.592
```

20.
```
 7.25
 ×0.5
3.625
```

21.
```
0.75
  ×4
3.00 or 3
```

22.
```
 12.50
 ×0.15
  6250
 12500
1.8750 or 1.875
```

23.
```
 6.5
×0.7
4.55
```

LESSON 8.1

Your Turn

2. $\frac{9}{10} = 9 \cdot \frac{1}{10}$
 $= 9 \cdot 10\%$
 $= 90\%$

3. $\frac{2}{5} = 2 \cdot \frac{1}{5}$
 $= 2 \cdot 20\%$
 $= 40\%$

4. 64% is close to $66\frac{2}{3}\%$, which equals $\frac{2}{3}$, so about $\frac{2}{3}$ of the animals are dogs.

Guided Practice

1. 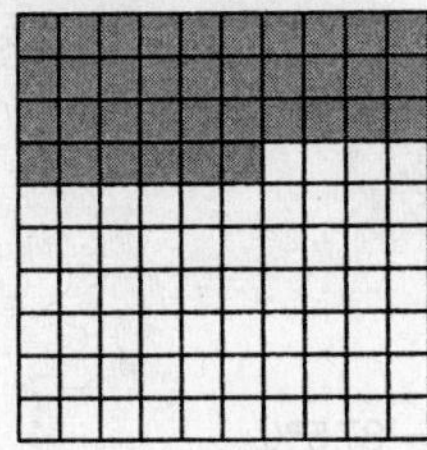

$\frac{9 \times 4}{25 \times 4} = \frac{36}{100} = 36\%$

2. 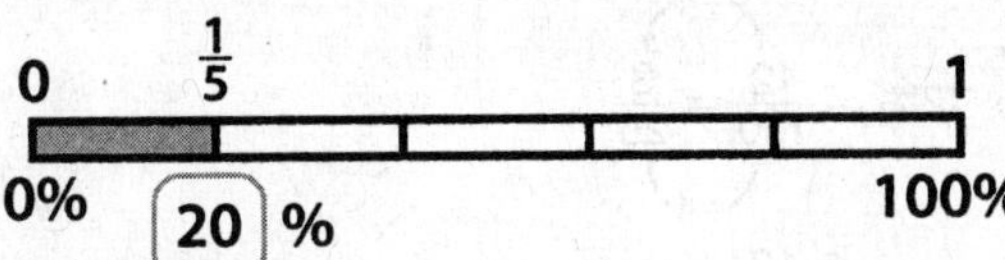

3. The benchmark for $\frac{6}{10}$ is $\frac{1}{10}$.

$\frac{6}{10} = 6 \cdot \frac{1}{10}$
$= 6 \cdot 10\%$
$= 60\%$

4. The benchmark for $\frac{2}{4}$ is $\frac{1}{4}$.

$\frac{2}{4} = 2 \cdot \frac{1}{4}$
$= 2 \cdot 25\%$
$= 50\%$

5. The benchmark for $\frac{4}{5}$ is $\frac{1}{5}$.

$\frac{4}{5} = 4 \cdot \frac{1}{5}$
$= 4 \cdot 20\%$
$= 80\%$

6. 41% is close to 40%, which equals $\frac{2}{5}$, so about $\frac{2}{5}$ of the students want to be graphic designers.

7. Write the ratio as a fraction. Then write an equivalent fraction with a denominator of 100, and use the numerator as the percent.

Independent Practice

8. $\frac{23}{50} = \frac{46}{100}$

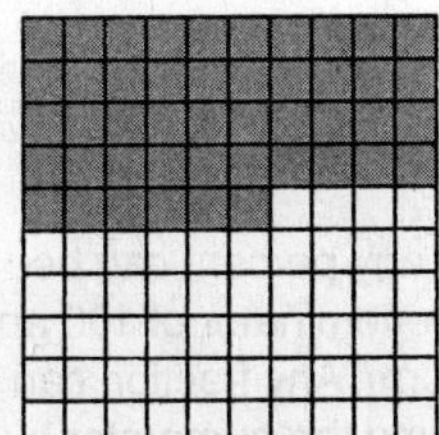

9. $\frac{11}{20} = \frac{55}{100}$

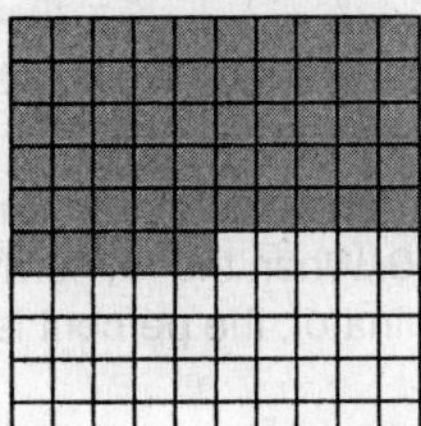

10. $66\frac{2}{3}$ squares which is $66\frac{2}{3}\%$

11. $\frac{9}{10} = 90\%$, $\frac{4}{5} = 80\%$, $\frac{17}{20} = 85\%$; from least to greatest 80%, 85%, 90%

12. $\frac{1}{3} = 33\frac{1}{3}\%$ and $50\% = \frac{1}{2}$;

$\frac{1}{3}$ of a box < 50% of a box

13. $30\% = \frac{3}{10}$ and $\frac{1}{4} = 25\%$;

30% of your minutes > $\frac{1}{4}$ of your minutes

14. Sample answer: 35% = 25% + 10% and

35% = 7 · 5%

15. 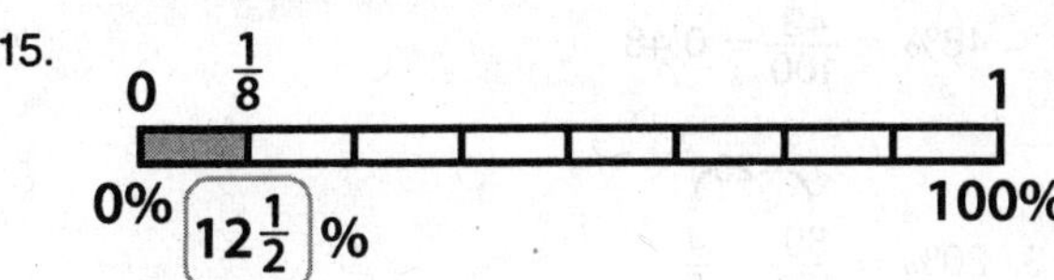

16. a. 15 Country songs
20 Rock songs
5 Classical songs
+10 World songs
50 songs

b. Country songs: $\frac{15}{50} = \frac{3}{10} = 30\%$

Rock songs: $\frac{20}{50} = \frac{2}{5} = 40\%$

Classical songs: $\frac{5}{50} = \frac{1}{10} = 10\%$

World songs: $\frac{10}{50} = \frac{1}{5} = 20\%$

Focus on Higher Order Thinking

17. No; the percent benchmark for $\frac{1}{3}$ is $33\frac{1}{3}\%$, so he used $50\% + 33\frac{1}{3}\% = 88\frac{1}{3}\%$ on rides and games. He used $100\% - 83\frac{1}{3}\% = 16\frac{2}{3}\%$ in the batting cage.

18.

Fraction	$\frac{1}{5}$	$\frac{2}{5}$	$\frac{3}{5}$	$\frac{4}{5}$	$\frac{5}{5}$	$\frac{6}{5}$
Percent	20%	40%	60%	80%	100%	120%

a. When the numerator and denominator are equal, the percent is equal to 100. When the numerator is greater than the denominator, the percent is greater than 100.

b. 150%; the pattern is

$\frac{1}{2} = 50\%, \frac{2}{2} = 100\%, \frac{3}{2} = 150\%.$

LESSON 8.2

Your Turn

1. $15\% = \frac{15}{100} = \frac{3}{20}$ (÷5)

$15\% = \frac{15}{100} = 0.15$

2. $48\% = \frac{48}{100} = \frac{12}{25}$ (÷4)

$48\% = \frac{48}{100} = 0.48$

3. $80\% = \frac{80}{100} = \frac{4}{5}$ (÷20)

$80\% = \frac{80}{100} = 0.8$

4. $75\% = \frac{75}{100} = \frac{3}{4}$ (÷25)

$75\% = \frac{75}{100} = 0.75$

5. $36\% = \frac{36}{100} = \frac{9}{25}$ (÷4)

$36\% = \frac{36}{100} = 0.36$

6. $40\% = \frac{40}{100} = \frac{2}{5}$ (÷20)

$40\% = \frac{40}{100} = 0.4$

8. $\frac{9}{25} = \frac{36}{100} = 0.36 = 36\%$ (×4)

9.
```
   0.875
8)7.000
 -64
   60
  -56
   40
  -40
    0
```

$\frac{7}{8} = 0.875 = \frac{875}{1{,}000} = \frac{87.5}{100} = 87.5\%$

Guided Practice

1. $12\% = \frac{12}{100} = \frac{3}{25}$ (÷4)

$12\% = \frac{12}{100} = 0.12$

2. 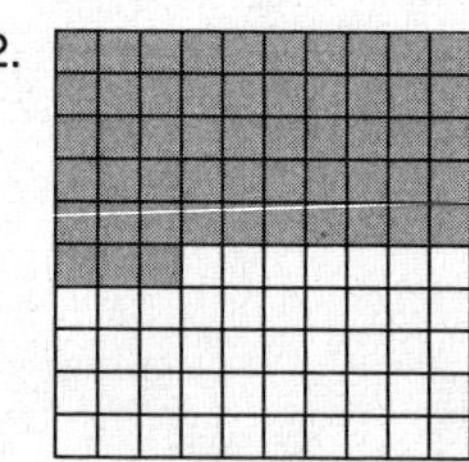

$0.53 = \frac{53}{100} = 53\%$

3. 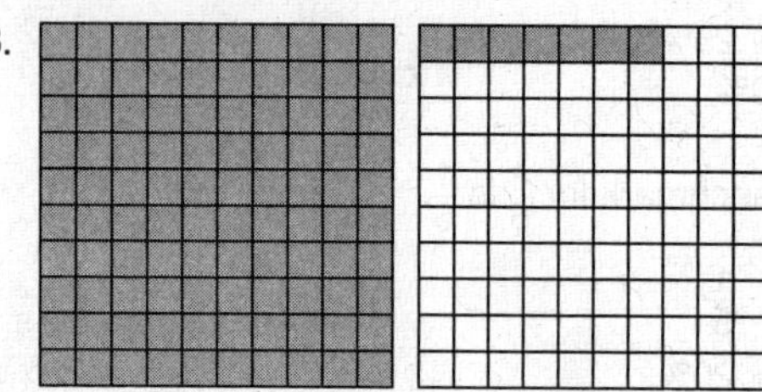

$1.07 = \frac{107}{100} = 1\frac{7}{100} = 107\%$

4. $\frac{7}{20} = \frac{35}{100} = 0.35 = 35\%$ (×5)

5.
```
   0.375
8)3.000
 -24
   60
  -56
   40
  -40
    0
```

$\frac{3}{8} = 0.375 = \frac{375}{1{,}000} = \frac{37.5}{100} = 37.5\%$

6. Percent means "per 100," so any percent can be written as a fraction with a denominator of 100 and then be written in simplest form. Any fraction can be written as a decimal by dividing the numerator by the denominator.

Independent Practice

7. $72\% = \frac{72}{100} = \frac{18}{25}$ (÷4)

$72\% = \frac{72}{100} = 0.72$

8. $25\% = \frac{25}{100} = \frac{1}{4}$ (÷25)

$25\% = \frac{25}{100} = 0.25$

9. $500\% = \frac{500}{100} = \frac{5}{1}$ (÷100)

$500\% = \frac{500}{100} = \frac{5}{1} = 5$

10. $5\% = \frac{5}{100} = \frac{1}{20}$ (÷5)

$5\% = \frac{5}{100} = 0.05$

11. $37\% = \frac{37}{100} = 0.37$

12. $165\% = \frac{165}{100} = \frac{33}{20} = 1\frac{13}{20}$ (÷5)

$165\% = \frac{165}{100} = 1.65$

13. $8\overline{)5.000}$ = 0.625

-48, 20, -16, 40, -40, 0

$\frac{5}{8} = 0.625 = \frac{625}{1{,}000} = \frac{62.5}{100} = 62.5\%$

14. $\frac{258}{300} = \frac{86}{100} = 0.86 = 86\%$ (÷3)

15. $\frac{350}{100} = \frac{7}{2} = 3.5 = 350\%$ (÷50)

16. $\frac{\text{wins}}{\text{total games}} = \frac{12}{15} = \frac{4}{5}$

$\frac{4}{5} = \frac{80}{100} = 0.8 = 80\%$ (×20)

17. $\frac{\text{correct answers}}{\text{total questions}} = \frac{68}{80} = \frac{17}{20}$

$\frac{17}{20} = \frac{85}{100} = 0.85 = 85\%$ (×5)

18. $75\% = \frac{75}{100} = \frac{3}{4} = \frac{12}{16}$. There are 16 pieces that make up the diagram. Shading 75% is the same as shading 12 of the 16 pieces.

19. $25\% = \frac{25}{100} = \frac{1}{4} = \frac{6}{24}$. There are 24 pieces that make up the diagram. Shading 25% is the same as shading 6 of the 24 pieces.

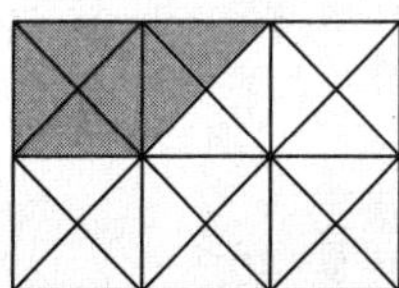

20. Children's books; Sample answer:

$0.3 = \frac{3}{10} = \frac{6}{20}$

$25\% = \frac{25}{100} = \frac{5}{20}$

$\frac{5}{20} < \frac{6}{20} < \frac{7}{20}$

Focus on Higher Order Thinking

21. If all the votes were for Smith or Murphy, then 60% plus $33\frac{1}{3}\%$ (the percent equivalent of $\frac{1}{3}$) should equal 100%, but $60\% + 33\frac{1}{3}\% = 93\frac{1}{3}\%$.

22. $\frac{\text{Food}}{\text{Total budget}} = \frac{500}{2{,}000}$

$\frac{\text{Rent}}{\text{Total budget}} = \frac{1{,}200}{2{,}000}$

$\frac{\text{Transportation}}{\text{Total budget}} = \frac{300}{2{,}000}$

	Food: $500	Rent: $1,200	Transportation: $300
Fraction	$\frac{1}{4}$	$\frac{3}{5}$	$\frac{3}{20}$
Percent	25%	60%	15%
Decimal	0.25	0.6	0.15

23. 1, 100%, 1
The fractions and decimals should add up to 1. The percents should add up to 100%. In each case, the three addends represent parts of Evan's $2,000.

24. $14.5\% = \frac{14.5}{100} = \frac{145}{1{,}000} = \frac{29}{200}$;

$14.5 = 14\frac{5}{10} = 14\frac{1}{2}$

$\frac{29}{200} < 14\frac{1}{2}$

LESSON 8.3

Your Turn

5. $\frac{38}{100} = \frac{?}{50}$

÷2

$\frac{38}{100} = \frac{19}{50}$

÷2

38% of 50 is 19.

6. $\frac{27}{100} \cdot 300 = \frac{8{,}100}{100} = 81$
27% of 300 is 81.

7. $75 \cdot 0.6 = 45$
60% of 75 is 45.

×4

9. $\frac{\text{part}}{\text{whole}} = \frac{19}{25} = \frac{76}{100} = 76\%$

×4

11. $\frac{6}{?} = \frac{30}{100}$

÷5

$\frac{30}{100} = \frac{6}{20}$

÷5

6 is 30% of 20.

12. $\frac{15}{100} = \frac{75}{?}$

×5

$\frac{15}{100} = \frac{75}{500}$

×5

15% of 500 is 75.

Guided Practice

1.

0%	10%	20%	30%	40%	50%	60%	70%	80%	90%	100%
0	30	60	90	120	150	180	210	240	270	300

240 televisions are high definition.

2. $\frac{65}{100} = \frac{?}{200}$

×2

$\frac{65}{100} = \frac{130}{200}$

×2

65% of 200 is 130.

3. $\frac{5}{100}$ of $180 = \frac{5}{100} \times 180$

$= \frac{900}{100} = 9$

5% of 180 is 9.

4. $\frac{?}{100} = \frac{21}{300}$

÷3

$\frac{21}{300} = \frac{7}{100}$

÷3

Alana spent 7% of her paycheck on the gift.

5. $\frac{9}{100} = \frac{27}{?}$

×3

$\frac{9}{100} = \frac{21}{300}$

×3

There were 300 pizzas made last week.

6. Read the problem to see whether you need to find a part of a whole, a whole, or a percent. Then use the proportion $\frac{\text{part}}{\text{whole}} = \frac{\text{percent part}}{\text{percent whole}}$ to find the unknown quantity.

Independent Practice

7. $\frac{64}{100} \cdot 75 = \frac{4{,}800}{100} = 48$
64% of 75 tiles is 48 tiles.

8. $70 \cdot 0.2 = 14$
20% of 70 plants is 14 plants.

9. $\frac{32}{100} = \frac{?}{25}$

$\frac{32}{100} = \frac{8}{25}$ (÷4)

32% of 25 is 8 pages.

10. $\frac{85}{100} \cdot 40 = \frac{3,400}{100} = 34$

85% of 40 e-mails is 34 e-mails.

11. $\frac{72}{100} = \frac{?}{350}$

$\frac{72}{100} = \frac{252}{350}$ (×3.5)

72% of 350 friends is 252 friends.

12. $220 \cdot 0.05 = 11$

5% of 220 files is 11 files.

13. $\frac{4}{20} = \frac{?}{100}$

$\frac{4}{20} = \frac{20}{100}$ (×5)

4 students is 20% of 20 students.

14. $\frac{2}{25} = \frac{?}{100}$

$\frac{2}{25} = \frac{8}{100}$ (×4)

2 doctors is 8% of 25 doctors.

15. $\frac{35}{50} = \frac{?}{100}$

$\frac{35}{50} = \frac{70}{100}$ (×2)

70% of 50 shirts is 35 shirts.

16. $\frac{150}{200} = \frac{?}{100}$

$\frac{150}{200} = \frac{75}{100}$ (÷2)

75% of 200 miles is 150 miles.

17. $\frac{56}{?} = \frac{4}{100}$

$\frac{4}{100} = \frac{56}{1,400}$ (×14)

4% of 1,400 days is 56 days.

18. $\frac{60}{?} = \frac{20}{100}$

$\frac{20}{100} = \frac{60}{300}$ (×3)

60 minutes is 20% of 300 minutes.

19. $\frac{32}{?} = \frac{80}{100}$

$\frac{80}{100} = \frac{32}{40}$ (÷2.5)

80% of 40 games is 32 games.

20. $\frac{360}{?} = \frac{24}{100}$

$\frac{24}{100} = \frac{360}{1,500}$ (×15)

360 kilometers is 24% of 1,500 kilometers.

21. $\frac{15}{?} = \frac{75}{100}$

$\frac{75}{100} = \frac{15}{20}$ (÷5)

75% of 20 peaches is 15 peaches.

22. $\frac{9}{?} = \frac{3}{100}$

$\frac{3}{100} = \frac{9}{300}$ (×3)

9 stores is 3% of 300 stores.

23. $\frac{15}{100} \cdot 60 = \frac{900}{100} = 9$

9 puppies

24. $\frac{24}{200} = \frac{?}{100}$

$\frac{24}{200} = \frac{12}{100}$ (÷2)

12%

25. $\frac{35}{?} = \frac{7}{100}$

$\frac{7}{100} = \frac{35}{500}$ (×5)

$500

26. $120 \cdot 0.6 = 72$
Ashton needs to save $\$120 - \$72 = \$48$.

27. $\frac{1.5}{?} = \frac{5}{100}$

$\times 0.3$

$\frac{5}{100} = \frac{1.5}{30}$

$\times 0.3$

\$30

28. School: $24 \cdot 0.25 = 6$ hours
Eating: $24 \cdot 0.1 = 2.4$ hours
Sleep: $24 \cdot 0.4 = 9.6$ hours
Homework: $24 \cdot 0.1 = 2.4$ hours
Free Time: $24 \cdot 0.15 = 3.6$ hours

Focus on Higher Order Thinking

29. Sample answer: I used the equation $\frac{30}{100} = \frac{75}{?}$ to find the cost of the rug, \$250. Since Marc made a \$75 deposit, I subtracted \$250 − \$75 to find out what he owes, \$175.

30. a. Mars: $\frac{56.55}{150} = \frac{?}{100}$

$\div 1.5$

$\frac{56.55}{150} = \frac{37.7}{100}$

$\div 1.5$

37.7%

Moon: $\frac{24.9}{150} = \frac{?}{100}$

$\div 1.5$

$\frac{24.9}{150} = \frac{16.6}{100}$

$\div 1.5$

16.6%

b. Mars: $0.377x$; Moon: $0.166x$

c. Moon: $0.166x$
$0.166\ (180) =$ about 29.88 pounds

d. $\frac{?}{180} = \frac{236.4}{100}$

$\times 1.8$

$\frac{236.4}{100} = \frac{425.52}{180}$

$\times 1.8$

about 425.52 pounds

31. To find 25% of 50, 50 represents the whole and you want to find the part, so the correct proportion is $\frac{25}{100} = \frac{?}{50}$. Then 25% of 50 is 12.5.

MODULE 8

Ready to Go On?

1. $\frac{19}{50} = \frac{38}{100} = 38\%$ ($\times 2$)

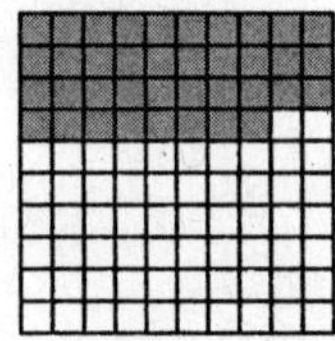

2. $\frac{13}{20} = \frac{65}{100} = 65\%$ ($\times 5$)

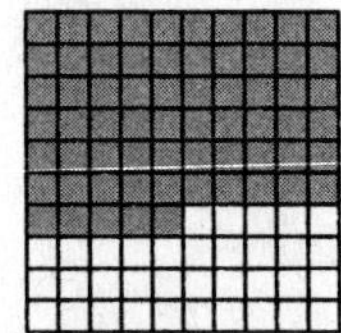

3. $\frac{3}{5} = \frac{60}{100} = 0.6 = 60\%$ ($\times 20$)

4. $62.5\% = \frac{62.5}{100} = \frac{5}{8}$ ($\div 12.5$)

$62.5\% = \frac{62.5}{100} = 0.625$

5. $0.24 = \frac{24}{100} = \frac{6}{25}$ ($\div 4$)

$0.24 = \frac{24}{100} = 24\%$

6. $\frac{31}{50} = \frac{62}{100} = 0.62 = 62\%$ ($\times 2$)

7. $\frac{7}{10} = \frac{70}{100} = 70\%$ ($\times 10$)

8. $\frac{12}{?} = \frac{30}{100}$

$\div 2.5$

$\frac{30}{100} = \frac{12}{40}$

$\div 2.5$

12 is 30% of 40.

9. $\frac{45}{100} = \frac{?}{20}$

$$\frac{45}{100} = \frac{9}{20} \quad (\div 5)$$

45% of 20 is 9.

10. $\frac{18}{30} = \frac{?}{100}$

$$\frac{18}{30} = \frac{60}{100} \quad (\div 0.3)$$

18 is 60% of 30.

11. $\frac{56}{?} = \frac{80}{100}$

$$\frac{80}{100} = \frac{56}{70} \quad (\times 0.7)$$

56 is 80% of 70.

12. The sales tax on the pencils is $4.32 − $4.00 = $0.32.

$\frac{32}{400} = \frac{?}{100}$

$$\frac{32}{400} = \frac{8}{100} \quad (\div 4)$$

The sales tax rate is 8%.

13. To find a percent of a number, multiply the number by the fraction or decimal equivalent of the percent. To find an unknown percent or part, solve a proportion comparing the percent to the ratio of part to whole.

UNIT 4

Solutions Key

Equivalent Expressions

MODULE 9 *Generating Equivalent Numerical Expressions*

Are You Ready?

1.
$$\begin{array}{r} 992 \\ \times 16 \\ \hline 5{,}952 \\ +9{,}920 \\ \hline 15{,}872 \end{array}$$
15,872

2.
$$\begin{array}{r} 578 \\ \times 27 \\ \hline 4{,}046 \\ +11{,}560 \\ \hline 15{,}606 \end{array}$$
15,606

3.
$$\begin{array}{r} 839 \\ \times 65 \\ \hline 4{,}195 \\ +50{,}340 \\ \hline 54{,}535 \end{array}$$
54,535

4.
$$\begin{array}{r} 367 \\ \times 23 \\ \hline 1{,}101 \\ +7{,}340 \\ \hline 8{,}441 \end{array}$$
8,441

5. $7 \times 7 \times 7$
49×7
343

6. $3 \times 3 \times 3 \times 3$
$9 \times 3 \times 3$
27×3
81

7. $6 \times 6 \times 6 \times 6 \times 6$
$36 \times 6 \times 6 \times 6$
$216 \times 6 \times 6$
$1{,}296 \times 6$
7,776

8. $2 \times 2 \times 2 \times 2 \times 2 \times 2$
$4 \times 2 \times 2 \times 2 \times 2$
$8 \times 2 \times 2 \times 2$
$16 \times 2 \times 2$
32×2
64

9. $20 \div 4 = 5$

10. $21 \div 7 = 3$

11. $42 \div 7 = 6$

12. $56 \div 8 = 7$

LESSON 9.1

Your Turn

2. The base is 4, and the exponent is 3.
$4 \times 4 \times 4 = 4^3$

3. The base is 6, and the exponent is 1.
$6 = 6^1$

4. The base is $\frac{1}{8}$, and the exponent is 2
$\frac{1}{8} \times \frac{1}{8} = \left(\frac{1}{8}\right)^2$

5. The base is 5, and the exponent is 6.
$5 \times 5 \times 5 \times 5 \times 5 \times 5 = 5^6$

6. $3^4 = 3 \times 3 \times 3 \times 3 = 81$

7. $1^9 = 1 \times 1 \times 1 \times 1 \times 1 \times 1 \times 1 \times 1 \times 1 = 1$

8. $\left(\frac{2}{5}\right)^3 = \left(\frac{2}{5}\right) \times \left(\frac{2}{5}\right) \times \left(\frac{2}{5}\right) = \frac{8}{125}$

9. $12^2 = 12 \times 12 = 144$

Guided Practice

1.

Exponential form	Product	Simplified product
5^1	5	5
5^2	5×5	25
5^3	$5 \times 5 \times 5$	125
5^4	$5 \times 5 \times 5 \times 5$	625
5^5	$5 \times 5 \times 5 \times 5 \times 5$	3,125

2. The base is 6, and the exponent is 3.
$\underbrace{6 \times 6 \times 6}_{\text{3 factors of 6}} = 6^3$

3. The base is 10, and the exponent is 7.
$10 \times 10 \times 10 \times 10 \times 10 \times 10 \times 10 = 10^7$

4. The base is $\frac{3}{4}$, and the exponent is 5.
$\frac{3}{4} \times \frac{3}{4} \times \frac{3}{4} \times \frac{3}{4} \times \frac{3}{4} = \left(\frac{3}{4}\right)^5$

5. The base is $\frac{7}{9}$, and the exponent is 8.
$\frac{7}{9} \times \frac{7}{9} \times \frac{7}{9} \times \frac{7}{9} \times \frac{7}{9} \times \frac{7}{9} \times \frac{7}{9} \times \frac{7}{9} = \left(\frac{7}{9}\right)^8$

6. $8^3 = 8 \times 8 \times 8 = 512$

7. $7^4 = 7 \times 7 \times 7 \times 7 = 2{,}401$

8. $10^3 = 10 \times 10 \times 10 = 1{,}000$

9. $\left(\frac{1}{4}\right)^2 = \left(\frac{1}{4}\right) \times \left(\frac{1}{4}\right) = \frac{1}{16}$

10. $\left(\frac{1}{3}\right)^3 = \left(\frac{1}{3}\right) \times \left(\frac{1}{3}\right) \times \left(\frac{1}{3}\right) = \frac{1}{27}$

11. $\left(\frac{6}{7}\right)^2 = \left(\frac{6}{7}\right) \times \left(\frac{6}{7}\right) = \frac{36}{49}$

12. $0.8^2 = 0.8 \times 0.8 = 0.64$

13. $0.5^3 = 0.5 \times 0.5 \times 0.5 = 0.125$

14. $1.1^2 = 1.1 \times 1.1 = 1.21$

15. $8^0 = 1$

16. $12^1 = 12$

17. $\left(\frac{1}{2}\right)^0 = 1$

18. $13^2 = 13 \times 13 = 169$

19. $\left(\frac{2}{5}\right)^2 = \left(\frac{2}{5}\right) \times \left(\frac{2}{5}\right) = \frac{4}{25}$

20. $0.9^2 = 0.9 \times 0.9 = 0.81$

21. You use an exponent to write a number that can be written as a product of equal factors.
    $16 = 4 \times 4$ (or $2 \times 2 \times 2 \times 2$), so it can be written as 4^2 (or 2^4).

Independent Practice

22. $100 = 10^2$

23. $8 = 2^3$

24. $25 = 5^2$

25. $27 = 3^3$

26. $\frac{1}{169} = \left(\frac{1}{13}\right)^2$

27. $14 = 14^1$

28. $32 = 2^5$

29. $\frac{64}{81} = \left(\frac{8}{9}\right)^2$

30. $1{,}000 = 10^3$

31. $256 = 4^4$

32. $16 = 2^4$

33. $9 = 3^2$

34. $\frac{1}{9} = \left(\frac{1}{3}\right)^2$

35. $64 = 8^2$

36. $\frac{9}{16} = \left(\frac{3}{4}\right)^2$

37. $729 = 9^3$

38. $3^3 = 27$ players

39. Tim will triple the number of pages he reads for 4 days, so he will read 3^4 pages, or 81 pages, on Thursday.

40. $10.5^2 = 10.5 \times 10.5 = 110.25$ in^2

41. 2^6 dollars, or \$64

42. 3^4 mm, or 81 mm

43. $\left(\frac{1}{3}\right)^3 = \frac{1}{3} \times \frac{1}{3} \times \frac{1}{3} = \frac{1}{27}$ in^3

44. Sample answer: $0.3^2 = 0.09$; $0.3 > 0.09$

Focus on Higher Order Thinking

45. The value of 1 raised to any power is 1. 1 multiplied by itself any number of times is 1. The value of 0 raised to any power is 0. 0 multiplied by itself any number of times is still 0.

46. 10; 100; 1,000; 10,000... Each term in the pattern is a 1 followed by the same number of zeros as the exponent. $10^6 = 1{,}000{,}000$

47. 2^6, 4^3, and 8^2

48. Disagree; the product of a number between 0 and 1 and itself is less than the original number. For example, $0.5 \times 0.5 = 0.25$, and $0.25 < 0.5$.

LESSON 9.2

Your Turn

1. $21 = 1 \cdot 21$
   $21 = 3 \cdot 7$
   The factors of 21 are 1, 3, 7, 21.

2. $37 = 1 \cdot 37$
   The factors of 37 are 1, 37.

3. $42 = 1 \cdot 42$
   $42 = 2 \cdot 21$
   $42 = 3 \cdot 14$
   $42 = 6 \cdot 7$
   The factors of 42 are 1, 2, 3, 6, 7, 14, 21, 42.

4. $30 = 1 \cdot 30$
   $30 = 2 \cdot 15$
   $30 = 3 \cdot 10$
   $30 = 5 \cdot 6$
   The factors of 30 are 1, 2, 3, 5, 6, 10, 15, 30.

Guided Practice

1. 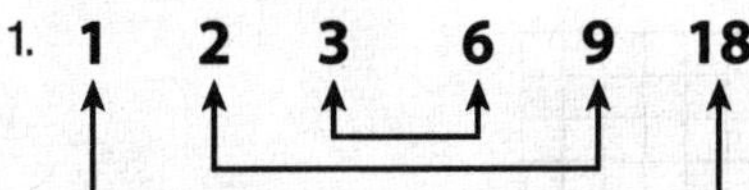

   The factors of 18 are 1, 2, 3, 6, 9, 18.

2. 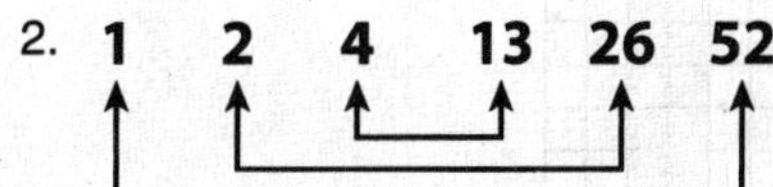

   The factors of 52 are 1, 2, 4, 13, 26, 52.

3. $72 = 1 \cdot 72$
   $72 = 2 \cdot 36$
   $72 = 3 \cdot 24$
   $72 = 4 \cdot 18$
   $72 = 6 \cdot 12$
   $72 = 8 \cdot 9$

Length	72	36	24	18	12	9
Width	1	2	3	4	6	8

4. 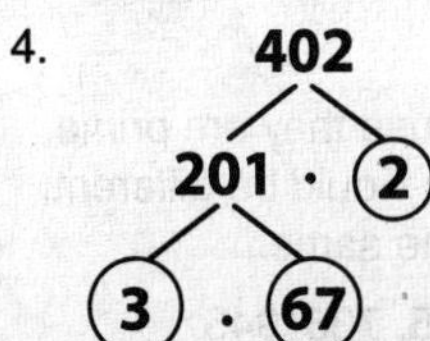

   $402 = 2 \cdot 3 \cdot 67$

5.

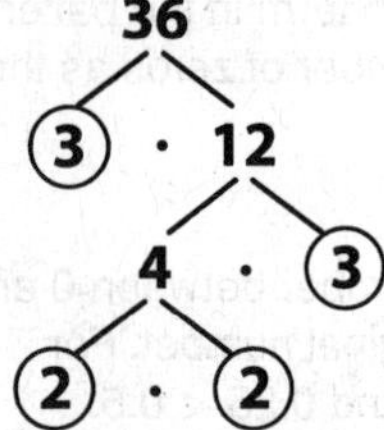

$36 = 3 \cdot 2 \cdot 2 \cdot 3 = 2^2 \cdot 3^2$

6.
```
2 | 32
  2 | 16
    2 | 8
      2 | 4
        2 | 2
              1
```

$32 = 2 \cdot 2 \cdot 2 \cdot 2 \cdot 2 = 2^5$

7.
```
3 | 27
  3 | 9
    3 | 3
          1
```

$27 = 3 \cdot 3 \cdot 3 = 3^3$

8. When all the factors are prime and their product is the original number, you have found the prime factorization.

Independent Practice

9.

1×12; 2×6; 3×4

10. 6 different ways: 1 row of 32 stamps; 2 rows of 16; 4 rows of 8; 32 rows of 1; 16 rows of 2; 8 rows of 4

11. When you find the factors of a number, you find all factors, some of which are prime; when you find the prime factorization, you find only the prime factors.

12. $891 = 3 \cdot 3 \cdot 3 \cdot 3 \cdot 11 = 3^4 \cdot 11$

13. $504 = 2 \cdot 2 \cdot 2 \cdot 3 \cdot 3 \cdot 7 = 2^3 \cdot 3^2 \cdot 7$

14. $23 = 23$

15. $230 = 2 \cdot 5 \cdot 23$

16. 3 and 11 can be chosen, because they are prime factors. The intermediate steps would be different, but the prime factorization is the same.

17. Sample answers: 105, 315, 525, 735, 945

18. 26; the prime factors of 25 are 5 and 5, the prime factors of 26 are 2 and 13, and the prime factors of 27 are 3, 3, and 3. The sums are 10, 15, and 9. The greatest sum is 15, so choose 26 to move 15 spaces.

19. 9 is not a prime number; the prime factorization of 27 is 3^3.

Focus on Higher Order Thinking

20. 36 has five factor pairs, so five different rectangles can be drawn. 15 has only two factor pairs, so only two different rectangles can be drawn.

21. Disagree; the factors that are being multiplied are all prime numbers, so the prime factorization of the number is $17 \cdot 13 \cdot 11 \cdot 7$.

22. one million: $5^6 \cdot 2^6$; one billion: $5^9 \cdot 2^9$

LESSON 9.3

Your Turn

2. $7 + 15 \times 9^2 = 7 + 15 \times 81$
$= 7 + 1{,}215$
$= 1{,}222$

3. $220 - 450 \div 3^2 = 220 - 450 \div 9$
$= 220 - 50$
$= 170$

5. $5 \times (20 \div 4)^2 = 5 \times 5^2$
$= 5 \times 25$
$= 125$

6. $8^2 - (5 + 2)^2 = 8^2 - 7^2$
$= 64 - 49$
$= 15$

7. $7 - \frac{(63 \div 9)^2}{7} = 7 - \frac{7^2}{7}$
$= 7 - \frac{49}{7}$
$= 7 - 7$
$= 0$

Guided Practice

1.

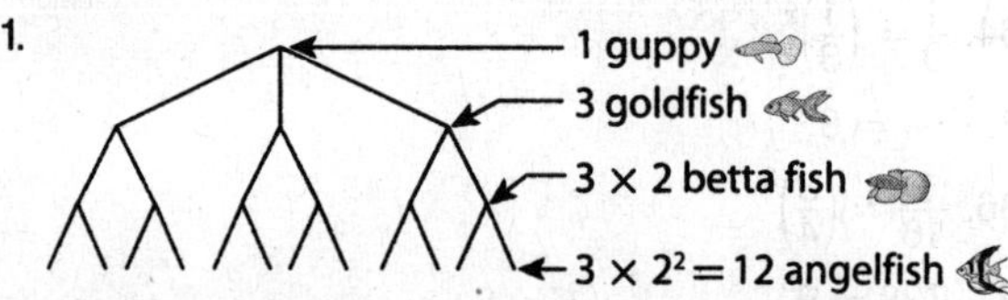

$3 \times 2^2 = 12$ angelfish

2. $89 - 4^2 \times 4 + 12 = 89 - 16 \times 4 + 12$
$= 89 - 64 + 12$
$= 25 + 12$
$= 37$

3. $6 \times (36 \div 12)^2 + 8 = 6 \times (3)^2 + 8$
$= 6 \times 9 + 8$
$= 54 + 8$
$= 62$

4. $12 \times \left(\frac{(4+2)^2}{4}\right) - 7 = 12 \times \left(\frac{(6)^2}{4}\right) - 7$
$= 12 \times \left(\frac{36}{4}\right) - 7$
$= 12 \times 9 - 7$
$= 108 - 7$
$= 101$

5. $320 \div \left(\frac{(11-9)^3}{2}\right) \times 8 = 320 \div \left(\frac{(2)^3}{2}\right) \times 8$
$= 320 \div \left(\frac{8}{2}\right) \times 8$
$= 320 \div 4 \times 8$
$= 80 \times 8$
$= 640$

6. Find the value of any expressions within parentheses first. Then evaluate all powers. Then multiply or divide from left to right, and finally add or subtract from left to right.

Independent Practice

7. $5 \times 2 + 3^2 = 5 \times 2 + 9$
$= 10 + 9$
$= 19$

8. $15 - 7 \times 2 + 2^3 = 15 - 7 \times 2 + 8$
$= 15 - 14 + 8$
$= 1 + 8$
$= 9$

9. $(11 - 8)^3 - 2 \times 6 = 3^3 - 2 \times 6$
$= 27 - 2 \times 6$
$= 27 - 12$
$= 15$

10. $6 + 3(13 - 2) - 5^2 = 6 + 3(11) - 5^2$
$= 6 + 3(11) - 25$
$= 6 + 33 - 25$
$= 39 - 25$
$= 14$

11. $12 + \frac{9^2}{3} = 12 + \frac{81}{3}$
$= 12 + 27$
$= 39$

12. $\frac{8 + 6^2}{11} + 7 \times 2 = \frac{8 + 36}{11} + 7 \times 2$
$= \frac{44}{11} + 7 \times 2$
$= 4 + 7 \times 2$
$= 4 + 14$
$= 18$

13. Jay worked inside the parentheses first, but he should have performed the division $12 \div 3$ first. The correct answer is 17.

14. a. $3 \times 12 + 2 \times 19 - 3$; \$71
b. $3 \times (12 - 3) + 2 \times (19 - 3)$; \$59
c. In part a, the \$3 discount is applied 1 time; in b it is applied 5 times.
d. Sample answer: If the shop owner wants to make more money, the sign should say "\$3 off your entire purchase." If customers can take the discount off every item, a lot more money is discounted from each purchase.

15. a. $3 \times 2 \times 2 \times 2 \times 2 = 3 \times 2^4$
b. $3 \times 2^4 - 7 = 3 \times 16 - 7 = 48 - 7 = 41$; 41

16. $2 \times 4 \times 4 = 2 \times 4^2 = 32$; 32 students receive a text.

Focus on Higher Order Thinking

17. a. Area of green square: 6^2 in^2
Area of blue rectangle: 24 in^2
Area of white rectangle: 2×6 in^2
$6^2 + 2 \times 6 + 24 = 72$ square inches
b. 8 in. by 9 in.

18. Lila is correct. Rob squared each of the numbers in the parentheses and then subtracted, instead of subtracting first and then squaring the difference.

19. $8 \times 4 - (2 \times 3 + 8) \div 2$

MODULE 9

Ready to Go On?

1. $7^3 = 7 \times 7 \times 7 = 343$
2. $9^2 = 9 \times 9 = 81$
3. $\left(\frac{7}{9}\right)^2 = \frac{7}{9} \times \frac{7}{9} = \frac{49}{81}$
4. $\left(\frac{1}{2}\right)^6 = \frac{1}{2} \times \frac{1}{2} \times \frac{1}{2} \times \frac{1}{2} \times \frac{1}{2} \times \frac{1}{2} = \frac{1}{64}$
5. $\left(\frac{2}{3}\right)^3 = \frac{2}{3} \times \frac{2}{3} \times \frac{2}{3} = \frac{8}{27}$
6. $\left(\frac{1}{3}\right)^4 = \frac{1}{3} \times \frac{1}{3} \times \frac{1}{3} \times \frac{1}{3} = \frac{1}{81}$
7. $12^0 = 1$
8. $1.4^2 = 1.4 \times 1.4 = 1.96$
9. $96 = 1 \cdot 96$
$96 = 2 \cdot 48$
$96 = 3 \cdot 32$
$96 = 4 \cdot 24$
$96 = 6 \cdot 16$
$96 = 8 \cdot 12$
The factors of 96 are 1, 2, 3, 4, 6, 8, 12, 16, 24, 32, 48, 96.
10. $120 = 1 \cdot 120$
$120 = 2 \cdot 60$
$120 = 3 \cdot 40$
$120 = 4 \cdot 30$
$120 = 5 \cdot 24$
$120 = 6 \cdot 20$
$120 = 8 \cdot 15$
$120 = 10 \cdot 12$
The factors of 120 are 1, 2, 3, 4, 5, 6, 8, 10, 12, 15, 20, 24, 30, 40, 60, 120.
11. 2|58
29|29
1
$58 = 2 \times 29$
12. 2|212
2|106
53|53
1
$212 = 2 \times 2 \times 53 = 2^2 \times 53$

13.
2|2,800
2|1,400
2|700
2|350
5|175
5|35
7|7
1

$2{,}800 = 2 \times 2 \times 2 \times 2 \times 5 \times 5 \times 7 = 2^4 \times 5^2 \times 7$

14.
2|900
2|450
5|225
5|45
3|9
3|3
1

$900 = 2 \times 2 \times 3 \times 3 \times 5 \times 5 = 2^2 \times 3^2 \times 5^2$

15. $(21 - 3) \div 3^2 = 18 \div 3^2$
$= 18 \div 9$
$= 2$

16. $7^2 \times (6 \div 3) = 7^2 \times 2$
$= 49 \times 2$
$= 98$

17. $17 + 15 \div 3 - 2^4 = 17 + 15 \div 3 - 16$
$= 17 + 5 - 16$
$= 22 - 16$
$= 6$

18. $(8 + 56) \div 4 - 3^2 = 64 \div 4 - 3^2$
$= 64 \div 4 - 9$
$= 16 - 9$
$= 7$

19. $7 \times 6 + 4 \times 3 = 42 + 12 = 54$ pounds

20. Write an expression to model the situation. Evaluate the expression using the order of operations: first perform operations in parentheses; then, find the value of each power, multiply or divide from left to right, and finally add or subtract from left to right.

MODULE 10 *Generating Equivalent Algebraic Expressions*

Are You Ready?

1. $11 + (20 - 13)$
   $11 + 7$
   18
2. $(10 - 7) - (14 - 12)$
   $3 - 2$
   1
3. $(4 + 17) - (16 - 9)$
   $21 - 7$
   14
4. $(23 - 15) - (18 - 13)$
   $8 - 5$
   3
5. $8 \times (4 + 5 + 7)$
   8×16
   128
6. $(2 + 3) \times (11 - 5)$
   5×6
   30
7. the difference between 42 and 19: $42 - 19$
8. the product of 7 and 12: 7×12
9. 30 more than 20: $20 + 30$
10. 100 decreased by 77: $100 - 77$
11. $3(8) - 15$
    $24 - 15$
    9
12. $4(12) + 11$
    $48 + 11$
    59
13. $3(7) - 4(2)$
    $21 - 8$
    13
14. $4(2 + 3) - 12$
    $4(5) - 12$
    $20 - 12$
    8
15. $9(14 - 5) - 42$
    $9(9) - 42$
    $81 - 42$
    39
16. $7(8) - 5(8)$
    $56 - 40$
    16

LESSON 10.1

Your Turn

1. The operation is multiplication; $7n$
2. The operation is subtraction; $4 - y$
3. The operation is addition; $x + 13$
4. Sample answer: the quotient of x and 12
5. Sample answer: 10 multiplied by y
6. Sample answer: c plus 3
7. 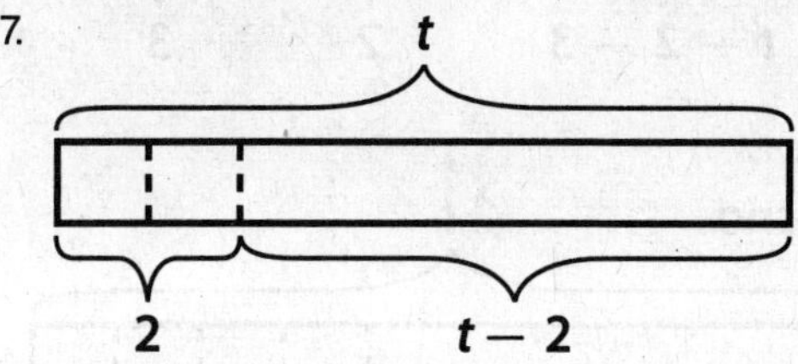

8. 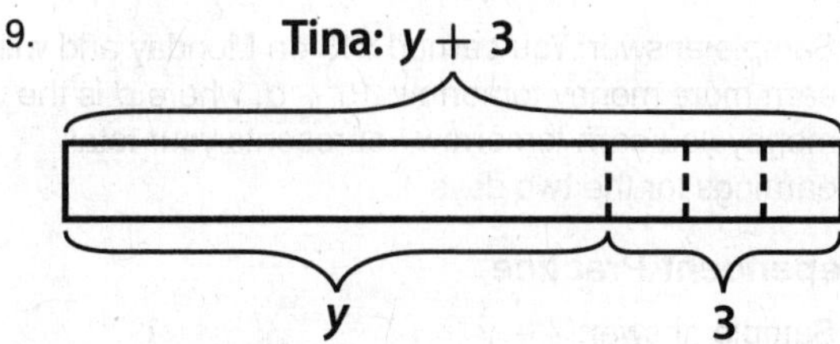

9. Tina: $y + 3$

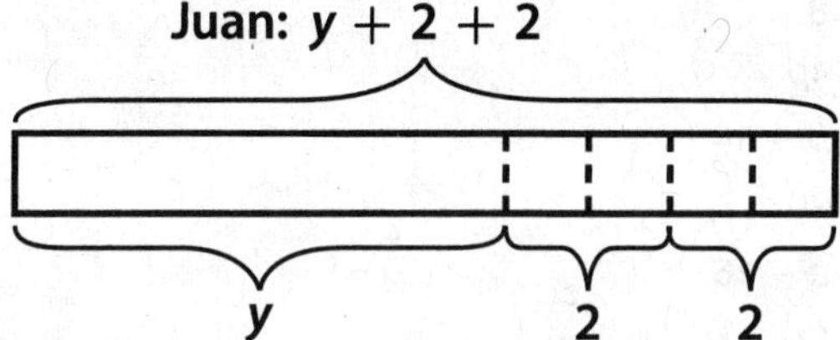

Juan: $y + 2 + 2$

No; the expressions are not equivalent.
10. The operation is division; $\frac{d}{4}$

Guided Practice

1. The operation is subtraction; $y - 3$
2. The operation is multiplication; $2p$
3. Sample answer: 12 added to y
4. Sample answer: 10 divided into p
5. 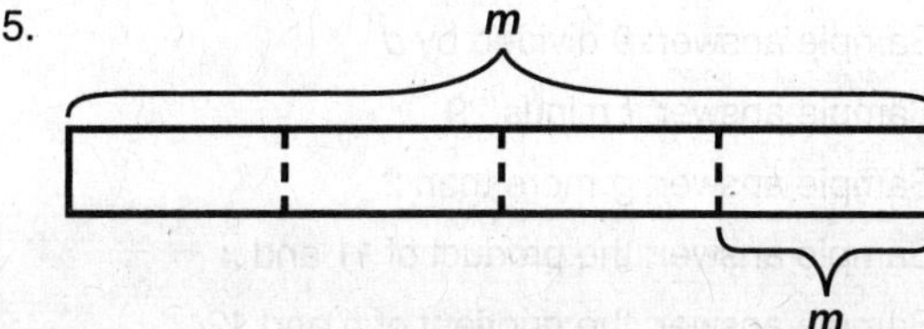

6. **Redding**

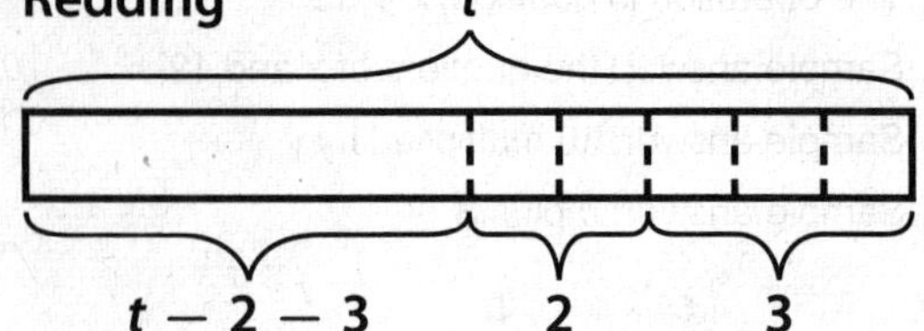

Fresno

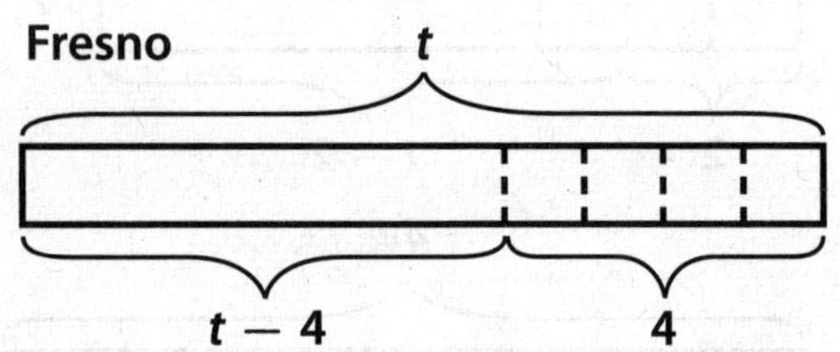

7. No; the models show that the temperature in Redding is 1 degree less than the temperature in Fresno.
8. The operation is multiplication; $24c$
9. Sample answer: You earned \$15 on Monday and will earn more money tomorrow. $15 + d$, where d is the money you earn tomorrow, represents your total earnings for the two days.

Independent Practice

10. Sample answer: $7 + y$
11. $\frac{n}{8}$
12. $4p$
13. $b + 14$
14. $90x$
15. $a - 16$
16. $24 - k$
17. $3w$
18. $1 + q$
19. $\frac{13}{z}$
20. $45 + c$
21. $w - 8$
22. Sample answer: 83 added to m
23. Sample answer: 42 times s
24. Sample answer: 9 divided by d
25. Sample answer: t minus 29
26. Sample answer: g more than 2
27. Sample answer: the product of 11 and x
28. Sample answer: the quotient of h and 12
29. Sample answer: k less than 5
30. $5w + 3w$
31. $8w$
32. Yes, Sarah and Noah got paid the same amount last week. Check students' models.
33. a. $3d$
    b. $3g$
    c. In Mia's expression, the numeral is the number of gallons and the variable represents cost per gallon. In Bob's expression, the numeral is the cost per gallon and the variable is the number of gallons.
34. $2b$
35. $\frac{t}{46}$
36. $15 - 2 + v$ or $13 + v$
37. Sample answer: m represents Meg's age; $m - 2$ represents Jill's age; $\frac{m}{2}$ represents Beth's age.
38. a. $3 + x$
    b. $5 - 2 + x$
    c. Yes; $5 - 2 + x = 3 + x$. The expressions are equivalent.
39. $g + 6$
40. $\frac{48}{b}$
41. $55h$

Focus on Higher Order Thinking

42. a. $3x$
    b. $5y$
    c. $3x + 5y$
43. a. $\frac{s}{2}$; there are half as many pairs of shoes as there are total shoes.
    b. $\frac{s}{2} + 1$ pairs
44. Sample answer: $2x - 8y + 7$.
45. Sample answer: Sam started the day with a box of pencils. During the day he gave out 8 pencils.
46. Yes; $1y$ is the product of 1 and y. Since 1 times any number is equal to the number, $1 \cdot y = y$. The expression $y + 4$ is equivalent to $1y + 4$.

LESSON 10.2

Your Turn

1. $4x$; $x = 8$
   $4(8)$
   32
   When $x = 8$, $4x = 32$.
2. $6.5 - n$; $n = 1.8$
   $6.5 - 1.8$
   4.7
   When $n = 1.8$, $6.5 - n = 4.7$.
3. $\frac{m}{6}$; $m = 18$
   $\frac{18}{6}$
   3
   When $m = 18$, $\frac{m}{6} = 3$.

4. $3(n + 1); n = 5$
$3(5 + 1)$
$3(6)$
18
When $n = 5$, $3(n + 1) = 18$.

5. $4(n - 4) + 14; n = 5$
$4(5 - 4) + 14$
$4(1) + 14$
$4 + 14$
18
When $n = 5$, $4(n - 4) + 14 = 18$.

6. $6n + n^2; n = 5$
$6(5) + 5^2$
$30 + 25$
55
When $n = 5$, $6n + n^2 = 55$.

7. $ab - c; a = 3, b = 4, c = 6$
$3(4) - (6)$
$12 - 6$
6
When $a = 3, b = 4, c = 6$,
$ab - c = 6$.

8. $bc + 5a; a = 3, b = 4, c = 6$
$4(6) + 5(3)$
$24 + 15$
39
When $a = 3, b = 4, c = 6$,
$bc + 5a = 39$.

9. $a^3 - (b + c); a = 3, b = 4, c = 6$
$3^3 - (4 + 6)$
$27 - (10)$
17
When $a = 3, b = 4, c = 6$,
$a^3 - (b + c) = 17$.

10. Surface Area: $6x^2; x = 2$
$6(2)^2$
$6(4)$
24
$S = 24\ m^2$
Volume: $x^3; x = 2$
$(2)^3$
8
$V = 8\ m^3$

11. $60m; m = 7$
$60(7)$
420
420 seconds

Guided Practice

1. $x - 7; x = 23$
$23 - 7$
16

2. $3a - b; a = 4, b = 6$
$3(4) - 6$
$12 - 6$
6

3. $\frac{1}{2}w + 2; w = \frac{1}{9}$
$\frac{1}{2}\left(\frac{1}{9}\right) + 2$
$\frac{1}{18} + 2$
$2\frac{1}{18}$

4. $5(6.2 + z); z = 3.8$
$5(6.2 + 3.8)$
$5(10)$
50

5. $\frac{8}{t} + t^2; t = 4$
$\frac{8}{4} + 4^2$
$2 + 16$
18

6. $5m - m^2; m = 3$
$5\,(3) - 3^2$
$15 - 9$
6

7. a. $12x + 5$
b. $12(3) + 5 = 36 + 5 = 41$
The family spent $41 to attend the game.

8. a. $2l + 2w$
b. $2(7) + 2(5) = 14 + 10 = 24$
Stan needs to buy 24 feet of trim.

9. Substitute for the variables and follow the order of operations that you would use for a numerical expression.

Independent Practice

10. a. $8.75a + 6.5c + 6.5s$ or $8.75a + 6.5(c + s)$
b. $8.75(2) + 6.5(3) + 6.5(1) =$
$17.5 + 19.5 + 6.5 = \$43.50$
c. No; $8.75(4) + 6.5(2) = \$48.00$
$\$48 > \$43.50$

11. $2x^2; 2(8)^2 = 2(64) = 128$ square feet

12. $\$2,340 + d - w; \$2,340 + \$100 - \$50 = \$2,390$

13.

x	0	1	2	3	4	5	6
$6x - x^2$	0	5	8	9	8	5	0

The value of $6x - x^2$ increases from 0 at $x = 0$ to 9 at $x = 3$, and then decreases back to 0 at $x = 6$. Also, the values are the same for $x = 0$ and 6, for $x = 1$ and 5, and for $x = 2$ and 4.

14. $\frac{1}{2}mv^2; m = 0.145, v = 40$
$\frac{1}{2}(0.145)(40)^2$
$E = 116$ joules

15. $\frac{1}{2}bh; b = 12, h = 7$
$\frac{1}{2}(12)(7)$
42
$A = 42\ in^2$

16. $\frac{1}{3}s^2h$; $s = 24$, $h = 30$

$\frac{1}{3}(24)^2(30)$

$V = 5{,}760$ ft^3

Focus on Higher Order Thinking

17. a. For $x = 2$, each expression has a value of 2. For $x = 7$, each expression has a value of 107. These results suggest that the expressions may be equivalent but do not prove that the expressions are equivalent.

    b. For $x = 5$, the first expression has a value of 47 and the second expression has a value of 53. Because the values are different, the expressions are not equivalent.

18. $3x$ means that 3 should be multiplied by the value of x; $3(5) + 2 = 15 + 2 = 17$

LESSON 10.3

Your Turn

3. Sample answer: $(ab)c = a(bc)$; Associative Property of Multiplication
4. Sample answer: $3y + 4y = (3 + 4)y$; Distributive Property
5. Sample answer: $6 + n = n + 6$; Commutative Property of Addition
6. $2(3x - 5) = 6x - 10$
   $6x - 10$ does not equal $6x - 8$; they are not equivalent expressions.
7. $2 - 2 + 5x = 5x$
   $2 - 2 + 5x$ and $5x$ are equivalent expressions.
8. Jamal bought $2x + 8$ stickers.
   $2(4 + x) = 8 + 2x = 2x + 8$; yes, they are equivalent expressions.

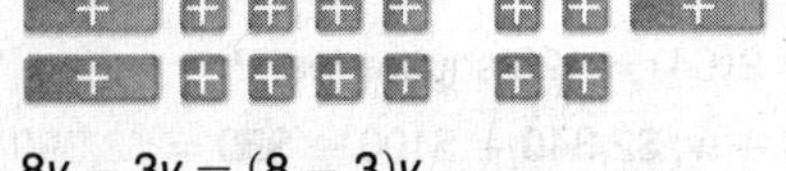

9. $8y - 3y = (8 - 3)y$
   $= 5y$
10. $6x^2 + 4(x^2 - 1) = 6x^2 + 4x^2 - 4$
    $= (6 + 4)x^2 - 4$
    $= 10x^2 - 4$
11. $4a^5 - 2a^5 + 4b + b = (4 - 2)a^5 + (4 + 1)b$
    $= 2a^5 + 5b$
12. $8m + 14 - 12 + 4n = 8m + 2 + 4n$

Guided Practice

1. $y = 5$
   $4 + 4y = 4 + 20 = 24$
   $4y - 4 = 20 - 4 = 16$
   $4(y - 1) = 4(4) = 16$
   $4(y + 1) = 4(6) = 24$
   $4y + 1 = 20 + 1 = 21$
   $1 + 4y = 1 + 20 = 21$

List A	List B
$4 + 4y =$ 24	$4y - 4 =$ 16
$4(y - 1) =$ 16	$4(y + 1) =$ 24
$4y + 1 =$ 21	$1 + 4y =$ 21

2. $x + 4$ and $2(x + 2) = 2x + 4$ are not equivalent.
3. Sample answer: $ab = ba$; Commutative Property of Multiplication
4. Sample answer: $5(3x - 2) = 5(3x) - 5(2)$; Distributive Property
5. $\frac{1}{2}(4 - 2x) = 2 - x$
   $2 - x$ does not equal $2 - 2x$; they are not equivalent expressions.
6. $\frac{1}{2}(6x - 2) = 3x - 1$
   $3x - 1$ does not equal $3 - x$; they are not equivalent expressions.
7. $32y + 12y = 44y$
8. $12 + 3x + 12 - x = 12 + 12 + 3x - x = 24 + 2x$
9. Use models to compare the expressions, or use properties of operations to rewrite one or both expressions.

Independent Practice

10. Sample answer: $cd = dc$; Commutative Property of Multiplication
11. Sample answer: $x + 13 = 13 + x$; Commutative Property of Addition
12. Sample answer: $4(2x - 3) = 4(2x) - 4(3)$; Distributive Property
13. Sample answer: $2 + (a + b) = (2 + a) + b$; Associative Property of Addition
14. 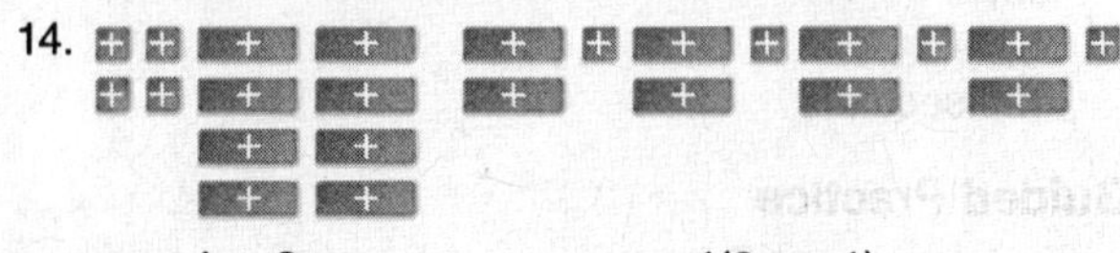

    $4 + 8x$ $4(2x + 1)$
15. $7x^4 - 5x^4 = 2x^4$
16. $32y + 5y = 37y$
17. $6b + 7b - 10 = 13b - 10$
18. $2x + 3x + 4 = 5x + 4$

19. $y + 4 + 3(y + 2) = y + 4 + 3y + 6$
$= 3y + y + 4 + 6$
$= 4y + 10$

20. $7a^2 - a^2 + 16 = 6a^2 + 16$

21. $3y^2 + 3(4y^2 - 2) = 3y^2 + 12y^2 - 6$
$= 15y^2 - 6$

22. $z^2 + z + 4z^3 + 4z^2 = 4z^3 + z^2 + 4z^2 + z$
$= 4z^3 + 5z^2 + z$

23. $0.5(x^4 + 3) + 12 = 0.5x^4 + 1.5 + 12$
$= 0.5x^4 + 13.5$

24. $\frac{1}{4}(16 + 4p) = 4 + p$

25. $3x + 12 + x = 12 + 3x + x$ (Commutative Property), and $12 + 3x + x = 12 + 4x$ (Distributive Property); $4(3 + x) = 12 + 4x$ (Distributive Property). So, $3x + 12 + x = 12 + 4x$.

26. $13h + 13(3h) = 13h + 39h = 52h$

27. $(46 + 38 + 29)g + (29 + 27 + 17)s + (29 + 23 + 19)b$; $113g + 73s + 71b$

28. $2(6) + 2(3x + 1) = 12 + 6x + 2$
$= 6x + 14$ mm

29. $2(10.2) + 4(x + 4) = 20.4 + 4x + 16$
$= 36.4 + 4x$ in.

Focus on Higher Order Thinking

30. a. $4 + 6x$; $2(2 + 3x)$
b. The expressions become $6 + 9x$ and $3(2 + 3x)$.

31. Sample answer: $3x^2 - 4x + 7$; it doesn't have any like terms.

32. Sample answer: $2(8y + 16)$

MODULE 10

Ready to Go On?

1. The operation is division; $\frac{p}{6}$
2. The operation is subtraction; $j - 65$
3. The operation is addition; $185 + h$
4. The operation is multiplication; $16g$
5. $4x$
6. $8p$; $p = 9$
$8(9)$
72
7. $\frac{60}{m}$; $m = 5$
$\frac{60}{5}$
12
8. $4(d + 7)$; $d = 2$
$4(2 + 7)$
$4(9)$
36
9. $1 + r^2 - r$; $r = 5$
$1 + 5^2 - 5$
$1 + 25 - 5$
21
10. $b \times h \div 2$; $b = 6$; $h = 8$
$6 \times 8 \div 2$
$48 \div 2$
24 cm^2
11. $7x + 14 = 7(x + 2)$
$7 + 7x = 7(1 + x)$
$7(x - 1) = 7x - 7$

List A	List B
$7x + 14$	$7(1 + x)$
$7 + 7x$	$7x - 7$
$7(x - 1)$	$7(x + 2)$

12. Model the expressions with bar models or algebra tiles to determine if the expressions are equivalent. Write equivalent expressions using properties of operations, the order of operations, and combining like terms.

UNIT 5

Solutions Key

Equations and Inequalities

MODULE 11 *Equations and Relationships*

Are You Ready?

1. $4(5 + 6) - 15$
   $4(11) - 15$
   $44 - 15$
   29
2. $8(2 + 4) + 16$
   $8(6) + 16$
   $48 + 16$
   64
3. $3(14 - 7) - 16$
   $3(7) - 16$
   $21 - 16$
   5
4. $6(8 - 3) + 3(7 - 4)$
   $6(5) + 3(3)$
   $30 + 9$
   39
5. $10(6 - 5) - 3(9 - 6)$
   $10(1) - 3(3)$
   $10 - 9$
   1
6. $7(4 + 5 + 2) - 6(3 + 5)$
   $7(11) - 6(8)$
   $77 - 48$
   29
7. $2(8 + 3) + 4^2$
   $2(11) + 4^2$
   $2(11) + 16$
   $22 + 16$
   38
8. $7(14 - 8) - 6^2$
   $7(6) - 6^2$
   $7(6) - 36$
   $42 - 36$
   6
9. $8(2 + 1)^2 - 4^2$
   $8(3)^2 - 4^2$
   $8(9) - 4^2$
   $8(9) - 16$
   $72 - 16$
   56
10. A number increased by 7.9 is 8.3: $x + 7.9 = 8.3$
11. 17 is the sum of a number and 6: $17 = x + 6$
12. The quotient of a number and 8 is 4: $x \div 8 = 4$
13. 81 is three times a number: $81 = 3x$
14. The difference between 31 and a number is 7:
    $31 - x = 7$
15. Eight less than a number is 19: $x - 8 = 19$

LESSON 11.1

Your Turn

1. $11 = n + 6; n = 5$
   $11 \stackrel{?}{=} 5 + 6$
   $11 \stackrel{?}{=} 11$
   Yes; 5 is a solution of $11 = n + 6$.
2. $y - 6 = 24; y = 18$
   $18 - 6 \stackrel{?}{=} 24$
   $12 \stackrel{?}{=} 24$
   No; 18 is not a solution of $y - 6 = 24$.
3. $\frac{x}{9} = 4; x = 36$
   $\frac{36}{9} \stackrel{?}{=} 4$
   $4 \stackrel{?}{=} 4$
   Yes; 36 is a solution of $\frac{x}{9} = 4$.
4. $15t = 100; t = 6$
   $15(6) \stackrel{?}{=} 100$
   $90 \stackrel{?}{=} 100$
   No; 6 is not a solution of $15t = 100$.
5. $\underbrace{\text{Other fish}}_{f} + \underbrace{\text{Gold fish}}_{9} = \underbrace{\text{Total fish}}_{38}$
   $f + 9 = 38$
6. $\underbrace{\text{Beads per necklace}}_{17} \times \underbrace{\text{Number of Necklaces}}_{n} = \underbrace{\text{Total beads}}_{102;}$
   $17n = 102$
7. $c - \frac{1}{2} = 12$
8. $2.5h = 20$
10. $24 + x = 62$ | $24 + x = 62$
    $24 + 38 \stackrel{?}{=} 62$ | $24 + 31 \stackrel{?}{=} 62$
    $62 \stackrel{?}{=} 62$ | $55 \stackrel{?}{=} 62$
    $24 + x = 62$; the amount earned on Saturday afternoon; \$38

Guided Practice

1. $23 = x - 9; x = 14$
   $23 \stackrel{?}{=} 14 - 9$
   $23 \stackrel{?}{=} 5$
   No; 14 is not a solution of $23 = x - 9$.
2. $\frac{n}{13} = 4; n = 52$
   $\frac{52}{13} \stackrel{?}{=} 4$
   $4 \stackrel{?}{=} 4$
   Yes; 52 is a solution of $\frac{n}{13} = 4$.
3. $25 = \frac{k}{5}; k = 5$
   $25 \stackrel{?}{=} \frac{5}{5}$
   $25 \stackrel{?}{=} 1$
   No; 5 is not a solution of $25 = \frac{k}{5}$.

4. $2.5n = 45; n = 18$
$2.5(18) \stackrel{?}{=} 45$
$45 \stackrel{?}{=} 45$
Yes; 18 is a solution of $2.5n = 45$.

5. $21 - h = 15; h = 6$
$21 - 6 \stackrel{?}{=} 15$
$15 \stackrel{?}{=} 15$
Yes; 6 is a solution of $21 - h = 15$.

6. $d - 4 = 19; d = 15$
$15 - 4 \stackrel{?}{=} 19$
$11 \stackrel{?}{=} 19$
No; 15 is not a solution of $d - 4 = 19$.

7. $w - 9 = 0; w = 9$
$9 - 9 \stackrel{?}{=} 0$
$0 \stackrel{?}{=} 0$
Yes; 9 is a solution of $w - 9 = 0$.

8. $5q = 31; q = 13$
$5(13) \stackrel{?}{=} 31$
$65 \stackrel{?}{=} 31$
No; 13 is not a solution of $5q = 31$.

9. $\frac{\text{Number of floors}}{} \times \frac{\text{Number of rooms on each floor}}{} = \frac{\text{Total number of rooms}}{}$;
$8r = 256$

10. $\frac{n}{16} = 3$

11. $4.5 + k = 26.2$

12. $\frac{f}{2} = 5$

13. $8x = 208$ | $8x = 208$
$8(26) \stackrel{?}{=} 208$ | $8(28) \stackrel{?}{=} 208$
$208 \stackrel{?}{=} 208$ | $224 \stackrel{?}{=} 208$
$8x = 208$; the cost of each ticket; \$26

14. $x + 24 = 92$ | $x + 24 = 92$
$62 + 24 \stackrel{?}{=} 92$ | $68 + 24 \stackrel{?}{=} 92$
$86 \stackrel{?}{=} 92$ | $92 \stackrel{?}{=} 92$
$x + 24 = 92$; the low temperature in °F; 68 °F

15. Substitute the number for the variable and simplify. If the final statement is true, the number is a solution.

Independent Practice

16. $4n = 76$ | $4n = 76$
$4(19) \stackrel{?}{=} 76$ | $4(22) \stackrel{?}{=} 76$
$76 \stackrel{?}{=} 76$ | $88 \stackrel{?}{=} 76$
$4n = 76$; Andy's age; 19 years old

17. $x + 8 = 31$ | $x + 8 = 31$
$25 + 8 \stackrel{?}{=} 31$ | $23 + 8 \stackrel{?}{=} 31$
$33 \stackrel{?}{=} 31$ | $31 \stackrel{?}{=} 31$
$x + 8 = 31$; weight of backpack in pounds; 23 pounds

18. $x - 23 = 48$ | $x - 23 = 48$
$61 - 23 \stackrel{?}{=} 48$ | $71 - 23 \stackrel{?}{=} 48$
$38 \stackrel{?}{=} 48$ | $48 \stackrel{?}{=} 48$
$x - 23 = 48$; number of students to begin with; 71 students

19. Sample answer: $4x = 20$; $20 \div x = 4$ or $x = 20 \div 4$

20. An expression represents one value, and an equation represents the relationship between two values. An equation is a statement that two expressions are equivalent.

21. a. $29 - 12\frac{1}{2} = x$; $12\frac{1}{2} + x = 29$; the distance between Hadley and Greenville.
b. Yes; $16\frac{1}{2}$ is a solution of both equations in **a**.

22. Sarah is correct. The earnings are the number of hours worked times the amount earned per hour, or $9h$.

23. The dog's ideal weight in pounds; both; another correct equation is $44 - 7 = x$.

24. a. $x - 26 = 18$; the age of Cindy's dad.
b. No; $42 - 26 = 16$; 16 is not equal to 18.
c. Cindy's father will not be 42 when she is 18.

Focus on Higher Order Thinking

25. Yes, because the solution to $4 + f = 12$ is 8. There are 8 flute players, and 8 is twice 4.

26. Yes, Ronald was overcharged; $6(26) = 156$, and $156 < 162$.

27. Yes; setting an expression equal to itself forms an equation that will always be true regardless of the value of the variable(s) or numbers in the expression.

LESSON 11.2

Your Turn

3. $5 = w + 1\frac{1}{2}$; $w = 3\frac{1}{2}$
$-1\frac{1}{2} \quad -1\frac{1}{2}$
$3\frac{1}{2} = w$

−5 −4 −3 −2 −1 0 1 2 3 4 5

5. $h - \frac{1}{2} = \frac{3}{4}$; $h = \frac{5}{4}$, or $1\frac{1}{4}$
$+\frac{1}{2} \quad +\frac{1}{2}$
$h = \frac{5}{4}$

6. The sum of an unknown angle and a 65° angle is 90°.
$x + 65 = 90$
$-65 \quad -65$
$x = 25$; unknown angle measure; $x = 25°$

7. The sum of an unknown angle and a 42° angle is 90°.
$x + 42 = 90$
$-42 \quad -42$
$x = 48$; measure of the complement; $x = 48°$

9. Check students' word problems. $x = 140$

Guided Practice

1. a. Let x represent the number of guests who left when the party ended.

b.

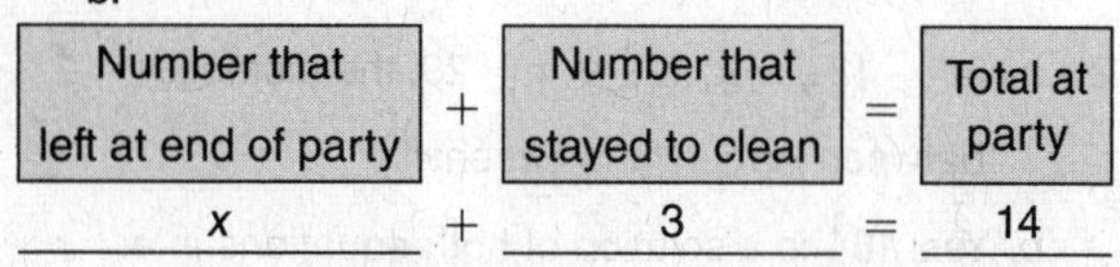

c. 11 friends left when the party ended.

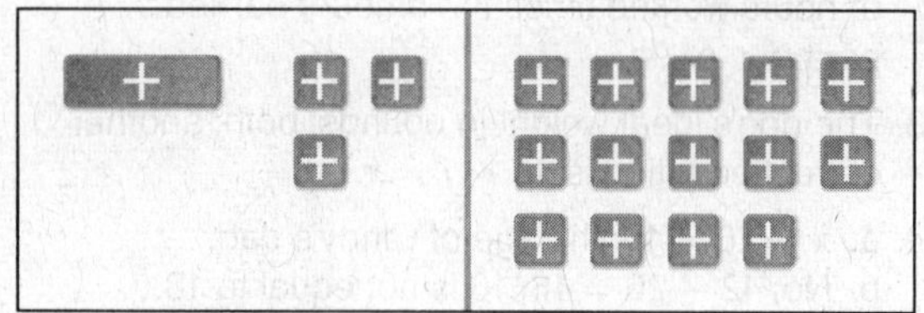

2. $2 = x - 3; x = 5$

$\underline{+3 \quad + 3}$

$5 = x$

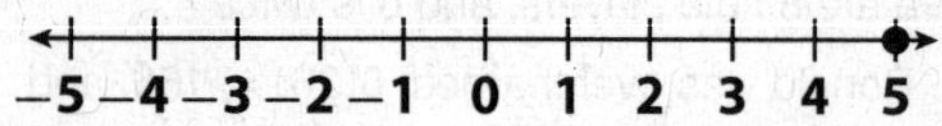

3. $s + 12.5 = 14; s = 1.5$

$\underline{-12.5 \quad -12.5}$

$s = 1.5$

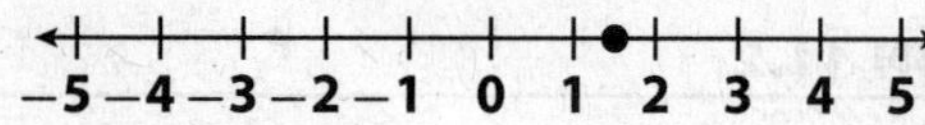

4. $h + 6.9 = 11.4; h = 4.5$

$\underline{-6.9 \quad -6.9}$

$h = 4.5$

5. $82 + p = 122; p = 40$

$\underline{-82 \quad -82}$

$p = 40$

6. $n + \frac{1}{2} = \frac{7}{4}; n = \frac{5}{4}$, or $1\frac{1}{4}$

$\underline{-\frac{1}{2} \quad -\frac{1}{2}}$

$n = \frac{5}{4}$

7. The sum of an unknown angle and a 45° angle is 180°.

$x + 45 = 180$

$\underline{-45 \quad -45}$

$x = 135$; $x = 135°$; unknown angle measure

8. Check students' answers; $x = 275$

9. Apply the inverse operation to both sides of the equation. Subtract for addition equations and add for subtraction equations.

Independent Practice

10. $e + 8 = 31$

$\underline{-8 \quad -8}$

$e = 23$; number of elephants before summer; 23 elephants

11. $14 = b - 12$

$\underline{+12 \quad +12}$

$26 = b$; brother's age; 26 years old

12. $x + 8.95 = 21.35$

$\underline{-8.95 \quad -8.95}$

$x = 12.40$; cost of colored pencils; \$12.40

13. $x + 8 = 37$

$\underline{-8 \quad -8}$

$x = 29$; number of compact cars; 29 compact cars

14. $73 + b = 95$

$\underline{-73 \quad -73}$

$b = 22$; amount Sandra needs; \$22

15. $m - 123.45 = 36.55$

$\underline{+123.45 \quad +123.45}$

$m = 160.00$; amount he originally had; \$160

16. $548 = t - 225$

$\underline{+225 \quad +225}$

$773 = t$; amount she originally had; \$773

17. Check students' answers. $c = 2.50$

18. She subtracted 7 from one side and added 7 to the other. She should have subtracted 7 from both sides to get $x = 3$.

19. a. $1.49 + a = 2.99$; $2.49 + r = 3.99$

b. Both a and r are equal to \$1.50, so the discounts are the same.

20. a. $w + b = 150$; $w = b + b = 2b$

b. $w = 100$; $b = 50$

21. a. $a = 1$; $b = 10$; $c = 100$; $d = 1{,}000$; ...

b. The value of each variable is 10 times that of the one before it.

c. $g = 1{,}000{,}000$

LESSON 11.3

Your Turn

2. $3x = 21$

$\frac{3x}{3} = \frac{21}{3}$

$x = 7$

0 1 2 3 4 5 6 7 8 9 10

3. $\frac{y}{9} = 1$

$9 \cdot \frac{y}{9} = 9 \cdot 1$

$y = 9$

0 1 2 3 4 5 6 7 8 9 10

4. $\frac{x}{5} = 9$

$5 \cdot \frac{x}{5} = 5 \cdot 9$

$x = 45$; the number of cards he gives away; 36 cards.

5. Check students' problems; $x = 35$

Guided Practice

1. a. Let x represent the number of miles run each day.

b.

Number of days	×	Number of miles run each days	=	Total number of miles
5	×	x	=	15

c.

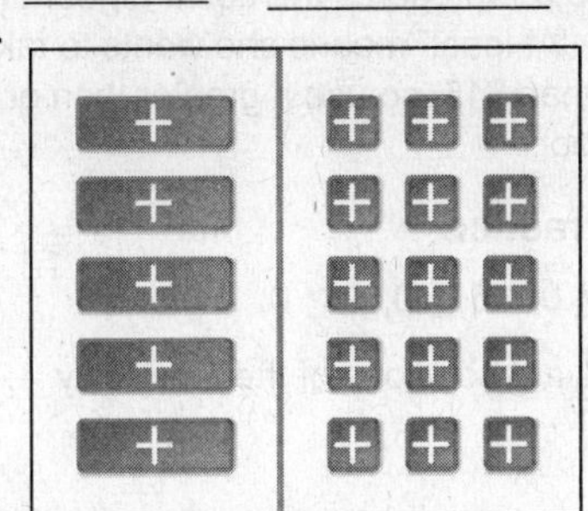

Caroline ran 3 miles each day.

2. $\frac{x}{3} = 3$

$3 \cdot \frac{x}{3} = 3 \cdot 3$

$x = 9$

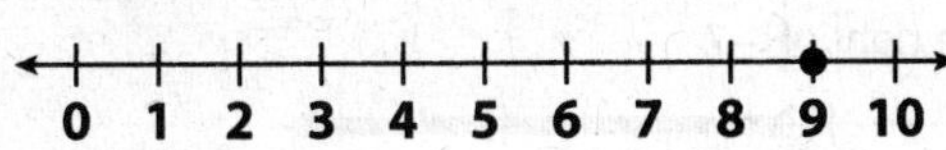

3. $4x = 32$

$\frac{4x}{4} = \frac{32}{4}$

$x = 8$

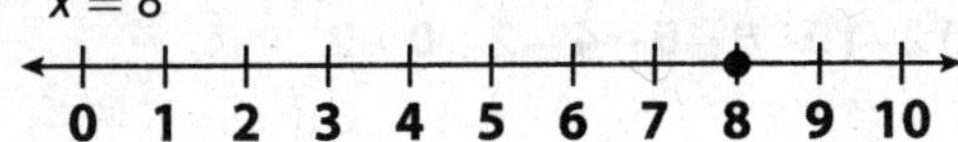

4. $24 = 6w$

$\frac{24}{6} = \frac{6w}{6}$

$4 = w$

The width is 4 inches; 2 inches longer.

5. Check students' problems; $w = 3$.

6. Apply the inverse operation to both sides of the equation. Divide for multiplication equations and multiply for division equations.

Independent Practice

7. $0.7x = 42$

$\frac{0.7x}{0.7} = \frac{42}{0.7}$

$x = 60$

8. $\frac{3}{4}x = \frac{1}{8}$

$\frac{4}{3} \cdot \frac{3}{4}x = \frac{1}{8} \cdot \frac{4}{3}$

$x = \frac{1}{6}$

9. $\frac{x}{4} = 2\frac{1}{4}$

$4 \cdot \frac{x}{4} = 4 \cdot \frac{9}{4}$

$x = 9$

10. $\frac{x}{5} = 2.3$

$5 \cdot \frac{x}{5} = 5 \cdot 2.3$

$x = 11.5$

11. $x \div 3.2 = 4.5$

$\frac{x}{3.2} \cdot 3.2 = 4.5 \cdot 3.2$

$x = 14.4$

12. $\frac{c}{28} = 3$

$28 \cdot \frac{c}{28} = 28 \cdot 3$

$c = 84$; cherry tomatoes they bought; 84 cherry tomatoes.

13. $4k = 44$

$\frac{4k}{4} = \frac{44}{4}$

$k = 11$; books she read; 11 books

14. $15m = 420$

$\frac{15m}{15} = \frac{420}{15}$

$m = 28$; 28 mi/gal

15. $3.5d = 14$

$\frac{3.5d}{3.5} = \frac{14}{3.5}$

$d = 4$; days commuted; 4 days

16. $4s = 132$

$s = 33$

The length of one side of the garden is 33 feet; square's side length; the area of the square garden is $33 \times 33 = 1{,}089$ square feet. Yes, the area of the garden is greater than 1,000 square feet.

17. $3d = 1\frac{1}{2}$; hours walking dog; $\frac{1}{2}$ h

18. Sample answer: Jayne earned $168 for babysitting over 6 weeks. If she earned the same amount each week, how much did she earn for one week?

$6x = 168$

$x = 28$; earnings per week

She earned $28.

19. Sample answer: Marcy split her income from last week equally between paying her student loans, rent, and savings. She put $450 in savings. How much did Marcy earn last week?

$\frac{x}{3} = 450$

$x = 1{,}350$

She earned $1,350.

Focus on Higher Order Thinking

20. $\frac{x}{7}$ is equivalent to $\frac{1}{7} \cdot x$. So, multiplying $7 \cdot \frac{x}{7}$ is the same as multiplying $7 \cdot \frac{1}{7} \cdot x$, which equals $1x$, or x. When you solve $\frac{x}{7} = 2$, you multiply both sides by 7 to get $x = 14$.

21. The number is 81.
$3(3x) = 729$
$9x = 729$
$x = 81$

22. a. $4p = 36$;
$p = 9$
Peter has 9 model cars.

b. $\frac{1}{3}j = 9$
$j = 27$
Jade has 27 model cars.

23. 31 inches; $42 = 12 \cdot x$, where x is the length of the other side of the rectangle; $x = 3.5$. So, the perimeter is $2(12) + 2(3.5) = 31$ inches.

LESSON 11.4

Your Turn

3. Draw a solid circle at −4 to show that −4 is a solution. Shade the number line to the left of −4 to show that numbers less than −4 are solutions.

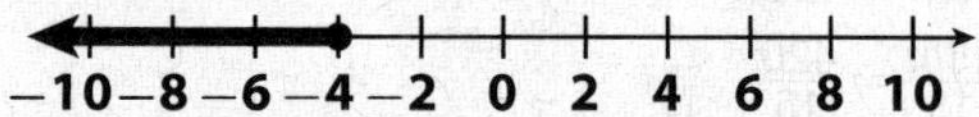

4. $1 + y \geq 3$; $y = 1$ is not a solution, because $1 + 1 = 2$ is not greater than or equal to 3.

5. $t \leq 6$; temperatures in °F
Draw a closed circle at 6, and shade the number line to the left of 6.

Guided Practice

1. Draw a solid circle at 1, and shade the number line to the right of 1.

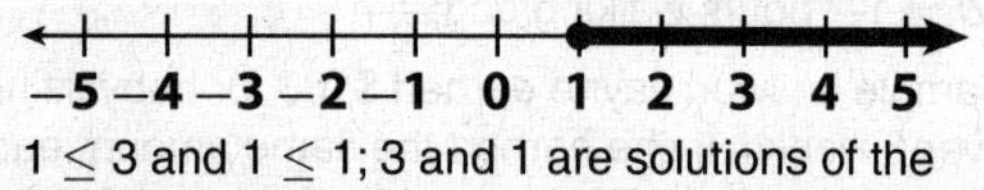

$1 \leq 3$ and $1 \leq 1$; 3 and 1 are solutions of the inequality $1 \leq x$.

2. Draw an open circle at −3, and shade the number line to the left of −3.

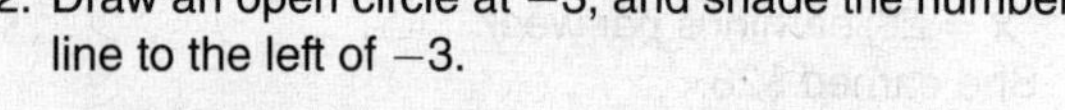

To check the graph, substitute a number from the shaded section of the number line into the inequality. $-3 > -4$; −3 is greater than −4, so −4 is a solution.

3. $3x > 6$; For $3x$ to be greater than 6, x must be greater than 2. Draw an open circle at 2, and shade the number line to the right of 2.

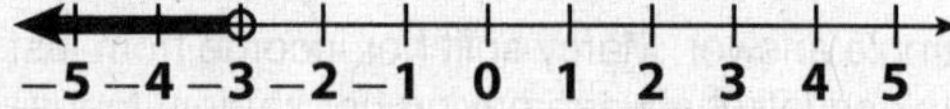

To check the graph, substitute a number from the shaded section of the number line into the inequality. $3(3) > 6$; 9 is greater than 6, so 3 is a solution.

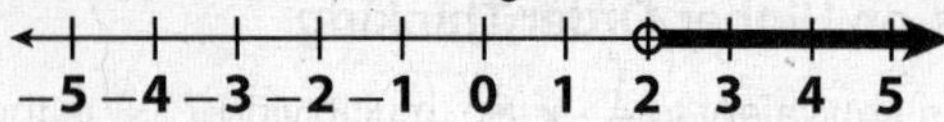

4. $t \geq 3$; temperatures in °C
Draw a closed circle at 3, and shade the number line to the right of 3.

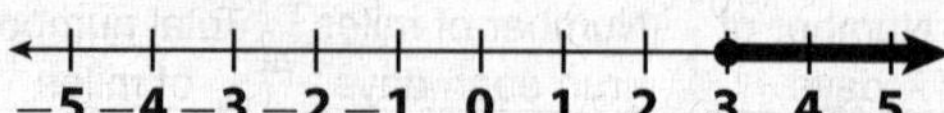

5. $d \geq 15$, where d represents the dollar amount Nina wants to take. "At least" means she wants to take \$15 or more than \$15, so use a greater than or equal to symbol.

Independent Practice

6. $0.03 \geq 0$, $0 \geq 0$, $1.5 \geq 0$, $\frac{1}{2} \geq 0$;
0.03, 0, 1.5, $\frac{1}{2}$ are solutions of the inequality $x \geq 0$.

7. $t - 8 \leq 0$
$t \leq 8$
Draw a solid circle at 8, and shade the number line to the left of 8.

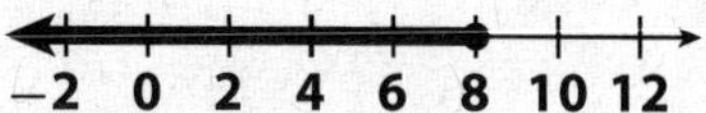

8. Draw an open circle at −7. Shade the number line to the right of −7.

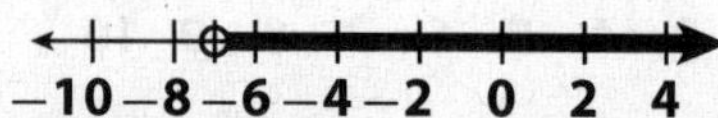

9. Draw a closed circle at −9. Shade the number line to the right of −9.

10. $2n > 5$
$n > \frac{5}{2}$
Draw an open circle at 2.5, and shade the number line to the right of 2.5.

11. Draw an open circle at $-4\frac{1}{2}$, and shade the number line to the left of $-4\frac{1}{2}$.

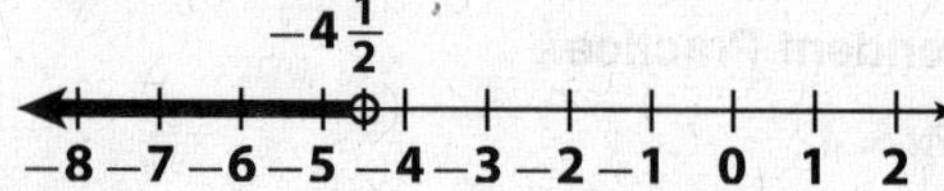

12. $x > 6$

13. $x \leq -3$

14. $x < 1.5$

15. $x \geq -3.5$

16. a. $c \geq 48$; heights in inches

b. No; 46 is not greater than or equal to 48.

17. $s \geq 14.5$; stock values

18. $t < 3.5$; temperatures in °F

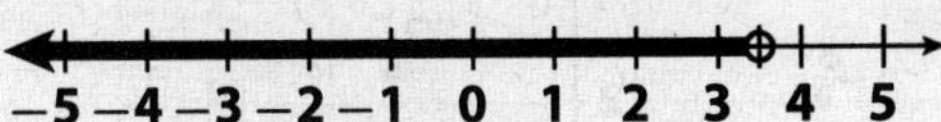

19. $g > 150$; money raised

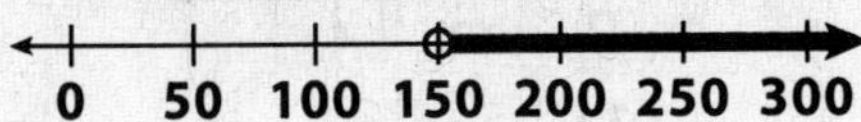

Focus on Higher Order Thinking

20. Make a solid circle at 8, because of the inequality symbol, greater than or equal to. Then shade in the numbers to the left of 8, which are the numbers that make the inequality $8 > y$ true.
21. Sample answer: Steve has more than $2.75 in his wallet.
22. The number line that shows only 0, 1, 2, 3, and 4 as solutions is correct. In this example, it does not make sense to have negative numbers of students or fractional parts of students.

MODULE 11

Ready to Go On?

1. $\frac{b}{12} = 5$; $b = 60$

$\frac{60}{12} \stackrel{?}{=} 5$

$5 \stackrel{?}{=} 5$

Yes; 60 is a solution of $\frac{b}{12} = 5$.

2. $7w = 87$; $w = 12$

$7(12) \stackrel{?}{=} 87$

$84 \stackrel{?}{=} 87$

No; 12 is not a solution of $7w = 87$.

3. $\underbrace{\text{Number of eggs in the refrigerator}}_{e} - \underbrace{\text{Number of eggs taken away}}_{5} = \underbrace{\text{Number of eggs left}}_{18}$

$e - 5 = 18$

4. $r - 38 = 9$; $r = 47$

$$\begin{array}{rcl} r - 38 & = & 9 \\ +38 & & +38 \\ \hline r & = & 47 \end{array}$$

5. $h + \frac{1}{2} = \frac{3}{4}$; $h = 2\frac{3}{4}$

$$\begin{array}{rcl} h + \frac{1}{2} & = & \frac{3}{4} \\ -\frac{1}{2} & & -\frac{1}{2} \\ \hline h & = & 2\frac{3}{4} \end{array}$$

6. $n + 75 = 155$; $n = 80$

$$\begin{array}{rcl} n + 75 & = & 155 \\ -75 & & -75 \\ \hline n & = & 80 \end{array}$$

7. $q - 17 = 18$; $q = 35$

$$\begin{array}{rcl} q - 17 & = & 18 \\ +17 & & +17 \\ \hline q & = & 35 \end{array}$$

8. $8z = 11.2$

$\frac{8z}{8} = \frac{11.2}{8}$

$z = 1.4$

9. $\frac{d}{14} = 7$

$14 \cdot \frac{d}{14} = 14 \cdot 7$

$d = 98$

10. $\frac{f}{28} = 24$

$28 \cdot \frac{f}{28} = 28 \cdot 24$

$f = 672$

11. $3a = 57$

$\frac{3a}{3} = \frac{57}{3}$

$a = 19$

12. $f < 8$

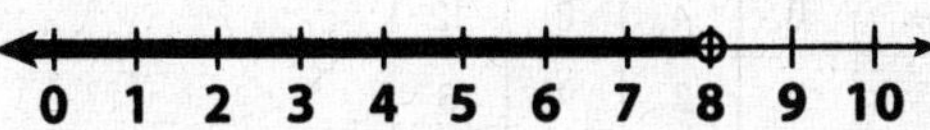

13. $p \geq 3$

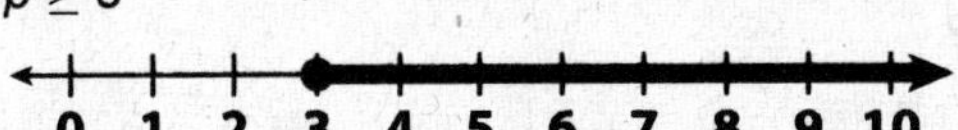

14. Write an equation for the situation. Then apply the inverse operation to get the variable alone on one side of the equation.

MODULE 12 *Relationships in Two Variables*

Are You Ready?

1. $7 \times 6 = 42$
2. $10 \times 9 = 90$
3. $13 \times 12 = 156$
4. $8 \times 9 = 72$
5.

x	1	2	3	4
y	7	14	21	28

y is 7 times x.

6.

x	1	2	3	4
y	7	8	9	10

y is 6 more than x.

7.

x	1	2	3	4
y	5	10	15	20

y is 5 times x.

8.

x	0	4	8	12
y	0	2	4	6

y is one-half x.

9–12.

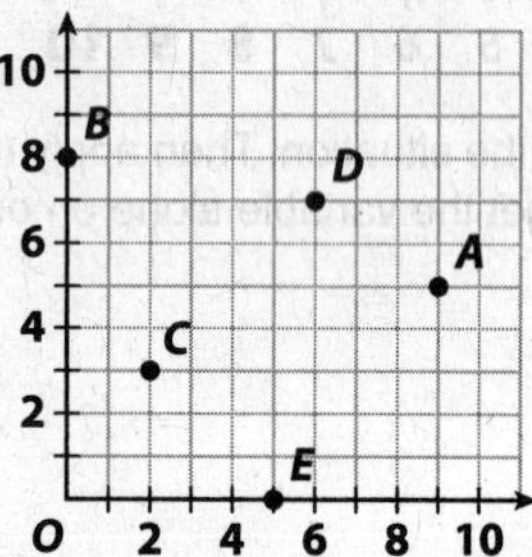

LESSON 12.1

Your Turn

4. Point G is 4 units right of the origin and 4 units down. It has x-coordinate 4 and y-coordinate -4, written $(4, -4)$; it is located in Quadrant IV.
5. Point E is 2 units left of the origin and 4 units up. It has x-coordinate -2 and y-coordinate 4, written $(-2, 4)$; it is located in Quadrant II.
6. Point F is 3 units right of the origin and 2 units up. It has x-coordinate 3 and y-coordinate 2, written $(3, 2)$; it is located in Quadrant I.
7. Point H is 1 unit left of the origin and 3 units down. It has x-coordinate -1 and y-coordinate -3, written $(-1, -3)$; it is located in Quadrant III.

8–12.

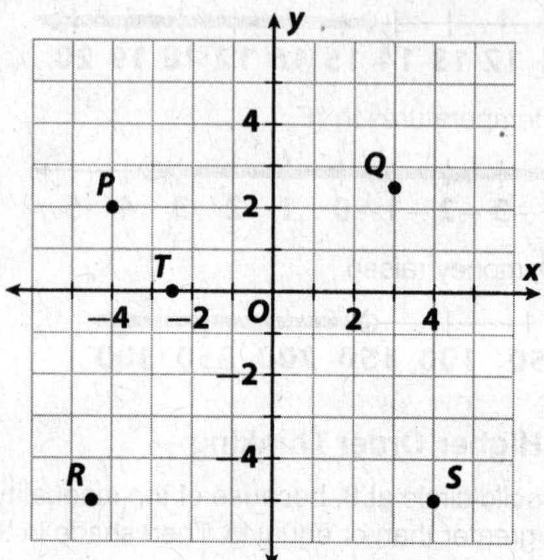

8. Point P, $(-4, 2)$, is 4 units left of the origin and 2 units up.
9. Point Q, $(3, 2.5)$, is 3 units right of the origin and 2.5 units up.
10. Point R, $(-4.5, -5)$, is 4.5 units left of the origin and 5 units down.
11. Point S, $(4, -5)$, is 4 units right of the origin and 5 units down.
12. Point T, $(-2.5, 0)$, is 2.5 units left of the origin.
13. Ted $(-20, -20)$. Ned's house is located 45 miles north of Ted's house, which is $-20 + 45 = 25$ miles above the y-axis; Ned $(-20, 25)$

Guided Practice

1. Point A is 5 units left of the origin and 1 unit up from the origin.

   Its coordinates are $(-5, 1)$. It is in quadrant II.
2. Point B is 2 units right of the origin and 3 units down from the origin.

   Its coordinates are $(2, -3)$. It is in quadrant IV.

3–4.

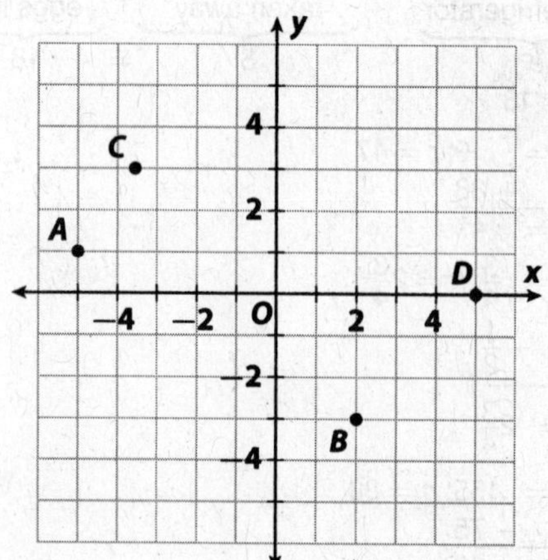

3. Point C at $(-3.5, 3)$ is 3.5 units left of the origin and 3 units up.
4. Point D at $(5, 0)$ is 5 units right of the origin.

5. Each grid square is $\frac{1}{2}$ unit on a side.

6–7.

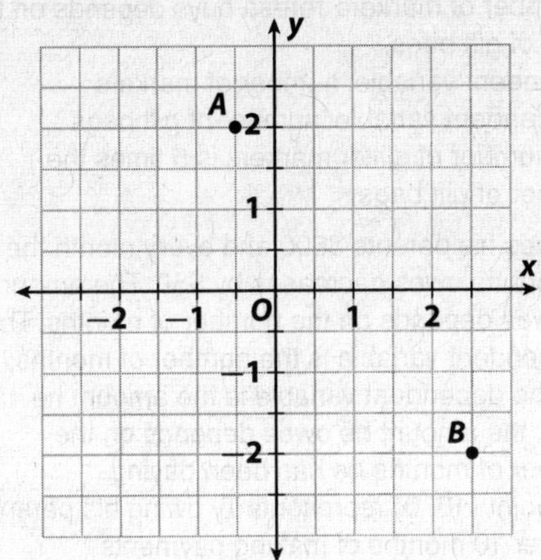

6. Point *A* at $\left(-\frac{1}{2}, 2\right)$ is $\frac{1}{2}$ unit to the left of the origin and 2 units up.
7. Point *B* at $\left(2\frac{1}{2}, -2\right)$ is $2\frac{1}{2}$ units to the right of the origin and 2 units down.
8. The first number, the *x*-coordinate, tells how many units to the right or left the point is located from the origin. The second number, the *y*-coordinate, tells how many units up or down the point is located from the origin.
9. Sample answer: Quadrant I: (2, 5); Quadrant II: (−3, 5); Quadrant III: (−3, −3); Quadrant IV: (5, −2). *x*-axis: (−3, 0); *y*-axis: (0, 5).

Independent Practice

10. Sam: (4, 2); Theater: (−3, 5)
11. Sam is 3 km south and 7 km east of the theater.

12–13.

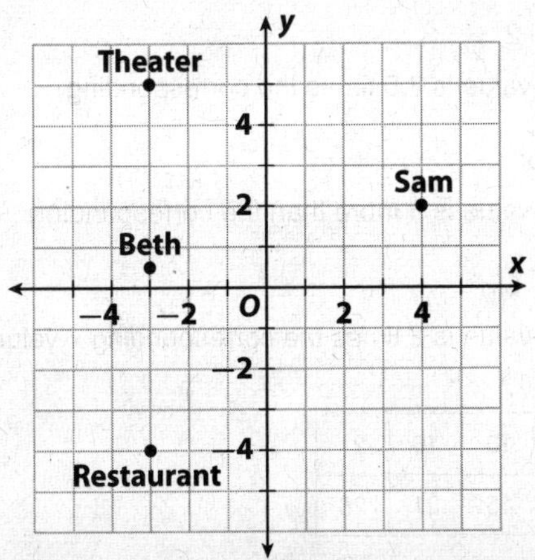

12. The restaurant is 9 km south of the theater, or $5 - 9 = -4$ units below the *y*-axis. The coordinates of the restaurant are (−3, −4).
13. The restaurant is 9 units south of the theater. Beth is halfway between the theater and the restaurant, so she is $9 \div 2 = 4.5$ units south of the theater. Beth: (−3, 0.5)

14–15.

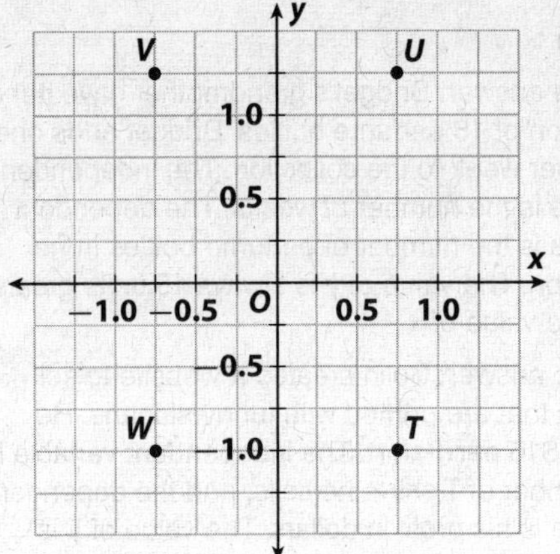

14. Each grid square is 0.25 units on a side. *T*(0.75, −1); *U*(0.75, 1.25); *V*(−0.75, 1.25)
15. To form a rectangle, point *W* must be directly below point *V* and directly across from point *T*; *W*(−0.75, −1)
16. Janine is describing points that lie on the *y*-axis. Ordered pairs that lie on the *x*-axis have a *y*-coordinate of 0. The origin lies on the *x*- and *y*-axis. Any other point with an *x*-coordinate of 0, such as (0, 3), lies on the *y*-axis.

Focus on Higher Order Thinking

17. The *x*-coordinates ranged from −5 to 3, and the *y*-coordinates ranged from −50 to 50. To graph all the points onto the given coordinate plane, on the *x*-axis I used a scale of 1 unit for the side of each grid square. On the *y*-axis I used a scale of 10 units for the side of each grid square.

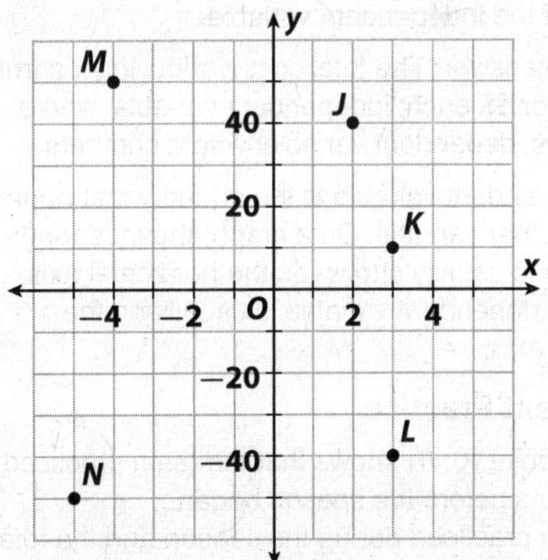

18. Count 18 grid squares to the right along the *x*-axis. Then count 12 grid squares down.
19. a. Quadrants I and IV; time is always positive, but temperatures can be positive or negative. In quadrants I and IV, the *x*-coordinate is always positive, but the *y*-coordinate can be positive or negative.
    b. In a region with a cold climate during the winter.

LESSON 12.2

Your Turn

8. Sample answer: Bridget's grandmother gave her a collection of 15 perfume bottles. Bridget adds one bottle per week to the collection. The independent variable is the number of weeks. The dependent variable is the number of perfume bottles in her collection. The value of y is always 15 units greater than the value of x.
9. Sample answer: Colin created a website to sell T-shirts that are printed with funny slogans. He makes $16 per T-shirt. The independent variable is the number of T-shirts he sells, and the dependent variable is his profit in dollars. The value of y is always 16 times the value of x.
10. Sample answer: Tickets to the school musical cost $3 each. The independent variable is the number of tickets purchased, and the dependent variable is the total cost. The value of y is always 3 times the value of x.

Guided Practice

1. Time is the independent variable, and cost is the dependent variable. Cost depends on the number of hours rented.
2. a.

Time x (h)	0	1	2	3
Distance y (ml)	0	60	120	180

   b. Time is the independent variable, and distance is the dependent variable. Distance depends on the number of hours the car travels.
   c. The value of y is always 60 times the value of x.
3. The value of the dependent variable is 5 times the value of the independent variable.
4. Sample answer: The total cost y of buying x carnival tickets for $5 each; independent variable: whole numbers; dependent variable: whole numbers.
5. The dependent variable is the quantity that depends on the other variable. On a graph, the independent variable is usually shown on the horizontal axis, and the dependent variable is usually on the vertical axis.

Independent Practice

6. a. The point (0, 6) shows that the team practiced 6 hours before the season began.
   b. hours practiced during the season and the total hours practiced for the year.
   c. The total practice time for the year depends on the practice time during the season. Independent variable: hours practiced during the season; Dependent variable: total practice time for year.
   d. independent, nonnegative numbers; dependent, Sample answer: nonnegative numbers greater than 6.
   e. The value of y is always 6 units greater than the value of x.
   f. The total practice time for the year is 6 hours more than the practice time during the season.
7. The number of markers Teresa buys depends on the number of gift bags.
   a. Dependent variable: number of markers
   b. Independent variable: number of gift bags
   c. The number of glitter markers is 5 times the number of gift bags.
8. a. Ty owes his parents $500 and every month the amount he owes decreases by $50. The amount he owes depends on the number of months. The independent variable is the number of months, and the dependent variable is the amount he owes; the amount he owes depends on the number of months he has been paying.
   b. The point (10, 0) represents Ty owing his parents $0 after 10 months of making payments.

Focus on Higher Order Thinking

9. I disagree, because the amount a shopper pays depends on the number of cans purchased. So, the number of cans is the independent variable, and the cost is the dependent variable.
10. Sample answer: Javonne has two dogs, Bud and Shadow. One eats more and is more active than the other. It may be that greater activity makes the dog hungrier; that is, food intake depends on energy expended. It may also be that greater food intake gives a dog more energy; that is, energy expended depends on food intake. It is also possible that neither variable depends on the other.

LESSON 12.3

Your Turn

2. Each y-value is 2 less than the corresponding x-value.
   $y = x - 2$
3. Each y-value is 2.5 times the corresponding x-value.
   $y = 2.5x$
4. Each y-value is 5 more than the corresponding x-value.
   $y = x + 5$
5. Each y-value is 2 times the corresponding x-value.
   $y = 2x$
6.

Ryan	10	16	21
Kyle	15	21	26

   Kyle's age is 5 years more than Ryan's age.
   $k = r + 5$
   $k = 52 + 5$
   $k = 57$; k = Kyle's age, r = Ryan's age; When Ryan is 52, Kyle is 57 years old.

Guided Practice

1. Each y-value is 4 less than the corresponding x-value.
   $y = x - 4$
2. Each y-value is 4 times the corresponding x-value.
   $y = 4x$
3. Each y-value is 3 more than the corresponding x-value.
   $y = x + 3$
4. Each y-value is corresponding x-value divided by 6.
   $y = \frac{x}{6}$
5.

Songs downloaded	1	2	5	10
Total cost ($)	1.35	2.70	6.75	13.50

   Each y-value is 1.35 times the corresponding x-value.
   $c = 1.35n$
   $c = 1.35 \cdot 25$
   $c = 33.75$; The cost of 25 songs is $33.75.
6. Compare the x- and y-values to find a pattern. Use the pattern to write an equation expressing y in terms of x.

Independent Practice

7. The variable y is on one side of the equation. The expression on the other side of the equation shows the relationship between x and y.
8. $l = 2w + 2$
9. The y-value is $\frac{1}{4}$ of the x-value. Write an equation that relates y to $\frac{1}{4}$ of x.
10. The student switched the variables; $y = 4x$
11. a. The amount Marvin earns is 8.25 times the number of hours he works.
    $e = 8.25h$
    b. $206.25 = 8.25h$
    $\frac{206.25}{8.25} = \frac{8.25h}{8.25}$
    $25 = h$; He needs to work 25 hours
12. The increase in Noah's test score depends on the number of hours Noah studies. The number of hours studied is the independent variable, and the increase in test score is the dependent variable. The increase in the score is 3 times the number of hours Noah studies.
    $s = 3h$

Focus on Higher Order Thinking

13. Not possible; there is no consistent pattern between the y-values and the corresponding x-values.
14. Sample answer: The distance Yasmine traveled in miles is equal to 50 times the number of hours she drove. This is a multiplicative relationship. $d = 50t$

Time (h)	2	3	4	5
Distance (mi)	100	150	200	250

15. No; with only one pair of values, Georgia cannot tell whether the value of x was added to or multiplied to get y so she cannot write an equation for the relationship.

LESSON 12.4

Your Turn

5.

x	$x + 2.5 = y$	(x, y)
0	$0 + 2.5 = 2.5$	(0, 2.5)
1	$1 + 2.5 = 3.5$	(1, 3.5)
2	$2 + 2.5 = 4.5$	(2, 4.5)
3	$3 + 2.5 = 5.5$	(3, 5.5)

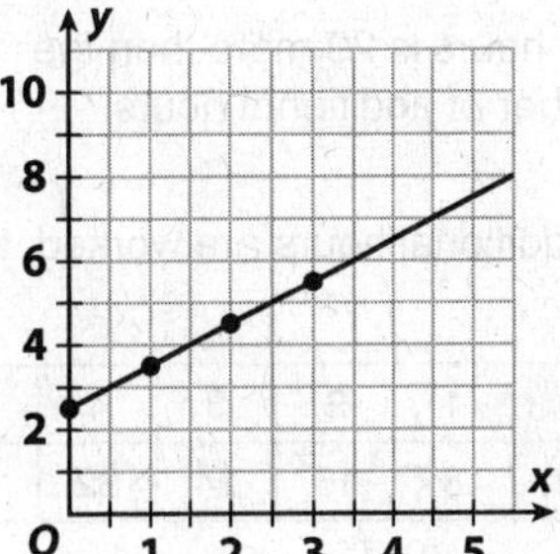

Guided Practice

1.

Hours worked	Lawns mowed
0	0
1	3
2	6
3	9

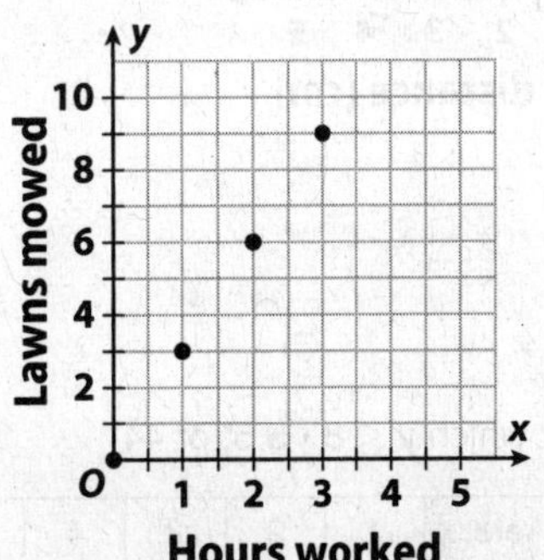

The number of lawns mowed is 3 times the number of hours worked.
$y = 3x$

2.

x	0	1	2	3
y	0	1.5	3	4.5

3.

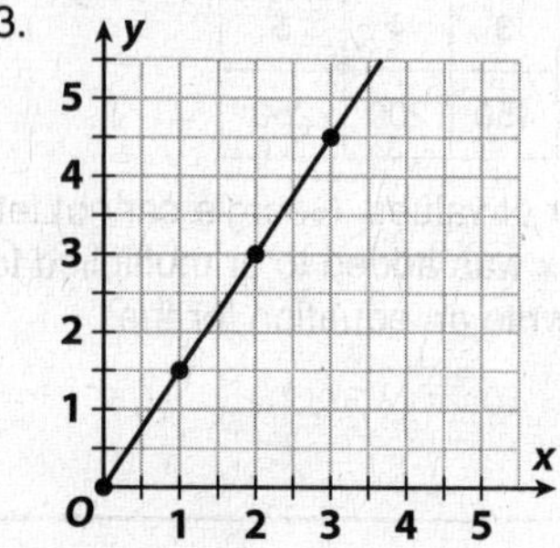

4. An equation gives information about all of the corresponding pairs of x and y values, rather than a few.

Independent Practice

5.

Additional hours	0	5	10	15	20
Total hours	20	25	30	35	40

6. The number of total hours is 20 more than the corresponding number of additional hours. $y = x + 20$; $y \geq 20$

7. 20 hours; when 0 additional hours are worked, the total is 20 hours.

8.

Map distance (cm)	1	2	3	4	5
Actual distance (km)	8	16	24	32	40

Sample answers are given.

9.

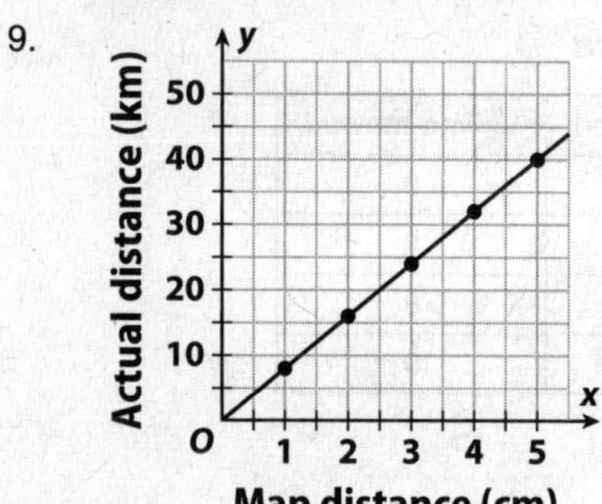

10. a. $y = 8x$

$64 = 8x$

$x = 8$

8 cm

b. Values of y for which $y \leq 8 \cdot 5.5$, or 44

11. a.

Number of tickets, x	1	2	3	4	5
Total cost ($), y	9	18	27	36	45

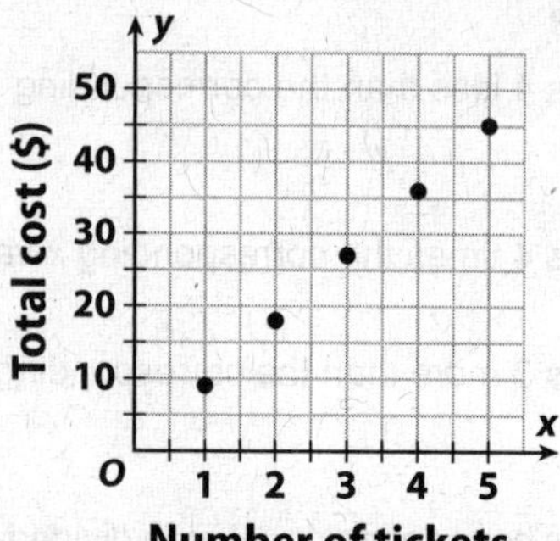

b. Dependent: total cost; independent: number of tickets; the total cost depends on how many tickets are purchased.

c. Sample answer: an equation; if the tickets cost $9 each, substitute 8 for x in $y = 9x$ to get $y = 9(8) = \$72$

Focus on Higher Order Thinking

12. The graph of $y = 5x$ would be steeper, because y increases more rapidly for each value of x.

13. Sample answer: (30, 10); every y value is $\frac{1}{3}$ of the x value. So, $10 = \frac{1}{3}(30)$.

14. Anna's equation does not show that every meal includes both a pizza and a drink; the correct equation is $y = 5x$.

MODULE 12

Ready to Go On?

1–6.

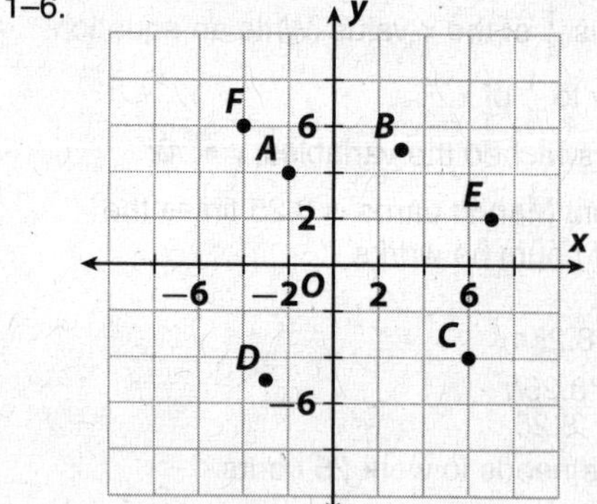

1. Point A, $(-2, 4)$, is 2 units left of the origin and 4 units up.
2. Point B, $(3, 5)$, is 3 units right of the origin and 5 units up.
3. Point C, $(6, -4)$, is 6 units right of the origin and 4 units down.
4. Point D, $(-3, -5)$, is 3 units left of the origin and 5 units down.

5. Point E, (7, 2), is 7 units right of the origin and 2 units up.
6. Point F, (−4, 6), is 4 units left of the origin and 6 units up.
7. The cost depends on the number of packages of pens Jon buys.
   The independent variable is the number of packages, and the dependent variable is the total cost.
8. Each y-value is 7 times the corresponding x-value.
   $y = 7x$
9. Each y-value is 12 more than the corresponding x-value.
   $y = x + 12$

10.

x	x + 3 = y	(x, y)
0	0 + 3 = 3	(0, 3)
2	2 + 3 = 5	(2, 5)
4	4 + 3 = 7	(4, 7)
6	6 + 3 = 9	(6, 9)

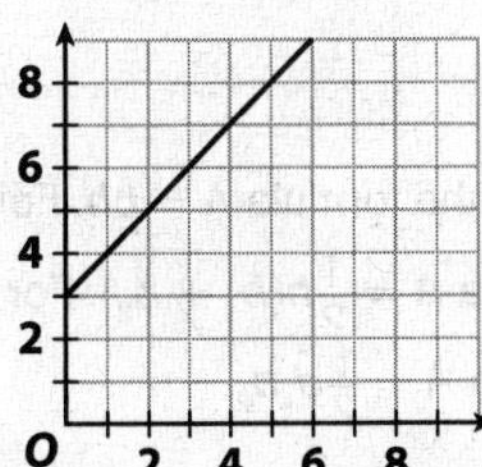

11.

x	y = 5x	(x, y)
0	5(0) = 0	(0, 0)
2	5(2) = 10	(2, 10)
4	5(4) = 20	(4, 20)
6	5(6) = 30	(6, 30)
8	5(8) = 40	(8, 40)

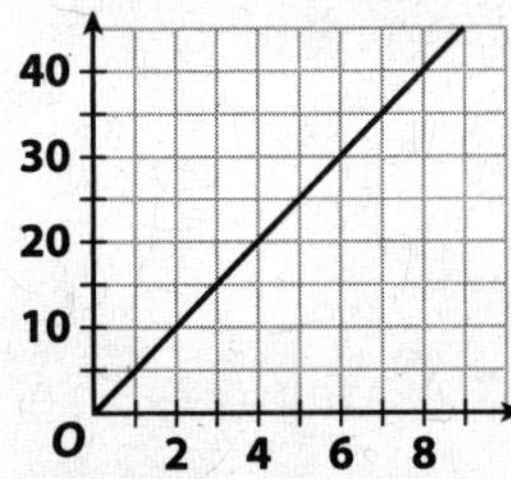

12. Decide which variable depends on the other. Use a table to find the relationship between the variables and write an equation.

UNIT 6 Solutions Key
Relationships in Geometry

MODULE 13 *Area and Polygons*

Are You Ready?

1. $9p = 54$
$\frac{9p}{9} = \frac{54}{9}$
$p = 6$

2. $m - 15 = 9$
$m - 15 + 15 = 9 + 15$
$m = 24$

3. $\frac{b}{8} = 4$
$\frac{b}{8} \cdot 8 = 4 \cdot 8$
$b = 32$

4. $z + 17 = 23$
$z + 17 - 17 = 23 - 17$
$z = 6$

5. $64 \text{ m} \cdot \frac{1{,}000 \text{ cm}}{1\text{m}} = 6{,}400 \text{ cm}$

6. $500 \text{ g} \cdot \frac{1 \text{ kg}}{1{,}000 \text{ g}} = 0.5 \text{ kg}$

7. $4.6 \text{ kL} \cdot \frac{1{,}000 \text{ L}}{1 \text{ kL}} = 4{,}600 \text{ L}$

8. $A = bh$
$= 5 \times 9\frac{1}{2}$
$= 47\frac{1}{2}$
The area of the rectangle is $47\frac{1}{2}$ ft².

LESSON 13.1

Your Turn

2. $A = \frac{1}{2}h(b_1 + b_2)$
$= \frac{1}{2} \cdot 12(27 + 34)$
$= \frac{1}{2} \cdot 12(61)$
$= 6(61)$
$= 366 \text{ ft}^2$

3. $A = \frac{1}{2}d_1d_2$
$= \frac{1}{2}(35)(12)$
$= 210 \text{ m}^2$

4. $A = \frac{1}{2}d_1d_2$
$= \frac{1}{2}(9.5)(14)$
$= 66.5 \text{ in}^2$

5. $A = \frac{1}{2}d_1d_2$
$= \frac{1}{2}(10)(18)$
$= 90 \text{ m}^2$

6. $A = \frac{1}{2}d_1d_2$
$= \frac{1}{2}\left(8\frac{1}{4}\right)(40)$
$= 165 \text{ ft}^2$

Guided Practice

1. $A = bh$
$= (13)(9)$
$= 117 \text{ in}^2$

2. $A = \frac{1}{2}h(b_1 + b_2)$
$= \frac{1}{2}(14)(9 + 15)$
$= 168 \text{ cm}^2$

3. $A = \frac{1}{2}d_1d_2$
$= \frac{1}{2}(18)(11)$
$= 99 \text{ in}^2$

4. For a parallelogram, use the formula $A = bh$. For a trapezoid, use the formula $A = \frac{1}{2}h(b_1 + b_2)$. For a rhombus, use the formula $A = \frac{1}{2}d_1d_2$.

Independent Practice

5. $A = bh$
$= 14 \cdot 6$
$= 84 \text{ cm}^2$

6. $A = bh$
$= 12\frac{3}{4} \cdot 2\frac{1}{2}$
$= 31\frac{7}{8} \text{ in}^2$

7. $A = \frac{1}{2}h(b_1 + b_2)$
$= \frac{1}{2} \cdot 24(42 + 36)$
$= \frac{1}{2} \cdot 24(78)$
$= 936 \text{ in}^2$

8. $A = \frac{1}{2}h(b_1 + b_2)$
$= \frac{1}{2} \cdot 10(11 + 14)$
$= \frac{1}{2} \cdot 10(25)$
$= 125 \text{ m}^2$

9. $A = \frac{1}{2}d_1d_2$
$= \frac{1}{2}(16)(9)$
$= 72 \text{ m}^2$

10. $A = \frac{1}{2}d_1d_2$

$= \frac{1}{2}(21)(32)$

$= 336 \text{ m}^2$

11. $A = \frac{1}{2}h(b_1 + b_2)$

$= \frac{1}{2} \cdot 1.5(6 + 5)$

$= \frac{1}{2} \cdot 1.5(11)$

$= 8.25 \text{ ft}^2$

12. $A = \frac{1}{2}d_1d_2$

$= \frac{1}{2}(25)(1.5)$

$= 187.5 \text{ in}^2$

13. $A = bh$
$= 36 \cdot 45$
$= 1{,}620 \text{ in}^2$

14. The area of the rectangle $= 12 \cdot 18 = 216 \text{ ft}^2$.
The area of the trapezoid $= \frac{1}{2} \cdot 6(10 + 18) = 84 \text{ ft}^2$.
The area of the figure is the sum of the area of the rectangle and the area of the trapezoid; $216 + 84 = 300 \text{ ft}^2$.

15. The area of the parking space $= 17 \cdot 9 = 153 \text{ ft}^2$. The area of the car $= 16 \cdot 6 = 96 \text{ ft}^2$. The area of the parking space minus the area of the car is 57 ft^2.

Focus on Higher Order Thinking

16. Yes; Simon uses the Distributive Property to multiply each base by the height. Then, he finds the sum. Multiplying by $\frac{1}{2}$ is the same as dividing by 2.

17. 9 in. and 15 in.; use the formula for the area of a trapezoid, and substitute 96 for A and 8 for h and simplify the equation to find $24 = (b_1 + b_2)$. Use guess and check to find two numbers that add up to 24 with one number 6 more than the other. The numbers are 9 and 15.

18. 9.6 in.; use the formula $A = \frac{1}{2}d_1d_2$ to find the area of the rhombus, which is 96 in^2. Since a rhombus is a parallelogram, use the formula for the area of a parallelogram to find the height of the rhombus; $96 = 10(h)$, so $h = 9.6$.

LESSON 13.2

Your Turn

3. $A = \frac{1}{2}bh$

$= \frac{1}{2}(8.5)(14)$

$A = 59.5 \text{ in}^2$

5. $A = \frac{1}{2}bh$

$= \frac{1}{2}(6)(4)$

$A = 12 \text{ ft}^2$

Guided Practice

1. $A = \frac{1}{2}bh$

$= \frac{1}{2}(14)(8)$

$= 56 \text{ in}^2$

2. $A = \frac{1}{2}bh$

$= \frac{1}{2}(12)(30)$

$= 180 \text{ in}^2$

3. Use the formula $A = \frac{1}{2}bh$. Substitute the known dimensions into the formula, and solve the equation.

Independent Practice

4. $A = \frac{1}{2}bh$

$= \frac{1}{2}(15)(10)$

$= 75 \text{ cm}^2$

5. $A = \frac{1}{2}bh$

$= \frac{1}{2}(24)(20)$

$= 240 \text{ ft}^2$

6. $A = \frac{1}{2}bh$

$= \frac{1}{2}(12)(17)$

$= 102 \text{ in}^2$

7. $A = \frac{1}{2}bh$

$= \frac{1}{2}(18)(32)$

$= 288 \text{ ft}^2$

8. $A = \frac{1}{2}bh$

$= \frac{1}{2}\left(15\frac{1}{4}\right)(18)$

$= 137\frac{1}{4} \text{ in}^2$

9. $A = \frac{1}{2}bh$

$= \frac{1}{2}(11)(13)$

$= 71.5 \text{ in}^2$

10. $A = \frac{1}{2}bh$

$= \frac{1}{2}(30)(20)$

$= 300 \text{ km}^2$

11. $A = \frac{1}{2}bh$

$= \frac{1}{2}(8)(5)$

$= 20 \text{ ft}^2$

12. $A = \frac{1}{2}bh$

$= \frac{1}{2}(3)(5)$

$= 7.5 \text{ cm}^2$

Each tile has an area of 7.5 cm^2.
The area of the mosaic is $7.5 \times 200 = 1{,}500 \text{ cm}^2$.

13. Monica forgot to multiply by $\frac{1}{2}$. The area of the fabric is 45 in^3.

14. The area of the rectangle $= 25 \cdot 12 = 300 \text{ ft}^2$.

The area of the triangle $= \frac{1}{2}(25)(8) = 100 \text{ ft}^2$.

The area of the side of the house is the sum of the area of the rectangle and the area of the triangle, $300 + 100 = 400 \text{ ft}^2$.

Focus on Higher Order Thinking

15. You can draw a diagonal in the parallelogram, forming two congruent triangles with the same base and height as the parallelogram. So, the area of the triangle is half the area of the parallelogram.

16. The height of the triangle is twice the height of the rectangle. For example, if both the rectangle and triangle have an area of 20 in^2 and both have a base of 10 in., the rectangle would have a height of 2 in., since $10 \cdot 2 = 20$. The triangle would have a height of 4 in., since $\frac{1}{2}(10)(4) = 20$.

17. a. $\frac{1}{2}(6)(6) = 18$; 6 in.

b. 1 in. and 36 in.; 2 in. and 18 in.; 3 in. and 12 in.; 4 in. and 9 in.

LESSON 13.3

Your Turn

1. $A = \frac{1}{2}bh$

$24 = \frac{1}{2}(6)b$

$24 = 3b$

$\frac{24}{3} = \frac{3b}{3}$

$8 = b$

The length of the base of each quilt piece is 8 in.

3. $A = \frac{1}{2}h(b_1 + b_2)$

$52 = \frac{1}{2}h(18 + 8)$

$52 = \frac{1}{2}h(26)$

$52 = 13h$

$\frac{52}{13} = \frac{13h}{13}$

$4 = h$

The height of the cross section is 4 ft.

4. $A = bh$

$= 21.5 \cdot 18$

$= 387$

The park needs 387 square meters of sod.
$387 \div 50 = 7.74$; 8 pallets are needed.

Guided Practice

1. $A = \frac{1}{2}bh$

$70 = \frac{1}{2}b\left(8\frac{3}{4}\right)$

$70 = 4\frac{3}{8}b$

$\frac{8}{35} \cdot \frac{70}{1} = \frac{8}{35} \cdot \frac{35}{8}b$

$16 = b$

The length of the base of bandana is 16 in.

2. $A = \frac{1}{2}h(b_1 + b_2)$

$791 = \frac{1}{2}h(26.5 + 30)$

$791 = \frac{1}{2}h(56.5)$

$791 = 28.25h$

$\frac{791}{28.25} = \frac{28.25h}{28.25}$

$28 = h$

The width of the desk is 28 cm.

3. Write an equation to find the area of the deck.
$A = bh$
$A = 42(28)$
$A = 1{,}176 \text{ ft}^2$
Write an equation to find the number of gallons of paint.
$n = 1{,}176 \div 350 = 3.36$
Taylor will need 4 gallons of paint.

4. Use the formula for the area of the figure to write an equation. Then solve the equation to find the missing dimension or the area of the figure.

Independent Practice

5. $A = bh$

$18\frac{1}{3} = b\left(3\frac{1}{3}\right)$

$\frac{55}{3} = \frac{10}{3}b$

$\frac{3}{10} \cdot \frac{55}{3} = \frac{3}{10} \cdot \frac{10}{3}b$

$5\frac{1}{2} = b$

The length of the base of the window is $5\frac{1}{2}$ ft.

6. $A = \frac{1}{2}bh$

$3.75 = \frac{1}{2}(2.5)h$

$3.75 = 1.25h$

$\frac{3.75}{1.25} = \frac{1.25}{1.25}h$

$3 = h$

The height of the sail is 3 m.

7. $A = \frac{1}{2}h(b_1 + b_2)$

$3.9 = \frac{1}{2}h(4 + 2.5)$

$3.9 = \frac{1}{2}h(6.5)$

$3.9 = 3.25h$

$\frac{3.9}{3.25} = \frac{3.25}{3.25}h$

$1.2 = h$

The section is 1.2 cm tall.

8. a. $A = \ell w$ $\quad$ $A = \ell w$

$A = 26 \cdot 9$ $\quad$ $A = 18 \cdot 9$

$A = 234$ $\quad$ $A = 162$

The total area of the walls is $2(234) + 162 = 630$ ft^2.

b. $g = 630 \div 250 = 2.52$

She should buy 3 gallons of paint.

9. $A = \frac{1}{2}bh$

$64 = \frac{1}{2}(2h)h$

$64 = h^2$

$8 = h$

The height is 8 in. and the base is $8 \times 2 = 16$ in.

10. a. $A = \ell w$

$A = 8 \cdot 3$

$A = 24$

He needs to varnish $24 \cdot 2 \cdot 12 = 576$ ft^2.

b. $p = 576 \div 125 = 4.608$

Alex needs to buy 5 pints of varnish, which will cost him $5 \cdot \$3.50 = \$17.50$.

11. $A = \ell w$

$A = 18 \cdot 10$

$A = 180$

The area of one piece of fabric is 180 cm^2, and the total area of the fabric is $180(32) = 5{,}760$ cm^2. Leia can cut $5{,}760 \div 45 = 128$ patches from the fabric.

12. $A = \frac{1}{2}h(b_1 + b_2)$ $\quad$ $A = \frac{1}{2}bh$

$A = \frac{1}{2}(26)(35 + 48)$ $\quad$ $A = \frac{1}{2}(39)(26)$

$A = 1{,}079$ $\quad$ $A = 507$

The total area of the fields is $1{,}079 + 507 = 1{,}586$ square yards.

$1{,}586 \div 150 = 10.573...$; The farmer needs to buy 11 bags of fertilizer.

13. Singles play court: $A = \ell w$

$A = 78 \cdot 27$

$A = 2{,}106$ ft^2

a. Doubles play court: $A = \ell w$

$A = 78 \cdot 36$

$A = 2{,}808$ ft^2

The doubles' court is $2{,}808 - 2{,}106 = 702$ ft^2, or $78 \cdot 9 = 702$ ft^2, larger than the singles' court.

b. Junior play court: $A = \ell w$

$A = 36 \cdot 18$

$A = 648$ ft^2

The singles' court is $2{,}106 - 648 = 1{,}458$ ft^2 larger than the junior's court.

c. 10 and under court: $A = lw$

$A = 60 \cdot 27$

$A = 1{,}620$ ft^2

The singles' court is $2{,}106 - 1{,}620 = 486$ ft^2 larger than the 10 and under court.

14. The length of the bottom base is 2 more than 12 cm, or 14 cm. To find the height of the metal ingot, solve the equation $A = \frac{1}{2}h(12 + 14)$ for h; $h = 3$. The height of the ingot is 3 centimeters.

Focus on Higher Order Thinking

15. a. $A = 2(bh)$

$9\frac{1}{3} = 2\left(1\frac{1}{3}b\right)$

$\frac{1}{2} \cdot \frac{28}{3} = \frac{1}{2} \cdot 2\left(\frac{4}{3}b\right)$

$\frac{3}{4} \cdot \frac{14}{3} = \frac{3}{4} \cdot \frac{4}{3}b$

$3\frac{1}{2} = b$

The base of each parallelogram is $3\frac{1}{2}$ yd.

b. $A = lw$

$A = 2\left(3\frac{1}{2} + \frac{1}{2}\right) \cdot 1\frac{1}{3}$

$A = 2(4) \cdot 1\frac{1}{3}$

$A = 10\frac{2}{3}$

The area of the wall is $10\frac{2}{3}$ yd^2.

16. The area of the painting is $20 \cdot 9 = 180$ in^2. The area of the painting and the mat is $22 \cdot 11 = 242$ in^2. The area of the mat is $242 - 180 = 62$ in^2.

LESSON 13.4

Your Turn

3. Draw a vertical line segment on the diagram that divides the polygon into two rectangles.

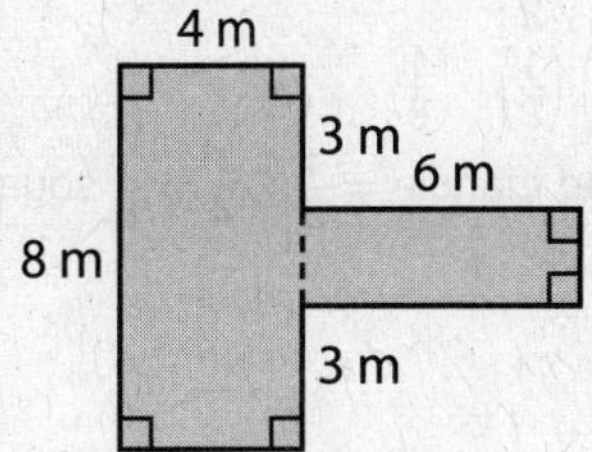

Find the area of the larger rectangle.
$A = bh = 4(8) = 32$ square meters.
Find the height of the smaller rectangle.
$8 - 3 - 3 = 2$ m
Find the area of the smaller rectangle.
$A = bh = 6(2) = 12$ square meters.
Add the areas of the two rectangles.
$32 + 12 = 44$ square meters
$A = 44$ square meters

4. Draw a vertical line segment on the diagram that divides the polygon into a square and a trapezoid.

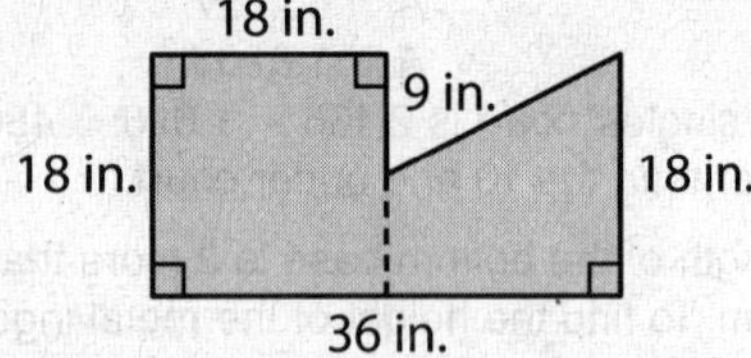

Find the area of the square.
$A = bh = 18(18) = 324$ square inches.
Find the smaller base of the trapezoid.
$18 - 9 = 9$ in.
Find the area of the trapezoid.

$A = \frac{1}{2}(b_1 + b_2)h$

$= \frac{1}{2}(18 + 9)18$

$= 243$ square inches

Add the areas of the square and the trapezoid.
$324 + 243 = 567$ square meters
$A = 567$ square meters

5. The center dashed line divided the figure into two identical trapezoids.
Find the area of one trapezoid.

$A = \frac{1}{2}(b_1 + b_2)h$

$= \frac{1}{2}(42 + 30)15.5$

$= \frac{1}{2}(72)15.5$

$= 558$ square feet

Multiply to find the area of the two trapezoids.
Total Area $= 2 \times 558 = 1{,}116$ square feet.
Find the cost of the carpet.
$1{,}116 \times 3 = \$3{,}348$
It will cost $3,348 to carpet the lobby.

Guided Practice

1. The area of the large square is 1 square unit, so the height and base of the square are each equal to 1.
Find the area of a small red triangle.

$A = \frac{1}{2}bh$

$b = \frac{1}{2}, h = \frac{1}{2}$

$A = \frac{1}{2}\left(\frac{1}{2}\right)\left(\frac{1}{2}\right) = \frac{1}{8}$

Area of red triangle $= \frac{1}{2} \times \frac{1}{4} = \frac{1}{8}$ square unit

2. Draw a vertical line segment on the diagram that divides the polygon into two rectangles.

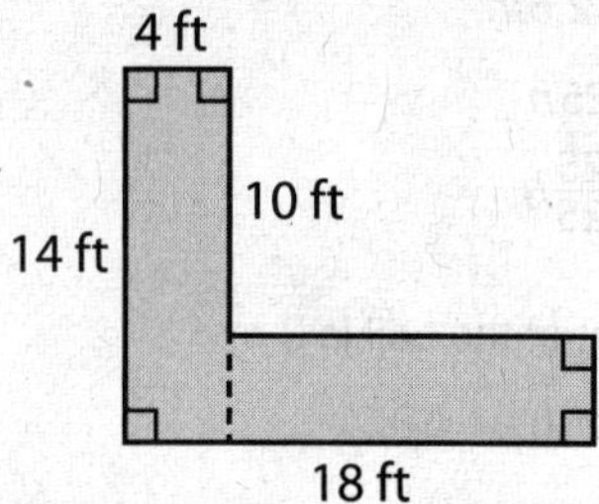

Find the area of the larger rectangle.
$A = bh = 4(14) = 56$ square feet.
Find the height of the smaller rectangle.
$14 - 10 = 4$ ft
Find the base of the smaller rectangle.
$18 - 4 = 14$ ft
Find the area of the smaller rectangle.
$A = bh = 14(4) = 56$ square feet.
Add the areas of the two rectangles.
$56 + 56 = 112$ square feet
$A = 112$ square feet

3. Extend the edges of the polygon to make a rectangle.

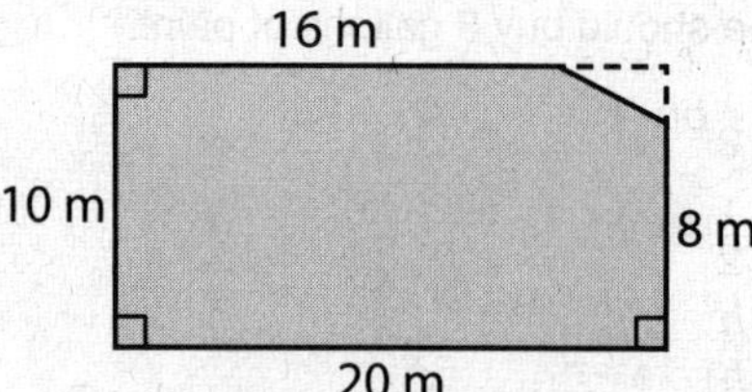

Find the area of the rectangle.
$A = bh = 20(10) = 200$ square meters.
Find the shorter leg of the right triangle formed by the extension.
$10 - 8 = 2$ m
Find the longer leg of the right triangle formed by the extension.
$20 - 16 = 4$ m
Find the area of the right triangle.

$A = \frac{1}{2}bh$

$= \frac{1}{2}(4)(2) = 4$ square meters

Subtract the area of the triangle from the area of the rectangle.
$200 - 4 = 196$ square meters
$A = 196$ square meters

4. Draw a vertical line segment on the diagram that divides the polygon into a rectangle and a triangle.

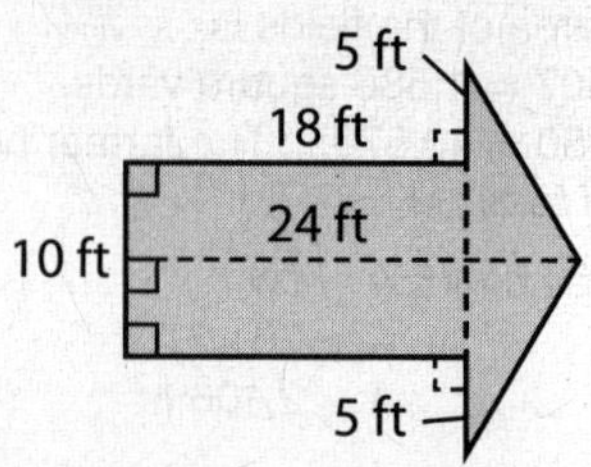

Find the area of the rectangle.
$A = bh$
$= 18 \times 10$
$= 180$ square feet
Find the base and height of the triangle.
$b = 5 + 10 + 5 = 20$
$h = 24 - 18 = 6$
Find the area of the triangle.
$A = \frac{1}{2}bh$
$= \frac{1}{2} \times 20 \times 6$
$= 60$ square feet
Add the area of the rectangle and the area of the triangle.
$180 + 60 = 240$
The area of the giant arrow is 240 square feet.
Find the number of cans of paint needed.
$240 \div 100 = 2.4$
2.4 cans of paint will be used to paint the giant arrow. Jess should buy 3 cans of paint.

5. Sample answer: You can break the large polygon into shapes such as rectangles and triangles, and then find the area of each of the smaller shapes using an area formula. Add the areas to find the area of the polygon.

Independent Practice

6. a. Draw a diagonal line to separate the polygon into 2 trapezoids.

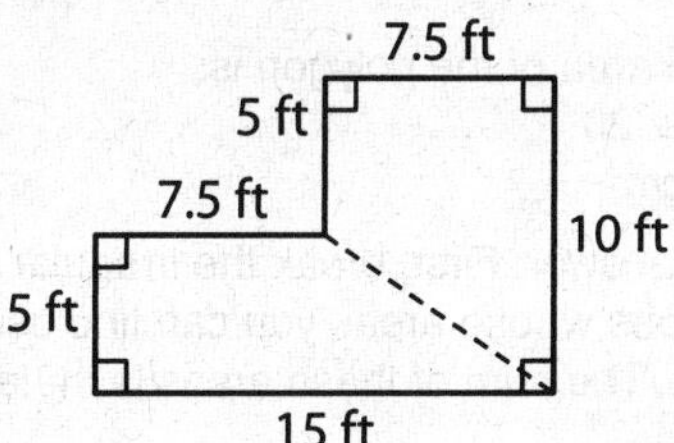

Find the area of the horizontal trapezoid.
$A = \frac{1}{2}(b_1 + b_2)h$
$= \frac{1}{2} \times (7.5 + 15) \times 5$
$= 56.25$ square feet
Find the area of the vertical trapezoid.
$A = \frac{1}{2}(b_1 + b_2)h$
$= \frac{1}{2} \times (5 + 10) \times 7.5$
$= 56.25$ square feet
Find the sum of the areas.
$56.25 + 56.25 = 112.5$ square feet
The area of the room:
$\frac{1}{2} \times (7.5 + 15) \times 7.5 + \frac{1}{2} \times (5 + 10) \times 7.5 =$
112.5 square feet

b. Sample answer: Divide the floor plan into two rectangles: $5 \times 15 + 7.5 \times 5 = 112.5$ square feet.

c. Find the cost of the carpet.
$112.5 \times \$4.5 = \$506.25$
Alice will pay \$506.25 for the carpet.

7. a. Find the base and height of the backyard.
$b = 8 + 9 = 17$ feet
$h = 3 + 5 = 8$ feet
Find the total area of the backyard.
$A = bh$
$= 17 \times 8 = 136$ square feet
Find the area of patio.
$A = bh$
$= 8 \times 5 = 40$ square feet
Find the base of the walkway.
$9 - 6 = 3$ feet
Find the area of the walkway.
$A = bh$
$= 3 \times 8 = 24$ square feet
Find the area of the garden.
$A = bh$
$= 6 \times 3 = 18$ square feet
Find the total area of the patio, walkway, and garden. $40 + 24 + 18 = 82$ square feet.
Find the percent of the backyard that is taken up by the patio, walkway, and garden.
$\frac{82}{136} \times 100 \approx 60$
The percent of the backyard that is taken up by the patio, walkway, and garden is about 60%.

b. Find the distance around 3 sides of the backyard.
$8 + 17 + 8 = 33$ feet
Find the cost of fencing for 33 feet.
$33 \times \$9.75 = \$321.75$
Hal will spend \$321.75 on the new fence.

8. a. Extend the sides to form a rectangle.

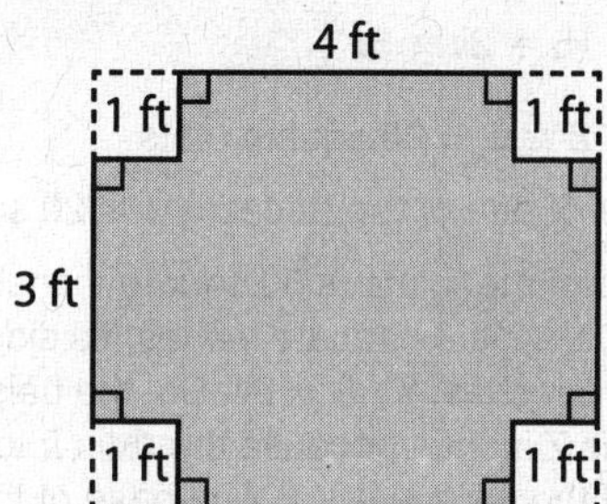

Find the base and height of the rectangle.
$h = 1 + 3 + 1 = 5$
$b = 1 + 4 + 1 = 6$
Find the area of the rectangle.
$A = bh$
$= 5 \times 6 = 30$ square feet
Subtract the area of the 4 corners to find the area of the tabletop.
area of tabletop: $30 - 1 - 1 - 1 - 1 =$
26 square feet
The area of the tabletop is 26 square feet.

b. Sample answer: 13 feet and 4 feet; the sides that meet at a right angle are the height and base of the triangle; $A = \frac{1}{2} \times 13 \times 4 = 26$ square feet.

9. a. Find the dimensions of the triangular banner.
$b = 7$ in. and $h = 21$ in.
Find the area of the banner.
$A = \frac{1}{2}bh$

$A = \frac{1}{2} \times 7 \times 21 = 73.5$ square inches

The area of a triangular banner is 73.5 square inches.

b. Find the base of the polygon left after the two banners are cut.

$28 - 7 = 21$ inches.

The dimensions of the fabric that is left over are 21 inches by 21 inches.

c. Find the number of rectangles with dimensions 7 inches by 21 inches that can be cut from the leftover fabric.

$21 \div 7 = 3$

So, 3 more rectangles can be cut, which would make 6 more banners.

Find the total number of banners.

$2 + 6 = 8$ banners

8 banners can be cut from the fabric; yes, she will use all the fabric.

Focus on Higher Order Thinking

10.

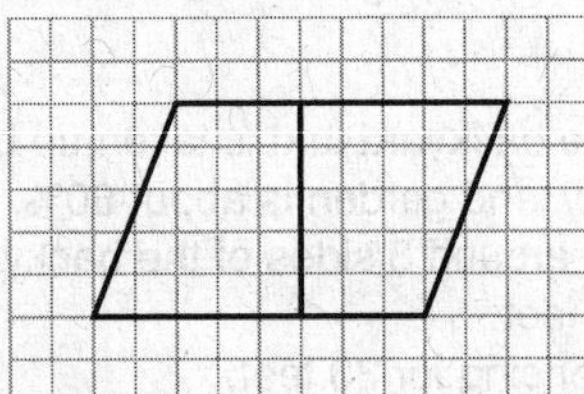

Find the area of one of the trapezoids.

$A = \frac{1}{2}(b_1 + b_2)h$

$= \frac{1}{2} \times (5 + 3) \times 5$

$= \frac{1}{2} \times 8 \times 5 = 20$ square units

The area of one of the trapezoids is 20 square units.

11. The area of the figure is 50 square inches; since the square's area is 64 square inches, its side length must be 8 inches: $8 \cdot 8 = 64$. So, the height of the triangle is 7 inches because the ratio h to the side length of the square is 7:8. The base of the triangle is 4 inches because 4 to 8 is equivalent to 1 to 2. The area of the shaded part $= 64 - \left(\frac{1}{2} \cdot 4 \cdot 7\right) = 50 \text{ in}^2$.

MODULE 13

Ready to Go On?

1. $A = bh$

$= 17\frac{1}{5} \cdot 12\frac{1}{2}$

$= 215 \text{ yd}^2$

2. $A = \frac{1}{2}bh$

$= \frac{1}{2}(17)(14)$

$= 119 \text{ ft}^2$

3. $A = \frac{1}{2}bh$

$270 = \frac{1}{2}b(30)$

$270 = 15b$

$\frac{270}{15} = \frac{15}{15}b$

$18 = b$

The length of the base is 18 inches.

4. $A = \frac{1}{2}h(b_1 + b_2)$

$6{,}550 = \frac{1}{2}h(115 + 85)$

$6{,}550 = \frac{1}{2}h(200)$

$6{,}550 = 100h$

$\frac{6{,}550}{100} = \frac{100}{100}h$

$65.5 = h$

The height is 65.5 centimeters.

5. The area of the square is:

$A = s^2$

$A = (5)^2$

$A = 25 \text{ cm}^2$

The area of the rectangle is:

$A = \frac{1}{2}bh$

$A = \frac{1}{2}(5)(8)$

$A = 20 \text{ cm}^2$

The total area of the polygon is:

$A = 25 + 20$

$= 45 \text{ cm}^2$

6. Sample answer: First, break the irregular polygon into shapes whose areas you can find using familiar formulas. The sum of these areas is the area of the polygon.

MODULE 14 *Distance and Area in the Coordinate Plane*

Are You Ready?

1. The x-coordinate is 1. The y-coordinate is 3. Point V (1, 3)
2. The x-coordinate is 7. The y-coordinate is 5. Point W (7, 5)
3. The x-coordinate is 4. The y-coordinate is 7. Point X (4, 7)
4. The x-coordinate is 3. The y-coordinate is 1. Point Y (3, 1)
5. The x-coordinate is 2. The y-coordinate is 2. Point Z (2, 2)
6. There are 6 sides. The figure is a hexagon.
7. There are 3 sides. One of the angles is a right angle. The figure is a right triangle.

LESSON 14.1

Your Turn

3. $|-4| + |5| = 9$ units
4. $|-10| - |-5| = 5$ units
5. $|10| + |-30| = 40$ miles.
   The truck drives 40 miles at 50 mi/h.
   40 miles $\div$ 50 mi/h $= 0.8$ hrs, or 48 minutes

Guided Practice

1. Reflecting $(5, -2)$ across the x-axis changes the y-value to its opposite: (5, 2)
2. Reflecting $(-6, 8)$ across the y-axis changes the x-value to its opposite: (6, 8)
3. $|5| + |-2| = 5 + 2 = 7$
4. $|5| - |1| = 5 - 1 = 4$
5. The reflection of C across the y-axis is $(-1, -3)$.
   $|-1| + |1| = 2$ units
6. The reflection of A across the x-axis is (5, 3).
   $|3| + |0| = 3$ units
7. $|-2| + |3| = 5$ blocks
8. $|4| + |-3| = 7$ blocks.
   7 blocks $\times$ 3 min/block $= 21$ minutes
   $|-3.5| - |2| = 1.5$ blocks
   1.5 blocks $\times$ 3 min/block $= 4.5$ minutes
9. If both y-coordinates have the same sign, find the difference of their absolute values to find the distance between the points. If the y-coordinates have different signs, find the sum of their absolute values.

Independent Practice

10. 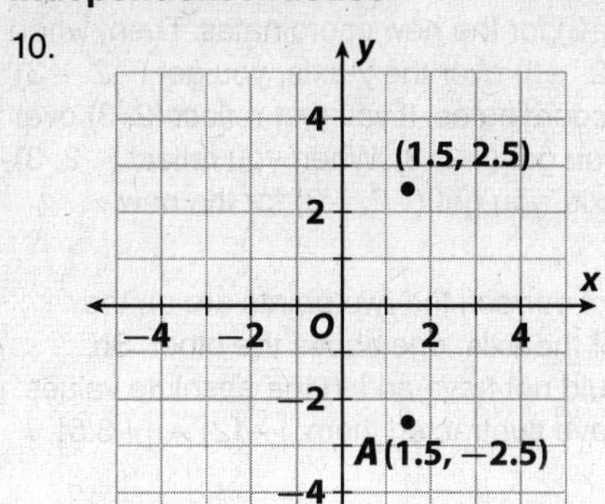

    Reflecting $(1.5, -2.5)$ across the x-axis changes the y-value to its opposite: (1.5, 2.5);
    $|2.5| + |-2.5| = 5$ units
11. Place another point on the other side of the y-axis the same distance from the y-axis as point A; $(-1.5, -2.5)$; 3 units
12. Reflecting $(-5, 8)$ across the x-axis changes the y-value to its opposite: $(-5, -8)$; $|8| + |-8| =$ 16 units
13. Reflecting $(-7, -3)$ across the y-axis changes the x-value to its opposite: $(7, -3)$;
    $|7| + |-7| = 14$ units
14. Reflecting (8, 2) across the x-axis changes the y-value to its opposite: $(8, -2)$; $|2| + |-2| = 4$ units
15. Reflecting $(2.4, -1)$ across the y-axis changes the x-value to its opposite: $(-2.4, -1)$;
    $|2.4| + |-2.4| = 4.8$ units
16. $\left|5\frac{1}{4}\right| + \left|-1\frac{3}{4}\right| = 7, 7 \div 2 = 3\frac{1}{2},$

    $5\frac{1}{4} - 3\frac{1}{2} = 1\frac{3}{4}, \left(-4\frac{1}{2}, 1\frac{3}{4}\right)$
17. $\left|5\frac{1}{4}\right| + \left|-1\frac{3}{4}\right| = 7, \left|-4\frac{1}{2}\right| + |2| = 6\frac{1}{2},$

    $7 + 6\frac{1}{2} = 13\frac{1}{2}, 13\frac{1}{2} \div 4\frac{1}{2} = 3$ hours
18. Reflecting $\left(2, -1\frac{3}{4}\right)$ across the x-axis changes the y-value to its opposite: $\left(2, 1\frac{3}{4}\right)$

Focus on Higher Order Thinking

19. Sample answer: $(4, -2)$ reflected across the y-axis to $(-4, -2)$. I chose this point because it has to have a positive x-coordinate and a negative y-coordinate to be in Quadrant IV. To reflect a point from Quadrant IV to Quadrant III, you have to reflect across the y-axis.
20. The method Jason is using only works if the two points have the same x-coordinate or the same y-coordinate. In this case, the two points have different x- and y-coordinates.

21. The same; if you first reflect (2, 3) over the x-axis, you get (2, −3) for the new coordinates. Then, when you reflect (2, −3) over the y-axis, you get (−2, −3) for the new coordinates. If you first reflect (2, 3) over the y-axis, you get (−2, 3). When you reflect (−2, 3) over the x-axis, you get (−2, −3) for the new coordinates.

22. Bentley is not correct; the two points are on the same side of the axis, one above the other. So, Bentley should not have added the absolute values, he should have subtracted them. $|-12| - |-3.5| =$ 8.5 units

LESSON 14.2

Your Turn

2. From (0, 0) to (0, 8) is $|8| - 0 = 8$ blocks. From (0, 8) to (7, 8) is $|7| - 0 = 7$ blocks. From (7, 8) to (7, 0) is $0 - |8| = 8$ blocks. From (7, 0) to (0, 0) is $|7| - 0 = 7$ blocks. $7 + 8 + 8 + 7 = 30$ blocks

3. ML $= |6| - |2| = 4$ units. LO $= |7| - |1| = 6$ units. The area of the rectangle is $6 \times 4 = 24$ units^2. QP $= |5| - |3| = 2$ units. The height of the trapezoid is $|2| - |0| = 2$ units. The area of the trapezoid is $2\left(\frac{6+2}{2}\right) = 8$ units^2. $24 + 8 = 32$ units^2.

Guided Practice

1.

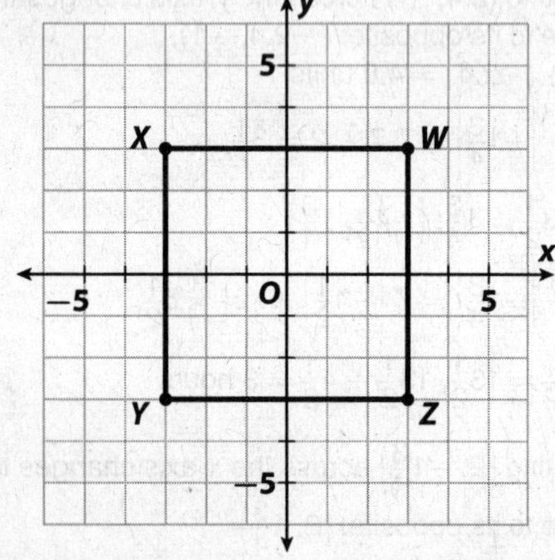

Since the shape has four equal sides and four right angles, it is a square.

2. Each side of the square is $|3| + |-3| = 6$ yards. $6 \times 4 = 24$ yards.

3. Since each side of the square is 6 yards, the area is $6 \times 6 = 36$ square yards.

4.

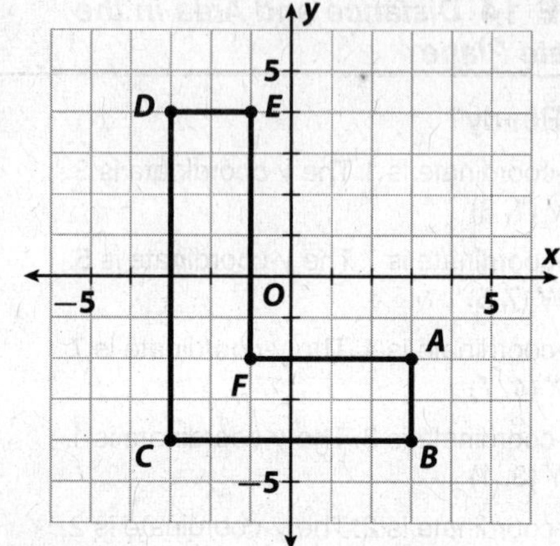

The letter formed is L.
DE $= |-3| - |-1| = 2$ units. DC $= |4| + |-4| =$ 8 units.
FA $= |-1| + |3| = 4$ units. AB $= |-4| - |-2| =$ 2 units.
The total area $= (2 \times 8) + (4 \times 2) = 24$ square inches.

5. Plot the polygon on the coordinate plane, find the length of the sides of the polygon, use known formulas to find area and perimeter, and convert from grid units to other units if necessary.

Independent Practice

6. a. F

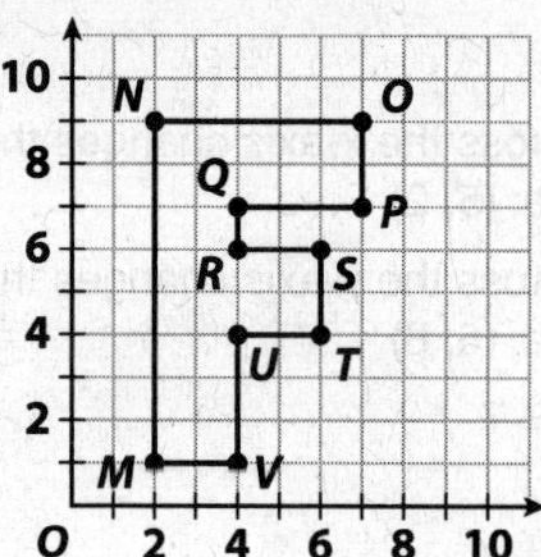

b. MN $= |9| - |1| = 8$ in., NO $= |7| - |2| = 5$ in., OP $= |9| - |7| = 2$ in., PQ $= |7| - |4| = 3$ in., QR $= |7| - |6| = 1$ in., RS $= |6| - |4| = 2$ in., ST $= |6| - |4| = 2$ in., TU $= |6| - |4| = 2$ in., UV $= |4| - |1| = 3$ in., VM $= |4| - |2| = 2$ in., $8 + 5 + 2 + 3 + 1 + 2 + 2 + 2 + 3 + 2 =$ 30 inches

c. The rectangle with sides VM and MN has an area of $2 \times 8 = 16$ square inches. The rectangle with sides OP and PQ has an area of $2 \times 3 = 6$ square inches. The rectangle with sides RS and ST has an area of $2 \times 2 = 4$ square inches. $16 + 6 + 4 = 26$ square inches

d. Sample answer: I divided the letter into four rectangles and added their areas.

7. a. The shape has 6 sides, so it is a hexagon.

b. From (3, 0) to (6, 0) is $|6| - |3| = 3$ units. $3 \times 6 = 18$ units

c. Trapezoid. Since the larger base is twice the smaller base, the larger base is $2 \times 3 = 6$ units. The perimeter of each trapezoid is $3 + 3 + 3 + 6 = 15$ units

8. a. Hexagon
   b. From (−1, 2) to (0, 2) is $|-1| + 0 = 1$ ft. From (0, 2) to (0, 0) is $|2| + 0 = 2$ ft. From (0, 0) to (4, −3) is 5 ft. From (4, −3) to (−5, −3) is $|4| + |-5| = 9$ ft. From (−5, −3) to (−5, −1) is $|-3| - |-1| = 2$ ft. From (−5, −1) to (−1, 2) is 5 ft. The perimeter of each trapezoid is $1 + 2 + 5 + 9 + 2 + 5 = 24$ feet.
   c. Divide the shape into 2 triangles that each have an area of $\frac{1}{2}(3)(4) = 6$ square feet, a rectangle with an area of $1 \times 5 = 5$ square feet, and a rectangle with an area of $2 \times 4 = 8$ square feet. The area of the shape is $6 + 6 + 5 + 8 = 25$ square feet.

Focus on Higher Order Thinking

9. The sides of the square are also the sides of three right triangles. Find the area of the square, and find the area of each triangle. Area of triangle *ABC* = Area of square − area of the other triangles: $= 25 - [(0.5)(2)(5) + (0.5)(2)(3) + (0.5)(3)(5)]$ $= 9.5$ square units.
10. Pentagon; five points are used to plot the polygon on a grid, so there will be five line segments connecting the points, and there will be five vertices. A figure with five sides and five vertices is a pentagon.
11. The octagon is a regular octagon, so all the sides will have the same length as the side whose endpoints are given. Since that side length = $|4| - |1| = 3$ units, the perimeter of the octagon is $8(3) = 24$ units.
12. Sample answer: Vertices at (0, 0), (0, 7), and (0, 10); Area = $(0.5)(7)(10) = 35$ square units

MODULE 14

Ready to Go On?

1–2.

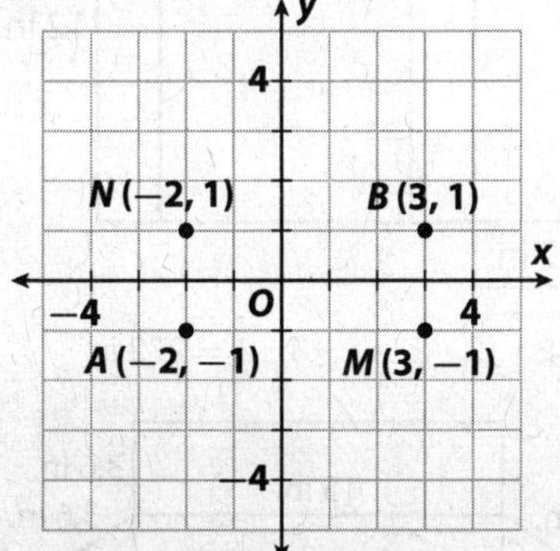

3. $|1| + |-1| = 2$ units
4. $|-2| + |3| = 5$ miles
5. Reflecting (−5, 7) across the *x*-axis changes the *y*-value to its opposite: (−5, −7)
6. Reflecting (2, 5.5) across the *y*-axis changes the *x*-value to its opposite: (−2, 5.5)
7. $|-2| + |1| = 3$ units
8. $|-4| - |-2| = 2$ units
9. $QR = |-10| + |10| = 20$ ft. $RS = |10| + |20| = 30$ ft.
   $ST = |-10| + |10| = 20$ ft. $TQ = |10| + |20| = 30$ ft.
   $20 + 30 + 20 + 30 = 100$, so the perimeter = 100 feet. $20 \times 30 = 600$, so the area = 600 square feet.
10. Plot the polygon on a grid using its vertices, and use absolute value to find the lengths of the sides; these lengths can be used to find the area.

MODULE 15 *Surface Area and Volume of Solids*

Are You Ready?

1. $\frac{1}{2}(3)(5+7) = \frac{1}{2}(3)(12)$ Within parentheses.
$= \frac{3}{2}(12)$ Multiply left to right.
$= 18$

2. $\frac{1}{2}(15)(13+17) = \frac{1}{2}(15)(30)$ Within parentheses.
$= \frac{15}{2}(30)$ Multiply left to right.
$= 225$

3. $\frac{1}{2}(10)(9.4+3.6) = \frac{1}{2}(10)(13)$ Within parentheses.
$= 5(13)$ Multiply left to right.
$= 65$

4. $\frac{1}{2}(2.1)(3.5+5.7) = \frac{1}{2}(2.1)(9.2)$ Within parentheses.
$= (1.05)(9.2)$ Multiply left to right.
$= 9.66$

5. Use the formula for the area of a triangle.
$A = \frac{1}{2}bh$
$= \frac{1}{2}(6)(3)$
$= 3(3)$
$= 9 \text{ in}^2$

6. Use the formula for the area of a square.
$A = s^2$
$= (7.6)^2$
$= 57.76 \text{ m}^2$

7. Use the formula for the area of a rectangle.
$A = bh$
$= \left(3\frac{1}{4}\right)\left(2\frac{1}{2}\right)$
$= \frac{13}{4}\left(\frac{5}{2}\right)$
$= \frac{65}{8}$
$= 8\frac{1}{8} \text{ ft}^2$

8. Use the formula for the area of a triangle.
$A = \frac{1}{2}bh$
$= \frac{1}{2}(8.2)(5.1)$
$= 4.1(5.1)$
$= 20.91 \text{ cm}^2$

LESSON 15.1

Your Turn

4.

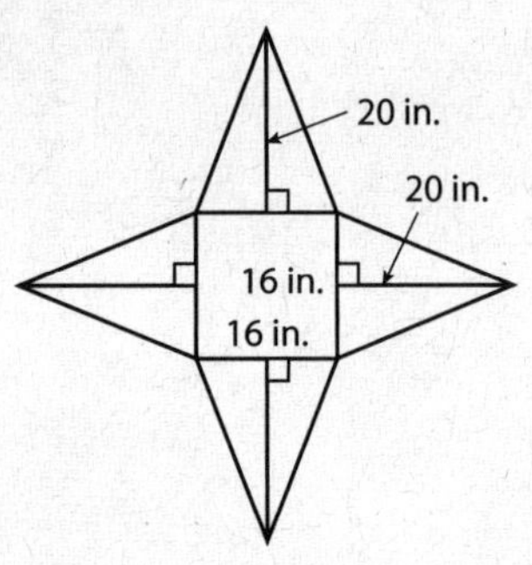

$16 \cdot 16 + 4 \cdot \frac{1}{2} \cdot 20 \cdot 16 = 896 \text{ in}^2$

6.

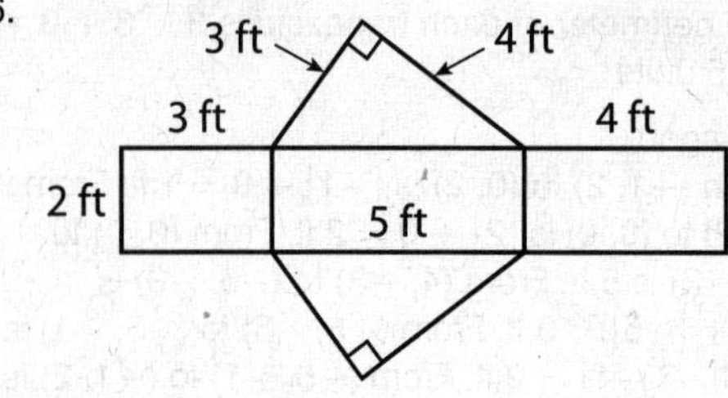

$2 \cdot 3 + 2 \cdot 4 + 2 \cdot 5 + 2 \cdot \frac{1}{2} \cdot 4 \cdot 3 = 36 \text{ ft}^2$
$36 \cdot 0.22 = \$7.92$

Guided Practice

1. 1, 4
2. $6 \cdot 6 = 36$
$4 \cdot \frac{1}{2} \cdot 6 \cdot 4 = 48$
$36 + 48 = 84$
3. a.

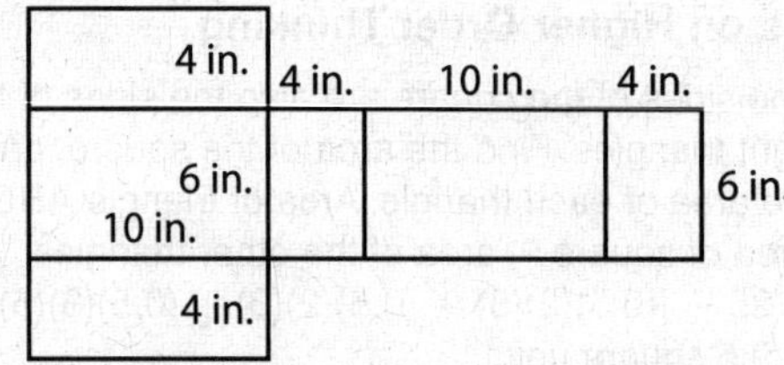

$2 \cdot 4 \cdot 6 + 2 \cdot 10 \cdot 6 + 2 \cdot 4 \cdot 10 = 248 \text{ in}^2$
b. $100 \cdot 248 = 24{,}800 \text{ in}^2$
c. $2 \cdot 14{,}000 = 28{,}000 \text{ in}^2$
2 cans
4. A net shows the three-dimensional figure as flat and two-dimensional, which makes it easier to visualize the shapes of the surfaces and add up their areas.

Independent Practice

5.

2 in.
2 in.
8 in.
2 in.
8 in.
12 in.
12 in.
2 in.

$2 \cdot 12 \cdot 8 + 2 \cdot 12 \cdot 2 + 2 \cdot 8 \cdot 2 = 272 \text{ in}^2$

6. a.

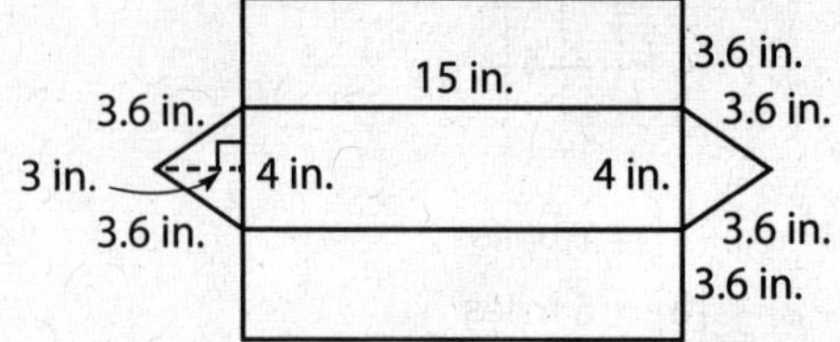

b. $4 \cdot 15 + 2 \cdot 3.6 \cdot 15 + 2 \cdot \frac{1}{2} \cdot 3 \cdot 4 = 180 \text{ in}^2$

7. $20 \cdot 20 \cdot 5 \div 5 \cdot 5 = 2000 \div 25 = 80$
He will need 80 tiles.

8. Box A: $8 \cdot 3 \cdot 2 + 8 \cdot 6 \cdot 2 + 6 \cdot 3 \cdot 2 = 180 \text{ in}^2$
$180 \cdot 0.03 = \$5.40$
$10 \cdot 3 \cdot 2 + 10 \cdot 4 \cdot 2 + 3 \cdot 4 \cdot 2 = 164 \text{ in}^2$
Box B: $164 \cdot 0.03 = \$4.92$
$\$5.40 - \$4.92 = \$0.48$
Box B will cost \$0.48 less than Box A.

9. Rectangular pyramid; triangular prism

10.

	5 in.		
8 in. / 6 in.	5 in.	8 in.	5 in. / 6 in.
5 in.			

$8 \cdot 6 \cdot 2 + 8 \cdot 5 \cdot 2 + 5 \cdot 6 \cdot 2 = 236 \text{ in}^2$

11. Sample answer: Decide whether the figure is a prism or a pyramid, and what the shapes of the bases and faces are. Make a net of the figure, and label the dimensions. Use appropriate area formulas to find the areas of the faces, and then find the sum of the areas.

Focus on Higher Order Thinking

12. a. $12 + 16 + 20 = 48$ cm
The distance around the base of the pedestal is 48 centimeters. The base is a triangle with perimeter $12 + 16 + 20$ cm.
b. $192 \div 48 = 4$ cm
Sample answer: The cloth is a rectangle whose longer side is 48 centimeters long; the width is the height of the pedestal.

13. Prism A: $5 \cdot 6 \cdot 2 + 5 \cdot 7 \cdot 2 + 6 \cdot 7 \cdot 2 = 214 \text{ cm}^2$
Prism B: $10 \cdot 12 \cdot 2 + 10 \cdot 14 \cdot 2 + 12 \cdot 14 \cdot 2 = 856 \text{ cm}^2$
$856 \div 214 = 4$
Robert is incorrect. B's surface area is 4 times as great as A's.

LESSON 15.2

Your Turn

4. $V = 7\frac{1}{2} \cdot 4 \cdot 2\frac{1}{2}$
$= \frac{15}{2} \cdot 4 \cdot \frac{5}{2}$
$= \frac{300}{4}$
$= 75$ cubic inches

5. $V = 5\frac{1}{4} \cdot 3\frac{1}{2} \cdot 3$
$= \frac{21}{4} \cdot \frac{7}{2} \cdot 3$
$= \frac{441}{8}$
$= 55\frac{1}{8}$ cubic inches

6. $B = 15 \cdot 10\frac{1}{2}$
$= 15 \cdot \frac{21}{2}$
$= \frac{315}{2} \text{ m}^2$
$V = \frac{315}{2} \cdot 2\frac{1}{2}$
$= \frac{315}{2} \cdot \frac{5}{2}$
$= \frac{1575}{4}$
$= 393\frac{3}{4}$ cubic meters

Guided Practice

1. $4 \times 4 \times 4 = 64$

2. $\frac{4}{5} \times \frac{4}{5} \times \frac{4}{5} = \frac{64}{125}$

3. $V = 10 \times 3.2 \times 5$
$= 160$ cubic meters

4. $B = 7\frac{1}{4} \times 4$
$= \frac{29}{4} \times 4$
$= 29 \text{ m}^2$
$V = 29 \cdot 8$
$= 232$ cubic meters

5. $V = 9.25 \cdot 4 \cdot 7.5$
$= 277.5$ cubic feet

6. $V = 18 \cdot 4\frac{1}{2} \cdot 6\frac{1}{2}$
$= 18 \cdot \frac{9}{2} \cdot \frac{13}{2}$
$= \frac{2106}{4}$
$= 526\frac{1}{2}$ cubic inches

7. $V = 8\frac{1}{2} \cdot 3\frac{1}{2} \cdot 12$
$= \frac{17}{2} \cdot \frac{7}{2} \cdot 12$
$= \frac{1428}{4}$
$= 357$ cubic inches

8. $V = lwh$ and $V = Bh$; The area of the base, B, is really lw (length times width), and since both B and lw are multiplied by h, the two are equivalent.

Independent Practice

9. $V = 4.5 \cdot 3.5 \cdot 7$
$= 110.25$ cubic inches

10. $V = 72\frac{1}{2} \cdot 24\frac{1}{2} \cdot 36$
$= \frac{145}{2} \cdot \frac{49}{2} \cdot 36$
$= \frac{255{,}780}{4}$
$= 63{,}945$ cubic inches

11. Prism A: $V = 6 \cdot 4 \cdot 5$
$= 120$ cubic inches
Prism B: $V = 12 \cdot 8 \cdot 10$
$= 960$ cubic inches
$960 \div 120 = 8$
Prism B's volume is 8 times as great as Prism A's volume.

12. $V = \frac{5}{8} \times \frac{5}{8} \times \frac{5}{8}$

$= \frac{125}{512}$ cubic inches

It could fit 125 smaller cubes.

13. $V = 6\frac{1}{2} \times 2\frac{1}{2} \times 4 \times \frac{9}{10}$

$= 6\frac{1}{2} \times 10 \times \frac{9}{10}$

$= 6\frac{1}{2} \times 9$

$= 58.5$ cubic inches

14. $19.3 = \frac{\text{mass}}{16 \cdot 2.5 \cdot 5}$

$19.3 = \frac{\text{mass}}{200}$

Mass = 3,860 grams

15. $V = 1\frac{1}{4} \cdot 1\frac{3}{4} \cdot 1\frac{1}{4}$

$= \frac{5}{4} \cdot \frac{7}{4} \cdot \frac{5}{4}$

$= \frac{175}{64}$

$= 2\frac{47}{64}$ cubic feet

16. a. Van: $V = 10\frac{1}{2} \cdot 6 \cdot 6$

$= \frac{21}{2} \cdot 6 \cdot 6$

$= \frac{756}{2}$

$= 378$ cubic feet

$\frac{94.5}{378} = \$0.25$ per cubic foot

Small truck:

$V = 12 \cdot 8 \cdot 6\frac{3}{4}$

$= 12 \cdot 8 \cdot \frac{27}{4}$

$= \frac{2{,}592}{4}$

$= 648$ cubic feet

$\frac{162}{648} = \$0.25$ per cubic foot

They cost the same per unit volume.

b. Large truck:

$V = 20 \cdot 8\frac{3}{4} \cdot 8\frac{1}{2}$

$= 20 \cdot \frac{35}{4} \cdot \frac{17}{2}$

$= \frac{11{,}900}{8}$

$= 1{,}487\frac{1}{2}$ cubic feet

$1{,}487.5 - 648 = 839.5$ cubic feet

c. They should rent the large truck.

Focus on Higher Order Thinking

17. Find a fraction that, when multiplied by itself 3 times, equals $\frac{1}{512}$.

The length of each side is $\frac{1}{8}$ m.

Surface area $= 6\left(\frac{1}{8}\right)\left(\frac{1}{8}\right) = \frac{3}{32}$

The surface area is $\frac{3}{32}$ m^2.

18. a. Prism *P*: $V = Bh$

Prism *Q*: $V = B2h = 2Bh$

The volume of *Q* is twice the volume of *P*.

b. Prism *P*: $V = Bh$

Prism *Q*: $V = 2Bh$

The volume of *Q* is twice the volume of *P*.

19. Lee: $B = 5 \cdot 2\frac{1}{2}$

$= 5 \cdot \frac{5}{2}$

$= \frac{25}{2}$

$= 12\frac{1}{2}\ \text{ft}^2$

$V = 12\frac{1}{2} \cdot 3\frac{1}{4}$

$= \frac{25}{2} \cdot \frac{13}{4}$

$= \frac{325}{8}$

$= 40\frac{5}{8}$ cubic feet

Lola: $B = 5 \cdot 3\frac{1}{4}$

$= 5 \cdot \frac{13}{4}$

$= \frac{65}{4}$

$= 16\frac{1}{4}\ \text{ft}^2$

$V = 16\frac{1}{4} \cdot 2\frac{1}{2}$

$= \frac{65}{4} \cdot \frac{5}{2}$

$= \frac{325}{8}$

$= 40\frac{5}{8}$ cubic feet

Both are correct. Lee used the $2\frac{1}{2}$ by 5-foot face as the base and $3\frac{1}{4}$ as the height, then multiplied the base area, $12\frac{1}{2}$, by the height. Lola used the $3\frac{1}{4}$ by 5-foot face as the base and $2\frac{1}{2}$ as the height, then multiplied the base area, $16\frac{1}{4}$, by the height.

LESSON 15.3

Your Turn

2. $V = \ell wh$

$\frac{15}{16} = \left(\frac{3}{4}\right)\left(\frac{1}{2}\right)h$

$\frac{15}{16} = \left(\frac{3}{8}\right)h$

$\frac{8}{3} \cdot \frac{15}{16} = \frac{8}{3}\left(\frac{3}{8}h\right)$

$\frac{5}{2} = h$

The height is $\frac{5}{2}$ ft or $2\frac{1}{2}$ ft.

3. One cubic foot of water equals approximately 7.5 gallons, so 33.75 gallons of water equal $33.75 \div 7.5 = 4.5$ cubic feet of water.

$V = \ell wh$

$4.5 = 2 \cdot w \cdot 1.5$

$4.5 = 3w$

$1.5 = w$

The width is 1.5 feet.

Guided Practice

1. $V = \ell wh$

$6{,}336 = 16 \cdot w \cdot 18$

$6{,}336 = 288w$

$\frac{6{,}336}{288} = \frac{288w}{288}$

$22 \text{ cm} = w$

2. $5.76 \div 0.08 = 72$ cubic inches

$V = 72 \text{ in}^3$

$V = \ell wh$

$72 = 8 \cdot 2\frac{1}{4} \cdot h$

$72 = 18h$

$\frac{72}{18} = \frac{18h}{18}$

$4 \text{ inches} = h$

Independent Practice

3. $V = \ell wh$

$3{,}758.75 = 24.25 \cdot 12.5 \cdot h$

$3{,}758.75 = 303.125h$

$\frac{3{,}758.75}{303.125} = \frac{303.125h}{303.125}$

$12.4 = h$

Height = 12.4 in.

4. $V = bh$

$18 = 4\frac{1}{2} \cdot h$

$h = 4$

The height of the box is 4 inches.

5. $V = \ell wh$

$3{,}600 = 20 \cdot w \cdot 30$

$3{,}600 = 600w$

$6 = w$

Width = 6 cm

6. $V = lwh$

$V = 3 \cdot 3\frac{1}{2} \cdot 1\frac{1}{2}$

$V = 15\frac{3}{4} \text{ ft}^3$

$15\frac{3}{4} \text{ ft}^3 \cdot \frac{7.5 \text{ gal}}{1 \text{ ft}^3} = 118\frac{1}{8} \text{ gal}$

It takes $118\frac{1}{8}$ gallons of water to fill the pool.

7. $V = \ell wh$

$V = 40 \cdot 25 \cdot 2$

$V = 2{,}000 \text{ mm}^3$

$w = 2{,}000 \times 0.0005 = 1 \text{ oz}$

The volume of the bar is 2,000 cubic millimeters, and the weight of the bar is 1 ounce.

8. $V = \ell wh$

$V = 5 \cdot 6 \cdot 5$

$V = 150 \text{ ft}^3$

Volume = 150 cubic feet

$w = 15 \div 150 = 0.1$ ton

Weight of 1 cubic foot of the stone = 0.1 ton

9. Height of cards:

$V = lwh$

$32 = 8 \cdot 4 \cdot h$

$32 = 32h$

$1 = h$

The cards are 1 inch tall.

Volume of box:

$V = lwh$

$V = 8 \cdot 4 \cdot 4$

$V = 128 \text{ in}^3$

Percent of box's volume = $32 \text{ in}^3 \div 128 \text{ in}^3 = 0.25$ or 25%.

10. a. 2.5 gallons

b. $V = \ell wh$

$V = 7 \cdot 5 \cdot 7$

$V = 245 \text{ in}^3$

c. No, the fish would need $231 \cdot 2.5 = 577.5$ cubic inches of water.

Focus on Higher Order Thinking

11. $V = \ell wh$

$V = 7 \times 3.5 \times 1.75$

$V = 42.875 \text{ in}^3$

Volume, rounded to the nearest tenth = 42.9 in^3

$b = 42.9 \times 0.1 = 4.29$

Weight of the brick = 4.3 pounds

$g = 42.9 \times 0.7 = 30.03$

Weight of the gold bar = 30.0 pounds

12. Sample answer: If the area of the base and the height are the same, the volume will also be the same. The length could be 50 cm and the width 44 cm, making the dimensions 50 cm by 44 cm by 30 cm. The volume of both ovens is 66,000 cubic centimeters.

13. 8 in. by 2 in.; $64 = 4B$, so $B = 16$. Since length : width = 4 : 1, I found two factors of 16 that are in this ratio, 8 and 2.

14. The length of an edge is 3 inches because $3 \cdot 3 \cdot 3 = 27$.

MODULE 15

Ready to Go On?

1.

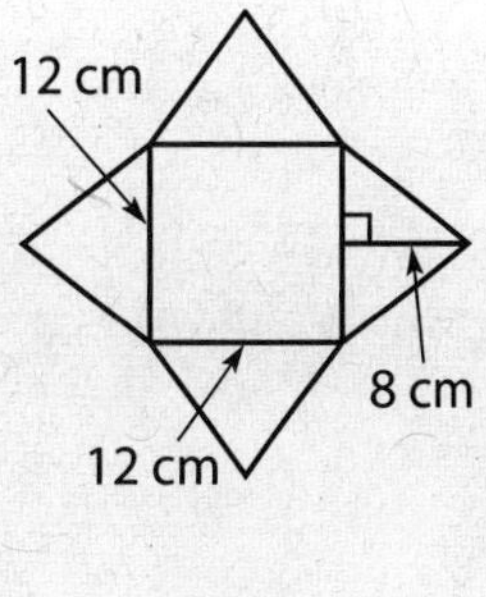

12 cm

8 cm

12 cm

2. There are four triangles with base 12 cm and height 8 cm.
Find the area of one triangle.
$A = \frac{1}{2}bh$
$= \frac{1}{2}(12)(8)$
$= 48 \text{ cm}^2$
Find the area of four triangles.
$4 \times 48 = 192 \text{ cm}^2$
Find the area of the base.
$A = 12 \times 12$
$= 144 \text{ cm}^2$
Add the area of the triangles and the area of the base.
$192 + 144 = 336 \text{ cm}^2$
The surface area of the pyramid is 336 square centimeters.

3. Use the formula for the volume of a rectangular prism.
$V = lwh$
$= 8\frac{3}{8} \cdot 6 \cdot 8\frac{1}{4}$
$= \frac{67}{8} \cdot 6 \cdot \frac{33}{4}$
$= \frac{6{,}633}{16} = 414\frac{9}{16}$
$V = 414\frac{9}{16}$ cubic meters

4. Use the formula for the volume of a rectangular prism.
$V = lwh$
$= 5 \cdot 6\frac{1}{2} \cdot 2\frac{1}{4}$
$= 5 \cdot \frac{13}{2} \cdot \frac{9}{4}$
$= \frac{585}{8} = 73\frac{1}{8}$
$V = 73\frac{1}{8}$ cubic feet

5. Use the formula for the volume of a rectangular prism to write an equation.
$V = lwh$
The area of the floor is equal to the length times the width.
$A = lw$
$V = Ah$
$2{,}025 = Ah$
$2{,}025 = A \cdot 9$
$\frac{2{,}025}{9} = \frac{A \cdot 9}{9}$
$225 = A$
The area of the floor is 225 ft^2.

6. Use the formula for the volume of a rectangular prism to write an equation.
$V = lwh$
$11.25 = lwh$
$11.25 = 2.5 \cdot 1.5 \cdot h$
$11.25 = 3.75 \cdot h$
$\frac{11.25}{3.75} = \frac{3.75 \cdot h}{3.75}$
$3 = h$
The depth of the aquarium is 3 ft.

7. A net shows faces and helps you find surface area; a drawing helps you choose a base and height when finding volume.

UNIT 7

Solutions Key

Measurement and Data

MODULE 16 *Displaying, Analyzing, and Summarizing Data*

Are You Ready?

1.
$$\begin{array}{r} 2.8 \\ 15\overline{)42.0} \\ -30 \\ \hline 12\,0 \\ -12\,0 \\ \hline 0 \end{array}$$

2.8

2.
$$\begin{array}{r} 1.24 \\ 75\overline{)93.00} \\ -75 \\ \hline 18 \\ -15 \\ \hline 3\,00 \\ -3\,00 \\ \hline 0 \end{array}$$

1.24

3.
$$\begin{array}{r} 1.75 \\ 52\overline{)91.00} \\ -52 \\ \hline 39\,0 \\ -36\,4 \\ \hline 2\,60 \\ -2\,60 \\ \hline 0 \end{array}$$

1.75

4.
$$\begin{array}{r} 2.375 \\ 24\overline{)57.000} \\ -48 \\ \hline 9\,0 \\ -7\,2 \\ \hline 1\,80 \\ -1\,68 \\ \hline 120 \\ -120 \\ \hline 0 \end{array}$$

2.375

5. Dion scored 3.
6. Ted scored 1 goal. Jeff scored 4. Ted and Dion scored $1 + 3 = 4$.
7. Cesar's score minus Alec's score: $6 - 5 = 1$

LESSON 16.1

Your Turn

3. Data in order from least to greatest:
   1 2 4 5 6 7 8 8 9 12
   The data set has two middle values: 6 and 7. The median is the average of these two values:
   $\text{Median} = \frac{6 + 7}{2} = 6.5$ minutes

Guided Practice

1. $\text{Mean} = \frac{\text{sum of data values}}{\text{number of data values}} = \frac{15}{5} = 3$
   The mean number of pets is 3.
2. a. Data in order from least to greatest:
   29 36 39 45 49 51
   $\text{Median} = \frac{39 + 45}{2} = 42$
   The median is 42.
   b. No; you can only find the median if you convert all the weights to the same units.
3. a. $\text{Mean} = \frac{\text{sum of data values}}{\text{number of data values}} = \frac{68}{8} = 8.5$;
   Data in order from least to greatest:
   3 4 5 6 6 7 9 28
   $\text{Median} = \frac{6 + 6}{2} = 6$
   b. The median; Sample answer: The median is closer to most of the data values than the mean is.
4. Sample answer: The mean and median can be used to represent or summarize the data.

Independent Practice

5. Ten students were asked because there are 10 data values in the list.
6. $\text{Mean} = \frac{\text{sum of data values}}{\text{number of data values}} = \frac{60}{10} = 6$;
   Data in order from least to greatest:
   0 0 1 2 3 7 9 10 13 15
   $\text{Median} = \frac{3 + 7}{2} = 5$
7. $\text{Mean} = \frac{471}{6} = 78.5$;
   Data in order from least to greatest:
   37 73 77 84 85 115
   $\text{Median} = \frac{77 + 84}{2} = 80.5$
8. Sample answer: Both can describe the number of points equally well.
9. Minutes and hours; convert all times to minutes
10. 0.5 hr = 30 min; 1 hr = 60 min
    $\text{Mean} = \frac{\text{sum of data values}}{\text{number of data values}} = \frac{152}{8} = 19$;
    Data in order from least to greatest:
    5 7 8 12 14 16 30 60
    $\text{Median} = \frac{12 + 14}{2} = 13$
11. Median; it is closer to most of the data values. The data value for 1 hour, or 60 minutes, raises the mean.

Focus on Higher Order Thinking

12. No; the sum is correct, but the sum should be divided by 10, not by 8. The mean is 5.5.

13. 95; Sample answer: the mean and the median of Lauren's scores are both 95. If she gets 95 on the next math test, the mean and median will remain at 95.

14. a. Mean:

$$\text{Company A} = \frac{96{,}000}{4} = \$24{,}000;$$

$$\text{Company B} = \frac{128{,}000}{4} = \$32{,}000$$

b. Median:

$$\text{Company A} = \frac{20{,}000 + 25{,}000}{2} = \$22{,}500;$$

$$\text{Company B} = \frac{23{,}000 + 36{,}000}{2} = \$29{,}500$$

c. Company B; both the mean and the median are greater at Company B, so Yuko will make a greater commission.

LESSON 16.2

Your Turn

2. Find the mean for Waiter A's smoothies:

$$\frac{19.1 + 20.1 + 20.9 + 19.6 + 20.9 + 19.5 + 19.2 + 19.4 + 20.3 + 20.9}{10} \approx 20$$

The mean is approximately 20 oz.
Find the mean for Waiter B's smoothies:

$$\frac{20.1 + 19.6 + 20.0 + 20.5 + 19.8 + 20.0 + 20.1 + 19.7 + 19.9 + 20.4}{10} \approx 20$$

The mean is approximately 20 oz.
Find the distance from the mean for each data set:

Waiter A										
Amount of Smoothie (oz)	19.1	20.1	20.9	19.6	20.9	19.5	19.2	19.4	20.3	20.9
Distance from mean	0.9	0.1	0.9	0.4	0.9	0.5	0.8	0.6	0.3	0.9

Waiter B										
Amount of Smoothie (oz)	20.1	19.6	20.0	20.5	19.8	20.0	20.1	19.7	19.9	20.4
Distance from mean	0.1	0.4	0	0.5	0.2	0	0.1	0.3	0.1	0.4

Calculate the MAD for each data set.

$$\frac{0.9 + 0.1 + 0.9 + 0.4 + 0.9 + 0.5 + 0.8 + 0.6 + 0.3 + 0.9}{10} \approx 0.6$$

$$\frac{0.1 + 0.4 + 0 + 0.5 + 0.2 + 0 + 0.1 + 0.3 + 0.1 + 0.4}{10} \approx 0.2$$

The MAD for Waiter A's smoothies is approximately 0.6 oz, and the MAD for Waiter B's smoothies is approximately 0.2 oz, so Waiter B's smoothies showed less variability.

3. The mean amount of aspirin in tablets made by Device A is 0.349875 g.
The mean amount of aspirin in tablets made by Device B is 0.34875 g.
The MAD for Device A is approximately 0.0017 g. The MAD for Device B is approximately 0.0063 g. Since the MAD for Device A is less than the MAD for Device B, Device A has less variability.

Guided Practice

1. a. $\frac{44.2 + 44.9 + 46.1 + 45.8 + 44.7 + 45.2 + 45.1 + 45.3 + 44.6}{9} = 45.1$

The mean is 45.1 min.

b.

Time (min)	44.2	44.9	46.1	45.8	44.7	45.2	45.1	45.3	44.6
Distance from mean	0.9	0.2	1	0.7	0.4	0.1	0	0.2	0.5

$$\frac{0.9 + 0.2 + 1 + 0.7 + 0.4 + 0.1 + 0 + 0.2 + 0.5}{9} = 0.\overline{4}$$

To the nearest tenth, the MAD is 0.4 min.
The bus driver did meet the company's goal.

2. The mean is 44.9 minutes, and the MAD is $0.7\overline{3}$ minutes. This time the bus driver did not meet the company's goal.

3. It is the mean of the distances between the data values and the mean of the data set. It can tell you how spread out from the mean the data values are.

Independent Practice

4. $\frac{1+6+2+4+4+3+5+5+2+8}{10} = 4$

   The mean is 4 people.

5. $\frac{3+2+2+0+0+1+1+1+2+4}{10} = 1.6$

   The MAD is 1.6 people.

6. Sample answer: The mean is 4, but the number of people varies greatly because the MAD is almost half the mean. For the sample, there is not really a typical household size.

7. Calculate the MAD of the serving sizes at the beginning of Week 1.

   $$\text{Mean} = \frac{76+81+85+79+89+86+84+80+88+79}{10} = 82.7$$

   $$\text{MAD} = \frac{6.7+1.7+2.3+3.7+6.3+3.3+1.3+2.7+5.3+3.7}{10} = 3.7$$

   Calculate the MAD of the serving sizes at the end of Week 1.

   $$\text{Mean} = \frac{79+82+84+81+77+85+82+80+78+83}{10} = 81.1$$

   $$\text{MAD} = \frac{2.1+0.9+2.9+0.1+4.1+3.9+0.9+1.1+3.1+1.9}{10} = 2.1$$

   Yes; The MAD at the beginning of Week 1 was 3.7, and at the end it was 2.1, so the serving sizes showed less variation.

8. All the serving sizes would be the same.

9. The mean for Austin is 31.855 in., while the mean for San Antonio is 30.459 in. Therefore, on average, it rains more in Austin in a year.

10. The MAD for Austin is 9.681 in., while the MAD for San Antonio is 10.925 in. The annual rainfall for San Antonio varies more from the mean than the rainfall for Austin.

11. Sample answer: Over many years, you should get more rainfall in Austin, but in any particular year, you can't predict which city will get more rainfall due to the variability.

12. Sample answer:

Life Spans of Ten Mayflies (h)									
1	1	2	2	4	4	4	6	6	10

   No; 24 hours represents a deviation of 20 hours from the mean. Because the MAD is 2 and there are 10 mayflies, the total amount of deviation for all of the mayflies is 20. If one mayfly lived for 24 hours, the others would have to all live for exactly 4 hours. This would result in a mean of 6 hours, not 4 hours, so it is not possible.

Focus on Higher Order Thinking

13. a. The mean is 1 and the MAD is 0. Because 1 is the only data value, it is the mean of the data set and does not deviate from the mean.

    b. The mean is 1.5, and the MAD is 0.5. This makes sense because $1 + 2 = 3$, $3 \div 2 = 1.5$, and both 1 and 2 are 0.5 away from 1.5.

    c. They increase. The values are getting larger, so the mean should increase, and they are getting more spread out, so the MAD should increase.

14. No, it does not affect the MAD of the data set. Since the mean also increases by 10, the distance between each data value from the mean remains the same.

15. No; the MAD is a mean of the distances of the various data values from the mean. When you find the MAD, you may not get a whole number value.

LESSON 16.3

Your Turn

2. Data in order from least to greatest:

   75 78 78 79 80 83 84 85 88 89 92 94

   Least value = 75; Greatest value = 94

   Median = $\frac{83 + 84}{2} = 83.5$

   Lower quartile = $\frac{78 + 79}{2} = 78.5$;

   Upper quartile = $\frac{88 + 89}{2} = 88.5$

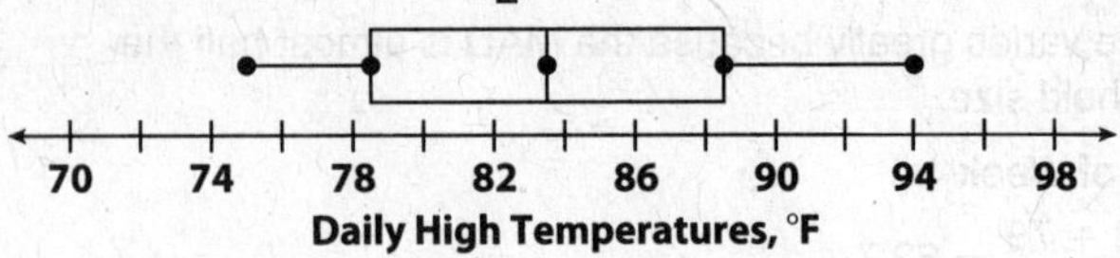

3. IQR = Upper quartile − Lower quartile
   Group A IQR = 1,800 − 1,100 = 700
   Group B IQR = 1,850 − 1,400 = 450
   Group A IQR = $700. Group B IQR = $450.
   Group A's IQR is greater, so the salaries in the middle 50% for group A are more spread out than those in group B.
4. Range = Greatest value − Least value
   Miami: Range = 91 − 76 = 15
   Chicago: Range = 84 − 31 = 53;
   Chicago has the greater range.

Guided Practice

1. Data in order from least to greatest:
   4 10 11 13 14 15 25 29 33 33 35 43 51 58 64
2. The median is 29.
3. The lower quartile is 13.
4. The upper quartile is 43.
5.

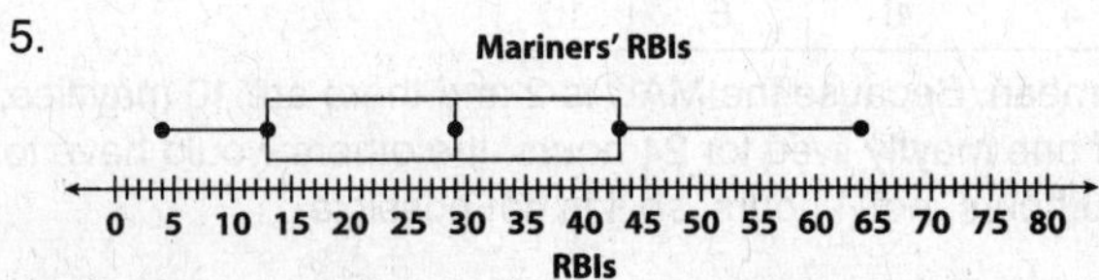

6. IQR = Upper quartile − Lower quartile
   IQR = 43 − 13 = 30
7. Range = Greatest value − Least value
   Range = 64 − 4 = 60
8. The range of a set of data is the difference of the greatest and least values in the data set. The IQR is the difference of the upper and lower quartiles.

Independent Practice

9. Data in order from least to greatest:

   45 46 46 47 48 48 48 52 52 56 57

   Least value: 45; Greatest value: 57
   Median: 48
   Lower quartile: 46; Upper quartile: 52;

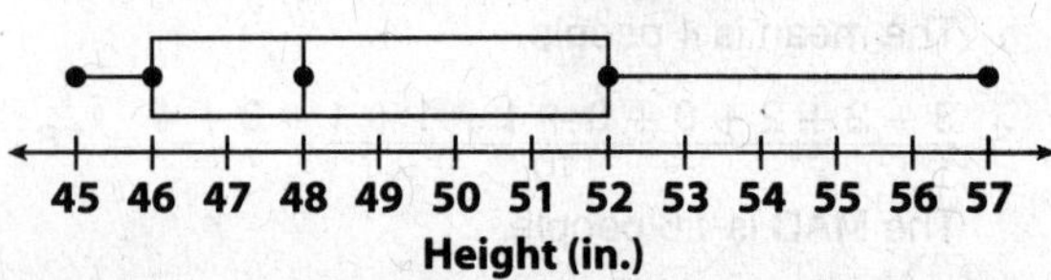

10. 11 students are included in the data set.
11. Sample answer: Students could have measured each others' heights.
12. Sample answer: You could collect test scores, shoe sizes, ages (years), etc.
13. IQR = Upper quartile − Lower quartile
    January: IQR = 2.0 − 1.7 = 0.3
    June: IQR = 2.3 − 2.0 = 0.3
14. Range = Greatest value − Least value
    January: Range = 2.5 − 1.3 = 1.2
    June: Range = 2.4 − 1.9 = 0.5
15. The IQRs are the same. The spreads of the middle 50% of the data values are the same for the two data sets.
16. The range for January is more than twice as great as the range for June.

Focus on Higher Order Thinking

17. Yes; sample example: One data set could range from 100 to 150, and another data set could range from 10 to 60. Both have a range of 50. The first data set could have quartiles at 120 and 130, and the second data set could have quartiles at 20 and 30. Both have an IQR of 10.
18. a.

Theater Group	Median	Range	IQR
Northside Players	39	50	37.5
Southside Players	32	38	28

    b. The box plot for the Northside Players will be longer overall because its data has a greater range. The box plot will also have a longer box portion because the IQR is greater.

    c. All box plots show only five values: the greatest and least values, the median, and the lower and upper quartile. You can't tell from looking at a box plot how many values were in the original data set.

LESSON 16.4

Your Turn

4. There are 14 dots, each of which represents a game, so the team played 14 games; the value with the greatest frequency is 4; there were 4 games in which the team scored 4 runs.

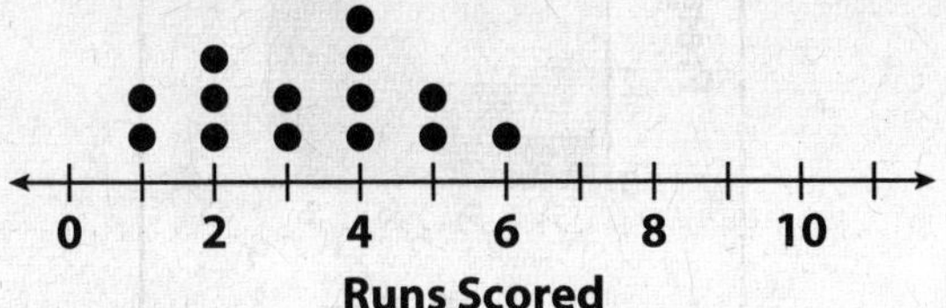

5. The data values are spread out from 0 to 11. 11 appears to be an outlier. The data has a cluster from 0 to 7 with one peak at 2. The distribution is not symmetric because the data is not clustered around the center of the distribution.

6. Mean $= \frac{2(1) + 3(2)... + 1(6)}{14} = \frac{46}{14} \approx 3.3$

   Median $= \frac{3 + 4}{2} = 3.5$

   Range $= 6 - 1 = 5$

   The typical number of runs is between 3 and 4 runs. The mean and median are close in value, and there are no outliers.

Guided Practice

1. Variable data; Sample answer: How many pounds of recyclable trash does each household generate?

2.

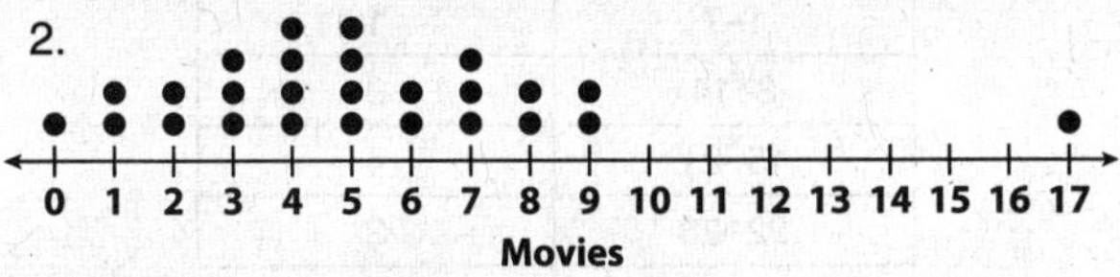

3. Mean $= \frac{1(0)... + 1(17)}{26} = \frac{135}{26} \approx 5.2$

   Median $= \frac{5 + 5}{2} = 5;$

   Range $= 17 - 0 = 17$

4. The data is spread from 0 to 17. 17 appears to be an outlier. The data has a cluster from 0 to 9 with peaks at 4 and 5. The distribution is not symmetric.

5. Mean, median, and range; you can see whether data are symmetric about a central value or clustered around a different value.

Independent Practice

6. A statistical question has many different, or variable, answers. Sample answer: How old are my friends' pets?

7. Not statistical

8. Statistical; feet and inches or centimeters

9. Not statistical

10. Statistical; dollars

11.

4 6 8 10 12 14

Days of Precipitation

12. The number of days of rain in one month; 12 months

13. All the data values are between 7 and 12 days with a peak around 9 days. There are no outliers.

14. Mean $= \frac{1(7)... + 2(12)}{12} = \frac{116}{12} \approx 9.7$ days

    Median $= \frac{9 + 10}{2} = 9.5$ days

    Range $= 12 - 7 = 5$ days

15. Mean $= \frac{1(3)... + 2(12)}{12} = \frac{112}{12} \approx 9.3$

    Median $= \frac{9 + 10}{2} = 9.5$

    Range $= 12 - 3 = 9$

    The mean would change from about 9.7 to about 9.3. The median would stay at 9.5. The range would change from 5 days to 9 days.

16. Mean $= \frac{2(5)... + 1(22)}{24} = \frac{246}{24} = 10.25$

    Median $= \frac{10 + 10}{2} = 10$

    Range $= 22 - 5 = 17$

17. Mean $= \frac{2(5)... + 2(15)}{23} = \frac{224}{23} \approx 9.7$

    Median $= 10$

    Range $= 15 - 5 = 10$

    The range; it changes from 17 to 10. The mean changes from 10.25 to about 9.7, and the median does not change.

18. 10 cars; The mean and median are both about 10.

19. $5(2) + 6(2) + 7 + 8(3) + 9(2) + 10(5) + 11 + 12(3) + 13(2) + 15(2) + 22$

20. Sample answer: The data values spread out from 5 to 22. The data value 22 appears to be an outlier. The data has a cluster from 5 to 15 with one peak at 10.

21. Count the number of dots above a data value.

22.

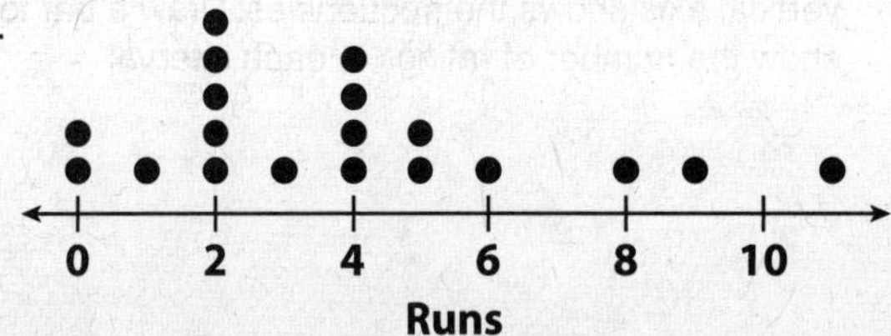

23. 19; Each dot represents one game.

24. 2 runs; 2 runs were scored against the Red Sox in 5 games in June 2010.

25. Mean: about 3.9 runs; median: 4 runs; range: 11 runs.

26. Sample answer: What was the typical number of runs scored by opponents of the Boston Red Sox in June 2010? The mean is 3.9 and the median is 4, so the typical number of runs is 4.

Focus on Higher Order Thinking

27. a. The units for the ages, which could be years, month, or weeks.

b. No; to make a dot plot or to find measures of center and spread, the doctor needs to use the same units for all the data.

28. a.

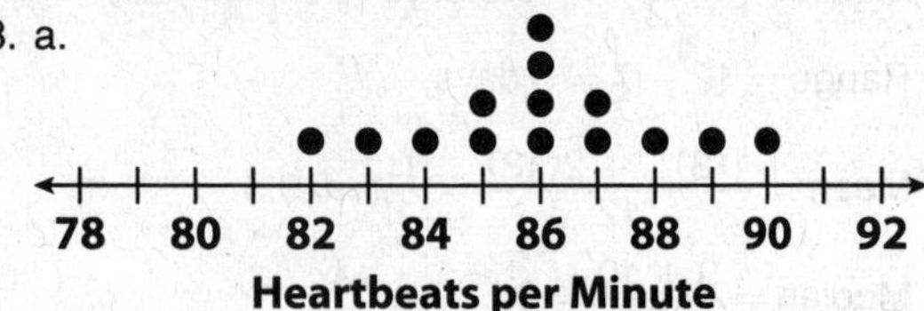

b. The data distribution is symmetric, and the data values are clustered around the median. There are no obvious outliers.

$\text{Mean} = \frac{1(82)... + 1(90)}{14} = \frac{1{,}204}{14} = 86$

$\text{Median} = \frac{86 + 86}{2} = 86$

$\text{Range} = 90 - 82 = 8$

$\text{IQR} = 87 - 85 = 2$

c. The heart rate might go up; the mean, the range, and the IQR could increase.

LESSON 16.5

Your Turn

4. Order the data from least to greatest.
1, 3, 4, 5, 5, 6, 7, 7, 7, 8, 8, 8, 8, 9, 10
Make a frequency table of the data.
Divide the data into intervals of 2.

Interval	Frequency
1–2	1
3–4	2
5–6	3
7–8	7
9–10	2

The intervals are listed along the horizontal axis. The vertical axis shows the frequencies. Draw a bar to show the number of ratings in each interval.

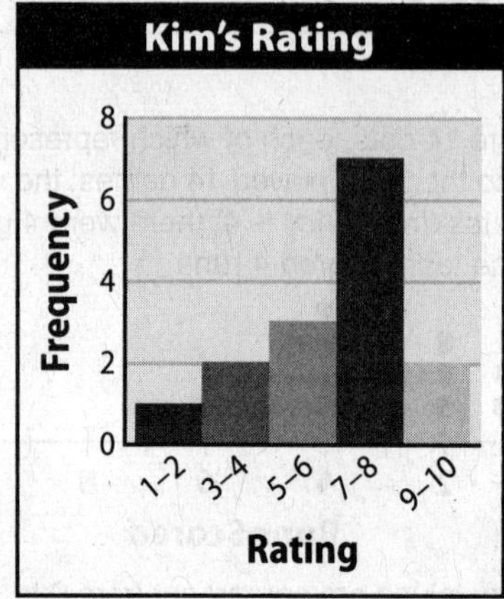

5. Sample answer: Kim gave ratings of 7 or 8 to 7 of 15 movies. She gave ratings of 9 or 10 to 2 of 15 movies.

Guided Practice

1.

Interval	Frequency
0–9	4
10–19	3
20–29	9
30–39	5

2. Order the data from least to greatest.
7, 8, 10, 12, 16, 18, 18, 20, 22, 26

Interval	Frequency
1–7	1
8–14	3
15–21	4
22–28	2

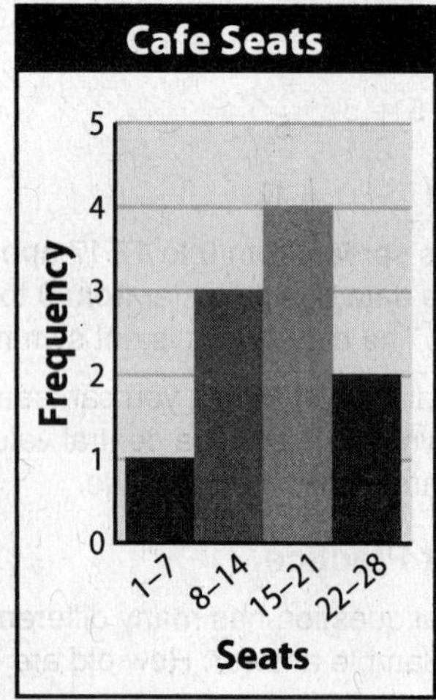

3. Sample answer: Only one cafe has less than 7 seats available. The bars increase in height until they reach the interval for 15–21 seats, and then they decrease in height, showing that most cafes have 21 or fewer seats.

4. Order the data from least to greatest. Organize the data in intervals of the same size, and make a bar graph of the frequencies for each interval.

Independent Practice

5. Order the data from least to greatest.
   11, 12, 16, 16, 17, 18, 18, 18, 18, 20, 21, 23, 23, 24, 29, 29, 31, 35, 38, 43, 45, 47, 48, 50, 56

Interval	Frequency
10–19	9
20–29	7
30–39	3
40–49	4
50–59	2

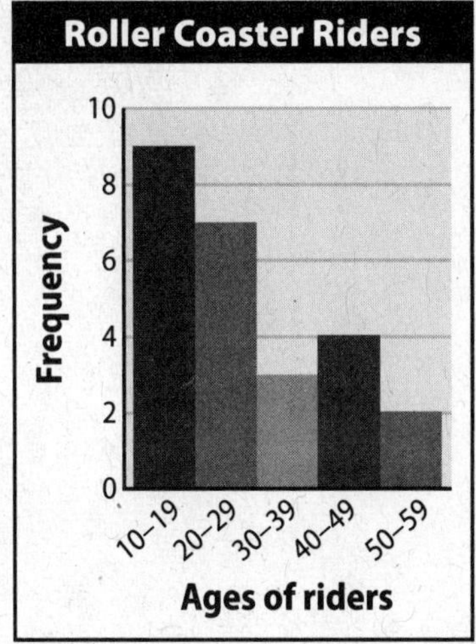

6. Sample answer: Out of 25 riders, no riders were younger than 10 or older than 59; the greatest number of riders were between 10 and 19 years old.

7. a. Order the data from least to greatest.
   7, 8, 9, 10, 12, 13, 14, 14, 18, 18, 18, 19, 20, 20, 21, 22, 23, 24, 26, 28
   Make a frequency table for Hank's histogram.

Interval	Frequency
6–10	4
11–15	4
16–20	6
21–25	4
26–30	2

   Hank's histogram has 6 bars. The height of the highest bar is 6.

   b. Frequency table for Lisa's histogram

Interval	Frequency
0–9	3
10–19	9
20–29	8

   Lisa's histogram has 3 bars. The height of the highest bar is 9.

   c. You could display these data in a box-and-whisker plot or a dot plot.

Focus on Higher Order Thinking

8. No; individual data values cannot be read from a histogram.

9. a.

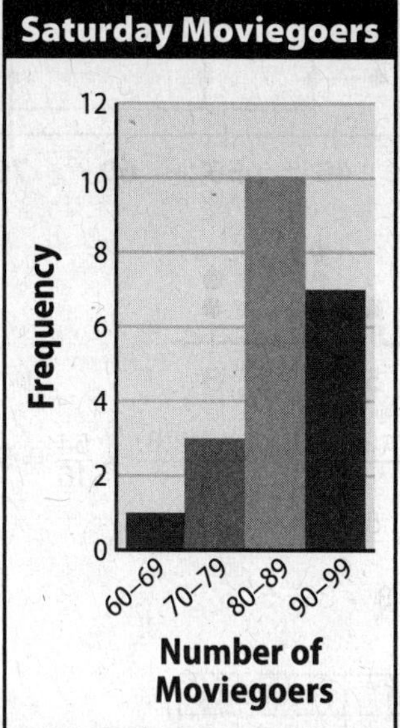

   b. Find the number of moviegoers in the two intervals with the greatest frequencies, 80–89 and 90–99.
   $10 + 7 = 17$
   Sample answer: You can expect somewhere between 80 to 99 people to come to the theater on a typical Saturday. The histogram shows that on 17 out of 21 Saturdays, the number of people who came to the theater was in that range.

   c. Yes; The number of people who come to the theater on Saturday varies.

10. No; Because a histogram groups data in intervals, you cannot see values in a given interval. So, you can't know the least and greatest data values.

MODULE 16

Ready to Go On?

1. Mean $= \frac{\text{sum of data values}}{\text{number of data values}} = \frac{63}{6} = 10.5$;
   The data set has two middle values: 9 and 11. The median is the average of these two values:
   Median $= \frac{9 + 11}{2} = 10$

2. $10.5 - 2 = 8.5$
   $10.5 - 5 = 5.5$
   $10.5 - 9 = 1.5$
   $11 - 10.5 = 0.5$
   $17 - 10.5 = 6.5$
   $19 - 10.5 = 8.5$

   $$\text{MAD} = \frac{\text{total absolute deviation}}{\text{number of data items}}$$
   $$= \frac{8.5 + 5.5 + 1.5 + 0.5 + 6.5 + 8.5}{6}$$
   $$= \frac{31}{6} = 5.17$$

3. Data in order from least to greatest:
   36 42 44 52 61 70 78
   Least value: 36; Greatest value: 78
   Median: 52
   Lower quartile: 42; Upper quartile: 70

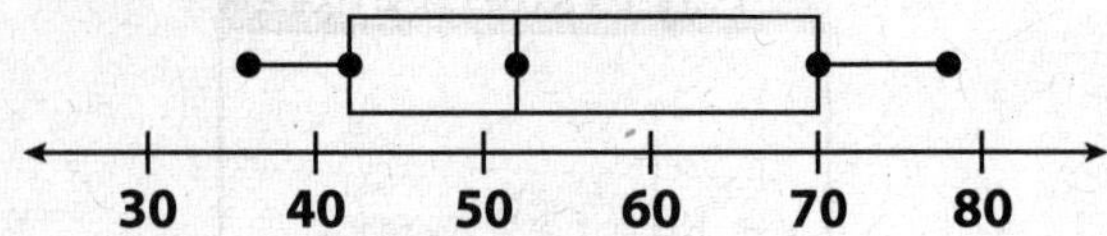

4.

5. Mean $= \frac{1(3) + 3(4)... + 2(8)}{10} = \frac{54}{10} = 5.4;$

   Median $= \frac{5 + 6}{2} = 5.5;$

   Range $= 8 - 3 = 5$

6.

Interval	Frequency
1–10	2
11–20	4
21–30	2
31–40	3
41–50	3
51–60	1
61–70	1

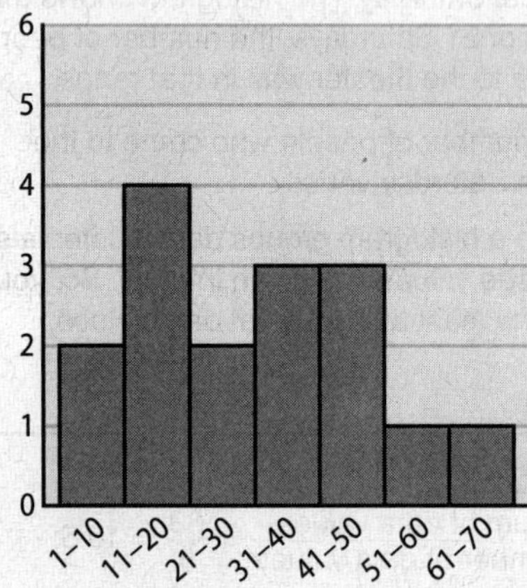

7. Make a number line and draw a dot above it for each data value. Summarize by describing the spread and shape of the data.